FASHION FOR MEN

An Illustrated History

FASHION FOR MEN

An Illustrated History

Diana de Marly

B. T. Batsford Ltd London

*Translations and transcriptions into modern
English are mainly by the author.*

© Diana de Marly 1985
First published 1985
Reprinted 1986
First paperback edition 1989

Printed and bound in Great Britain by
Courier International Ltd
Tiptree, Essex
for the publishers
B. T. Batsford Ltd
4 Fitzhardinge Street
London W1H 0AH

ISBN 0 7134 4493 2 (*hardback*)

ISBN 0 7134 4494 0 (*paperback*)

Contents

Illustrations

Acknowledgements for photographs

Austin Reed, 91, 94, 95, 96, back jacket
    illustration
Batsford archive, 53, 60, 63, 67, 86, 87, 88, 90
British Library, 2, 5, 7, 9, 11, 13, 38, 54
Burrell Collection, Glasgow, 12
Central Press Photos Ltd, 75
Chrysalis Records, 93
Country Life, 70
W. and D. Downey, 69
Greater London Council, front jacket illustration
John G. Johnson Collection, Philadelphia, 49
Keystone Press Agency, 78, 82
Kunsthistorisches Museum, Vienna, 16, 18, 19,
    43
Leeds City Art Gallery, 45

Lord Lichfield, 89
Museum of London, 42, 44
National Gallery, London, 4, 6, 8, 10, 14, 31
National Portrait Gallery, London, 1, 15, 17, 20,
    21, 22, 23, 24, 25, 26, 27, 28, 29, 30, 35, 36,
    37, 39, 40, 41, 47, 48, 52, 56, 57, 58, 59, 62,
    64, 65, 66, 68, 71, 72, 73, 77, 79, 80, 81, 85
Tate Gallery, London, 33
Topical Press Agency, 74, 76
Trinity College, Cambridge, 3
United Press International, 84
Victoria and Albert Museum, London, 32, 34,
    46, 50, 51, 55, 61
Warner/Reprise Records, 92

Chapter One

A VERRAY PARFIT GENTIL KNIGHT

History shows that human society swings between the male and the female principle, so that some periods consider themselves to be masculine, while others regard themselves as more feminine. This redefinition of identity affects the way society determines its ideal males, for a masculine age will insist on heroic and martial qualities, while a feminine one will allow more sophisticated and artistic attitudes. Consequently the changes to be seen in men's clothes reflect the changes in the definition of what is masculine, which successive periods promote. Thus the question of whether a man ought to wear frills and jewels will depend upon how far a given period in history considers them appropriate for the image of masculinity in which it believes.

In the Middle Ages there were four ways in which a man could hope to rise in society, through service to a court, or to the Church, or through the law or trade. Of these it was the court, whether of the local baron or the king, which could lead most quickly to glory and title. Courts competed with each other to be more famous than their rivals, and all courtiers were expected to assist the king or lord by dressing in a splendid manner. Indeed, it was considered an insult to the Crown and to a man's peers not to wear one's best clothes in their presence because it showed a lack of respect. Richness of attire added to the court's reputation for magnificence and triumph. At an important occasion the court would entertain the nobility, or a lord his tenants, in a manner intended to impress the known world. The anonymous author of *Sir Gawayne and the Grene Knight*, c. 1375, describes such an occasion:

This king lay at Camelot upon Christmas,
With many fine lords, men of the best,
Reckoned of the Round Table, all the rich brothers,
With rich revel outright and reckless mirth.
These men tournayed by times full many,
Jousted full jolly these gentle knights
Then carried on to the court to make dances
For the feast was all of full fifteen days,
With all the meat and mirth that men could devise:
Such clammer and glee glorious to hear,
The din by day and the dancing at nights.
All was happy and high in halls and chambers,
With lords and ladies as he believed,
With all the well of the world they stayed there
     together,
The most famous knights under Christ's self,
And the loveliest ladies that life ever had,
And he the comeliest king.

These legendary knights were a rich brethren and it would behove their reputation to dress accordingly. When the mysterious Grene Knight enters the hall his attire is as fine as any knight's should be:

All was gowned in green this man and his clothes,
A narrow cote full straight that stuck to his sides,
Above that a marvelous mantle lined within
With the finest fur, the feel full clean,
Proudly displayed and bright, and his hood
That was flung back from his locks and lay on his
     shoulders;
Neat fitting hose of the same green
Might be spied on his calves, with fine spurs under
Of bright gold embroidered on a silk base richly,
And soles under shanks, there the fellow rides,
All his vesture was verily as green as grass.

This rich ideal also occurs in another anonymous work, *The Parlement of the Thre Ages* of c. 1350, where youth has both physical perfection and plenty of finery:

The first was a fierce fellow, fairer than these others,
A bold man on a horse ready for riding,
A hero on a high horse with a hawk upon his hand.
He was round in the breast and broad in the shoul-
     ders,
His shoulders and his arms were of equal length,
And in the middle like a maiden he was handsomely
     shaped,
Long legs and large, attractive to show.
He straightened him in the stirrups and stood upright.
He had no hood nor hat but on his hair
A chaplet of his curls, chosen for the Nones,
Decorated with red roses richest of flowers,
With trefoils and trueloves of perfect pearls
With a chief carbuncle shown in the middle.
He was garbed all in green with gold work
Embroidered with besants and coins full rich,
His collar with quartz was clustered full thick,
With many diamonds set on his sleeves,
The seams set with sapphires full many,
With emeralds and amethysts upon each side,
With full rich rubies round the hems;
The price of that bejewelled outfit was full many
     pounds worth.
His saddle was of sycamore that he sat in,
His bridle all of beaten gold with silk braided reins,
His saddle cloth was of silk of Tartary that trailed to
     the earth,
And he excellently was thrived of thirty years of age,
And thereto young and frisky, and Youth was his
     name.

In contrast, Middle Age, at 60, was attired in

russet and grey, while Old Age, at 100, was dressed all in black – not that many people in that period reached such an age. The knight's horse was part of his *raison d'être* as a mounted warrior, so it too was attired in finery. The Grene Knight's mount was, of course, in green decked with precious stones, and this was an accurate reflection of reality. When Richard II summoned Henry of Lancaster and the Duke of Norfolk to appear at a tourney, Lancaster and his charger both arrived in green and blue velvet embroidered with swans and antelopes in gold, while Norfolk and his mount were both in crimson velvet embroidered with silver lions.[1] Taking part in such contests was considered a fundamental part of military training; this rule had been laid down in one of the most important books on knighthood, Ramon Lull's *Le Libre del Ordre de Cavayleria* of 1275–6. Two hundred years later this work was still considered important enough for William Caxton to translate it and produce it on his new printing press, dedicating the book to Richard III in 1483–5. 'Knightes ought to take coursers to juste and to go to tornoyes to holde open table to hute at hertes at bores & other wyld bestes. For in doynge these thynges the knyghtes exercyse them to armes for to maytene thordre of knighthode.'[2] The fine physique that the author of *The Parlement* described for Youth was essential if the knight was to carry the weight of armour and wield a heavy sword or axe in battle or a tournament. The Grene Knight was also suitably built: 'for his back and his brest all his body was broad, but his middle and his waist were worthily small'. This importance of physique was stressed in another work translated and printed by Caxton, *The Book of Fayttes of Armes and of Chyvalrye*, which Christine de Pisan wrote in 1408–9. The only female author in France at the time to live exclusively by her writings, Christine wrote a very practical study covering training, how much food was needed to feed a garrison, how to conduct an ambush, and the importance of regular pay, as well as considering the ideal physique of the warrior: 'a streyght hede a large brest, grete sholders & wel shapen armes long & bigge wel made, longe handes & grete bones, small bely & the reynes wel formed bigge thyes leggis streyght wel shapen full of synewis & drye, brode fete and streyght'.[3] The knight's pride in his physique was shown by Henry, Duke of Lancaster, a veteran of Sluys and Calais, who would stretch out his legs at jousts so that the ladies could admire them. Armour became heavier when plate armour

began to be added to chain mail in the late fourteenth century, so the wearer had to be very fit. A fat knight who donned an equally large suit of armour would put considerable strain on his heart. It was essential to keep fit by hunting and by training in the use of arms. Knighthood was

1 Edward, Prince of Wales *c.* 1377. The ideal shape for knightly heroes, with the chest well padded out and the waist and hips of maidenly slenderness. The Black Prince's surcoat is of leather embossed with the arms of England and France. Its dagged hemline is of a shortness that shocked the moralists, and the ornate belt drew eyes to the sexual region, in flagrant masculine display.

the ideal to aim for, and the yeoman farmer or impoverished gentleman who wanted to see his son rise in society would send him into the service of the local baron or bishop, or even of a duke or cardinal, to be trained as a page or groom, then to see war as a squire, and hopefully win his spurs and be translated into a physically fit, richly dressed and magnificently mounted knight. The household of a magnate could number from 100 to 500 persons and was known as his family. To serve in such a family and to wear its livery was distinction, while attaining knighthood would entail a grant of land in return for military service to one's overlord, or king.

To fight was to be noble, for Ramon Lull argued that arms had a spiritual meaning: the sword was like the cross, the haubergeon was a defence against vice and the dagger showed trust in God. A knight should also be a sober character, not a weakling given to drink or lechery, for 'the strong courage of a noble knight fyghteth with the ayde of Abstynence, prudence and attemperaunce'. This was the code of chivalry, and as the knight was intended for warfare, some argued that there should be permanent wars to give every knight his heroic opportunity. Such supporters gave little thought to the poor peasants and townsfolk who were heavily taxed to pay for these wars, but the martial knights got their way with the Hundred Years' War between England and France, the huge expense of which resulted in peasant revolts in France, England and Flanders. All Europe marvelled at the spectacle of England, with her population under 4,000,000, defeating mighty France, population 20,000,000, not just once but several times at Crécy, Sluys, Poitiers and Agincourt, but the commoners groaned beneath the strain. In his poem *Le Songe du Vieil Pelerin* of 1389, Philipe de Mezières argued that chivalry had failed. Modern knights were not the equals of the heroes of the past. They did not honour their own code, they did not protect the population. The poor lived in terror of their own knights who would pillage and murder just like any invader. One of the aims of war might be to gain loot and sack cities, he conceded, but why should knights attack their own compatriots? French chivalry was defeated by the English because French knights objected to fighting more than two hours at a time. Given the weight of their armour that is understandable, but de Mezières was disgusted. Others argued that the disgrace of France was due to clothes. Attire had become so immodest that God had sent the English to ravage France in punishment, an argument which overlooked the fact that the English wore the same clothing as the French.

It was allowed that courts had to dress in a luxurious manner. In his poem de Mezières makes Queen Truth rule that a prince's habits should be rich to conform with his estate, to impress people, and to ensure the respect due to rank, but she condemns very short habits, long pointed shoes and lavish expenditure on the toilette. Courts should restrain the money spent on pleasure, she maintains, as it is a burden on the people.[4] Thus the court and nobility could dress richly but the clothes should not be immodestly short. The subject concerned many moralists, for the fourteenth century saw the biggest change in European clothes that menswear had ever experienced. After being worn for thousands of years, the tunic, which was pulled on over the head, now faced a challenge from the buttoned cote, which could be opened and closed, and donned more simply. The tunic was a rectangle which did not waste any cloth, while the new cote had to be cut in sections, which required more skill, and resulted in a great advance in tailoring techniques. The word 'tailor' comes from the French *tailler*, to cut, and for the new cote cut was all-important. Any peasant family could make their own simple tunics, for little cutting or fitting was necessary, but cotes had to be tailored by experts. This meant, of course, that only the aristocracy could afford the new garment, and fashion was the prerogative of the upper classes, showing who was important and who was not by the quality and

2 Philippe de Mezières presenting his treatise *The Crown of Thorns* to Richard II in 1395–6. The shocking short cote can be seen on the macebearer on the left with the low belt. The men on the right are mainly in houpelandes which could be long or short, but one wears a buttoned cote with modest skirts. The poet was pleading for peace between England and France.

the novelty of their clothes.

Although button and loop fastenings had been used in Coptic Egypt, buttonholes seem to have arrived in the thirteenth century. The origins of the new garment in Europe can be found in two sources. The fitted look had long been a characteristic of gowns in the Byzantine Empire, and as early as 1078 the Emperor Nicephoros Botiniates was portrayed in a low-waisted gown which was much narrower than western tunics. This Byzantine style affected neighbouring states, and during the Second Bulgarian Empire the Sebastocrator Kaloian was depicted in 1259 on a mural of a church at Boiana near Sofia, in a narrow long-waisted gown with narrow sleeves. But it was possible to produce this slim look by using lacing, and buttons seem to have come to Europe via the Arabs and Moors, rather than Byzantium. In the *Book of Chess* of Alfonso the Wise of Castile, written in the mid-thirteenth century, the Castilians are shown with narrow clothes achieved by lacing, but the Moor is portrayed in a long gown with a tailored collar and a row of buttons from neck to waist. This was clearly a traditional form of dress, for on the painted ceilings of the Hall of Justice in the Alhambra Granada of about 1354 the Moors have buttoned necks. By this date, however, Europeans had taken to buttons, and the first mention of buttons in the accounts of the Great Wardrobe for Edward III occurs in 1337.[5] The introduction of buttons was, of course, a gradual process, and it would have been below Edward III's dignity as a king to be the first European to wear them. A survey of trades in Paris in 1292 shows that there were 16 button-makers in the city at that time, along with 197 tailors, 366 shoemakers, 46 seamstresses, 5 linen underwear seamstresses, 70 mercers, 19 drapers, 21 glovers, 54 hatters, 214 furriers, 14 embroiderers, 3 wool-carders, 11 fabric-weavers, 13 wool merchants, 45 purse-makers, 6 lace-makers, 10 pin-makers, and 36 buckle-makers.[6] Thus it took buttons over 40 years to reach the very top, from being a strange novelty copied from the Moors to being tasteful enough to appeal to the court. There buttons became jewels; they had to be richer than the Moorish originals in order to appear at court, so buttons were decorated with precious stones. The French royal dress accounts for 1352 mention pearl buttons, and there were also gold ones and diamond ones, which no peasant could have copied.

The big impact on menswear was that they now had front-opening garments which were a male monopoly, for womens' gowns continued to be laced up for centuries to come. Buttoned cotes were very much a masculine garment. Women wore buttons only on sleeves or else as decorations down the front of their garments. Not until Zuccaro's drawing of Queen Elizabeth I in 1575 do we have an example of a woman's skirt buttoned in front, and when women started wearing coats in the seventeenth century they had to copy men's ones. The other big change brought about by buttons was that they could make clothes very tight. A tunic-style garment must not be too narrow to be pulled on over the head, but buttons would allow the garment to be opened and slid on. As this was something which buttons could do, it was made a major feature of the new cotes, producing a very slim line. This was regarded as very elegant and youthful, and reflected the long, narrow lines of Gothic art and architecture.

The new garment fulfilled artistic ideals, but the Church began to frown. Religions both Christian and Mohammedan said that bodies were sinful and should be covered, but now that fashion had discovered the body it was not going to give is up. Cotes became even tighter and were made very obvious by using wide stripes and big checks, (an early form of Op Art!). They were so bright and new that even young clergymen started to wear them, a practice which the Archbishop of Canterbury condemned in 1342, saying the clergy were dressing like laymen in red and green checks, scanty cotes, excessively wide sleeves lined with fur or silk, extremely long hoods and tippets, pointed and slashed shoes, bejewelled belts with gilt purses, and long hair and beards instead of the tonsure.[7] In fact, they were dressing just as richly as the court. What annoyed the Church even more was that cotes grew much shorter than tunics. To create a very long look it was necessary to drop the waistline to the hips to make the body look longer, and to shorten the hemline to show the legs in order to make them longer. From being on the knee in 1340, men's hems rose to mid-thigh by 1360, which was shocking, for it meant that when a man was sitting down or mounting his horse there was a clear view all the way up his hose to his drawers. In Chaucer's *Canterbury Tales* the Parson criticises these short garments very strongly because they show far too much:

Alas! some of them show the very boss of the penis and the horrible pushed-out testicles that look like the malady of hernia in the wrapping of their hose, and the buttocks of such persons look like the hinder parts

a ymago·

3 John Foxton, *Liber Cosmographiae*, 1408. Sinful worldly pride and vanity is here shown by a very short houpelande with a buttoned collar. It exposes the genitals in their hose, showing how little courtly fashion cared about morality. The vogue for floral embroidery and curled hair was damned as effete, while the flames about the wearer's feet indicate his ultimate destination.

of a she-ape in the full of the moon. And moreover, the hateful proud members that they show by the fantastic fashion of making one leg of their hose white and the other red, make it seem that half of their privy members are flayed. And if it be that they divide their hose in other colours, as white and black, or white and blue, or black and red, and so forth, then it seems, by the variation of colour, that the half of their privy members are corrupted by the fire of Saint Anthony, or by cancer, or by other such misfortune.[8]

For the first time in western fashion, the male sex organs were being flaunted for all to see.

Formerly, rich and aristocratic men had worn long garments when in civilian dress to underline the fact that they did not work in the fields like peasants, who had to wear their tunics knee-length for practical reasons, yet now fashionable men were wearing cotes and tunics which were even shorter than those worn by workers. It was not a signal of fellow feeling, for it went way beyond anything worn by the labouring classes. Amongst primitive peoples today it is normal for the warrior class to flaunt its masculinity; for example, in Papua New Guinea headhunters wear bamboo extensions to the penis to make it much longer than nature allows. A similar phenomenon occurred in the fourteenth century; the male 'bulge' was to be built up in the years to come, and was still being displayed two hundred years later. For extra emphasis, the hanging money-pouch was moved round from its usual place at the side, and located at the centre over the sex organs like the Scottish Highlander's sporran. These purses could be of gilded or coloured leather, which was another way of drawing the eye to the sexual region. The dagger and the sword were also moved round from the side and tucked behind the purse in centre front. What could be more sexual than the sight of a man walking about with a sword hanging between his legs? So it was that the knightly class which was supposed to be all things modest and moral displayed its sex in an obvious manner, advertising its valour in the field and in bed. Perhaps it was a sign that they were not so sure of their masculinity as they claimed to be.

Of course, when the Black Death hit Europe in 1347 the Church declared that this was a divine punishment for the sinful clothes men were wearing; for the mi-parti (the contrast of two colours in an outfit), for the short cotes, and for the exposure of the private parts; but in fact cotes grew shorter after the Plague. The objections of Chaucer's Parson to colour contrasts were written about 1386 or later, so the Plague, terrible though it was, did not put a stop to the fashion. Indeed, after such a disaster the psychological need for colour and a youthful look was increased, to counter the shock. So the display went on, growing ever more fanciful. The long line produced by dropping the waist and belt to the hips was further emphasized by elaborating the belt. It was enriched with gold or silver plates, the leather was gilded and stamped with designs, trinkets were hung from it, fringes were cut from it in leaf-shapes. The belt became the most glittering, decorated, fanciful item in the male wardrobe, and many a poor young man must have sighed with covetousness. It was absolutely essential to own such a belt to be in the fashion.

The great popularity of the short cote did not put an end to every form of long gown. For official court events long robes were still regarded as the most suitable wear, but a new version was produced, the 'houpelande', first noticed in the French royal accounts in 1359. It was all the rage by 1364, for Froissart wrote a pastoral poem in which a shepherd calls his companions to see the knights riding past in that brand new fashion, the houpelande, and each verse ends with the desire *'A vestir une houpelande'*.[9] The

4   The Wilton Diptych (detail), Richard II with his patron saints, *c*. 1395. Richard II was considered an extravagant fop. His golden houpelande is lavishly embroidered with his symbol, the white hart, and lined with white fur. The lower orders were not allowed to wear such luxury even if they could afford it. His over-fondness for fashion was one of the reasons Richard lost the throne.

shape was very new, for it was not the straight up and down of the long tunic, but the result of the new sophisticated tailoring techniques which specialized in fit. The bodice was cut to fit closely, but the skirts were cut in sections so that they swung out at the bottom in a flare. There was a standing collar, and the sleeves were either the wide-mouthed ducal sleeve reserved for royalty and heads of state like the Doge of Venice, or else the bag sleeve which was very full but narrowed where it met the wrist. These sleeves could be decorated very richly with embroidery and jewels, and the garment could be any length the wearer pleased, from thigh to mid-calf or ankle. Were the moralists pleased that the houpelande offered an alternative to the flagrant short cote? On the contrary, Chaucer's Parson denounced the decoration under the heading of *De Superbia*, on pride. The first sin lies in superfluity of clothing, not only costly embroidery, but 'the elaborate notching or barring, the waved lines, the stripes, the twists, the diagonal bars, and similar waste of cloth in vanity, but there is also the costly furring of gowns, so much perforating with scissors to make holes, so much slashing with shears, and then the superfluity in length of the aforesaid gowns, trailing in the dung and the mire'. Thomas Occleve was another writer who condemned houpelandes, claiming to have seen one in scarlet which was 12 yards wide in the skirts, with the sleeves long enough to sweep the ground.[10] The court may well have felt that there was no pleasing some people; whether it promoted a semi-naked or a covered-up style somebody would criticize it on moral grounds.

The celebration of the male physique represented by short cotes and a narrow line reached its apogee over the years 1360–1400. As not all knights and noblemen were physically perfect, some assistance was devised to give the impression of muscular perfection. Padding was introduced to build up the chest in front, creating a pronounced curve like a pigeon breast. What nature did not supply, the tailor could. The result was an elongated *S* shape, pouting out over the chest in front and over the buttocks at the back. It had the effect of making the waist look smaller, and both *Sir Gawayne and the Grene Knight* and *The Parlement of the Thre Ages* had stressed that the ideal knight should have a waist as small as a maiden. The hero became very curvaceous, but it was not a feminine shape, for women were not padded out in this way. Padding had an effect on armour, for when men's clothes changed shape armour had to change to fit over them, and many an English brass of a knight in full armour shows him with the padded chest, narrow waist, curved hips and rich belt of high fashion in the second half of the fourteenth century. Where one's eternal image was concerned every country knight wanted to look as superbly shaped as the Black Prince, Edward Prince of Wales.

The actual business of dressing such princes was in the hands of their chamberlains. John Russell, servant to Henry V's brother Humphrey, Duke of Gloucester in the early fifteenth century, described the duties in his *Boke of Nurture*. The chamberlain should start the day by preparing his lord's underwear, a clean shirt, breeches, tunic, doublet, as well as his cote, hose, socks, shoes or slippers. The linen should be warmed by the fire and then handed to the lord when he dresses, first the shirt and breeches (drawers), then the doublet (at that time a sort of long-sleeved waistcoat). Smooth the hose up his legs, and lace them to the doublet. Next place a kerchief over the lord's shoulders and comb his hair; wash his hands and face in warm water. Kneel, and ask which gown his lordship wishes to wear that day and send a groom to fetch it. Help the lord into the gown, settle his belt in place, and hand him his hat or hood. Before he leaves brush him down. Let all be plain and pure, whether in satin, velvet or scarlet or grey wool. Looking after the clothes was the duty of the wardrober, who should brush all the robes clean once a week and should be present when the lord retires at night, to put away the clothes. The chamberlain was advised to put a cloak around the lord when removing his shoes, socks, breeches and hose, and hand him a kerchief and a nightcap. (There was no nightshirt as people slept in the nude until the sixteenth century.) When his lordship required a bath, the chamberlain should prepare it and hang sheets around the tub to ward off draughts.[11] The ordering of royal clothes was handled by the Great Wardrobe in England which had its own tailors, and by the Treasury L'Argenterie in France. Extracts from Edward III's clothing accounts have been reproduced by Stella Mary Newton.[12] The accounts of Etienne de la Fontaine, treasurer to Jean II, cover the year 1352 which was just four years before that king was captured by Edward III and taken prisoner to London. They include orders for several males in the French royal family:

Jehan Perceval draper, for 10½ ells of scarlet cloth vermillion shade delivered to the said Martin de Coussy, tailor to the Dauphin, to make 2 surcoats, 2 cloaks and 2 hats, all lined with miniver, for the persons of my lord Dauphin and the Duc d'Orléans, 64 *sols* the ell, 33 *livres* 12 *sols*.

Edouart Thadelin, for 3 bundles of scarlet silk, containing 18 pieces, delivered to Eustace de Brulle tailor to the King our sire, by his relation rendered below, to line the robes of my lord the Dauphin, of my lord the Duc d'Orléans, of my lords Jehan and Philippe of France, my lord the Count of Anjou, my lord the Duke Louis of Bourbon, the Duke of Burgundy, the Count of Alençon, and the Count of Estampes, for their livery at Pentecost, 65 *escus* the bundle, 195 *escus*.

At this time robe meant a suit of clothes, while *cote/cotte hardie* was the French term for cote, which occurs in the King's orders:

Jehan Prime, draper of Brussels, for a dark greenish multicolour cloth of Brussels to make the said lord a robe of 4 garments, lined with miniver, for the eve of Easter, 35 *livres*.

Jehan Perceval for wood green half-cloth of the great measure of Brussels to make the said lord for the season of summer, *cotes hardies* and riding jackets, at special rate, 20 *livres*.

Pierre le Flamenc, draper of Paris, for a fine multicolour brownish cloth of the great measure of Brussels, to make the said lord a robe of 4 garments, lined with miniver, for the season of Lent at 14 *escus*.

Jacques le Flamenc draper, for a fine multicolour dark greenish pink of the said measure of Brussels, to make the said lord another similar robe for the festival of Floral Easter, 42 *livres*.

Godefrey Miltin for 4 multicolour cloths of Brussels of two kinds, delivered to Eustace de Brulle, the king's tailor, by his relation rendered below, to make robes for my lord the Dauphin and his brothers, for the festival of Christmas recently passed, 53 *escus* the cloth, the one by the other piece of 14 *sols*, equals 145 *livres* 12 *sols*.

Godefrey Miltin, merchant and draper of Brussels for a vermillion scarlet of Brussels to make the said lord a surcoat and a *cote hardie* lined with miniver, two other surcoats lined with white silk, a narrow train lined with another cloth, and hats lined and unlined; for this, 100 *escus* of gold.[13]

Brussels cloth was famous as being the best quality stuff woven in northern Europe, usually with English wool, which had the best body.

For most of history men had to do the family shopping in town or capital because they were the ones to travel. This can be seen in the letters of the Paston family over the years 1422–1509.[14]

John Paston was often away from Norfolk on legal business, so one finds his wife Margaret writing to him in 1448 to get some frieze cloth for the children's gowns, and a yard of broad blackcloth at 4s. a yard to make a hood, as the local shops are no good. In September 1465 John wrote back to his wife 'mine own dear sovreign lady' that the weather was growing cold so would she send two ells of worsted for doublets, and find out where William Paston got his fine worsted tippet which is almost like silk. If it costs over 7 or 8s. she is only to get a little for collars, as he would prefer the bulk of his doublet to be local worsted, being a Norfolk man. The biggest demands came when a member of the family was staying in London. In 1471 John Paston III received a list from his brother Edward back at home, asking for:

3 yards of purple camlet at 4s. a yard
a bonnet of deep murray at 2/4d.
hose cloth of yellow kersey at 2s. an ell
a girdle of plunket ribbon at 6d.
4 silk laces
3 dozen points in red, white and yellow, 6d.
3 pairs of pattens about $2\frac{1}{2}d.$ a pair

He added that their mother wanted some malmsey wine but advised his brother to put it in canvas to stop the carriers from sampling it. John also received a shopping list from his brother William at Eton College in 1478. He wanted some hose cloth, plain for workdays and coloured for holidays, a stomacher, two shirts and a pair of slippers. In 1458 Agnes Paston checked the wardrobe of Clement Paston who was 16. He had a short green gown, a short *muster-de-villers* gown (grey wool from that town in Normandy), a short blue gown made from a wide gown when she was last in London, a wide russet gown furred with beaver two years old, and an ample murray gown twelve months old. The Pastons were a middle-class family; in 1468 John III was in Bruges when Princess Margaret of England married Charles the Bold, Duke of Burgundy, and he was dazzled by the finery worn by the upper class. The groom's father, the Count of Roche, was actually in real cloth of gold, embroidered with silver and silk, and bedecked with goldsmith's work. Where most people could only afford wool, the aristocrat gleamed in silks, satins and brocades.

The wardrobe of a wealthy merchant can be seen in an inventory taken in 1397 for the wool merchant Francesco di Marco Datini of Prato, who was the equivalent of a modern millionaire, with business houses in Avignon, Prato, Florence, Pisa, Genoa, Spain and Majorca. He was worth 70,000 gold florins when he died in August 1410. His underwear consisted of 6 linen shirts, 6 pairs of breeches, 3 pairs of long blue hose with leather soles, and 2 pairs in black to wear with slippers, 10 pairs of white linen undersocks, 1 vermillion doublet and 3 in fine linen. His outerwear consisted of 5 gowns for everyday, an undyed one for writing in (quill pens tended to splutter), two with fur linings for cold days, one of dark cloth lined with vermillion, one of cloth lined with green taffeta, one of dark camlet lined with blue taffeta, and in addition there were a riding gown of grey cloth lined with Sardinian sheepskin, and two grand gowns, a red lined with squirrel fur, and a scarlet lined with scarlet taffeta. For outdoors he had 5 cloaks: a grey with a shepherd's hood, two old blue ones, one of scarlet and one of pale cloth, two short riding capes in pale blue and grey, and a long white pilgrim's cloak. He owned 9 hoods and 5 round beretta hats. The absence of velvets and brocades will be noticed. Despite his great wealth, Datini was not allowed to wear the richer stuffs which were the prerogative of the aristocratic classes by law. Despite this Datini demanded good quality, and when a tailor, Antonio, came from Florence he insisted that not only did he do the cutting and fitting in Prato, but also the sewing and finishing, so Datini could keep an eye on what he was getting.[15] When garments had to be sent to relations the Italian used mule trains, while the English employed pack horses, a very common sight on the roads leading out of the metropolis.

While courts spent on finery whatever they pleased, they restricted what the rest of the population could wear. In 1294 Philipe le Bel of France ruled that bourgeois persons might not wear squirrel or grey fur, ermine, precious stones, gold or crowns. Dukes, counts and barons with incomes of 6,000 *livres* a year from their estates could have 4 robes (suits) a year. Knights and bannerets with incomes of 3,000 *livres* from their lands might have 3 pairs of robes of which one had to be for summer. Boys and girls were entitled to only one pair of robes a year. No prelates or barons were to have robes costing over 25 Tours *sols* the Parisian ell, no bourgeois was to spend over 10 *sols* the ell for cloth, and their wives 12 *sols*.[16] These sumptuary laws were a mixture of class distinction and trade protection. In 1337 Edward III ruled that nobody below the rank of knight should wear fur in England, but he also decreed that

5 Thomas Hoccleve presenting his *Regement of Princes* to Henry, Prince of Wales, 1411–12. Under the martial Lancastrians curled hair and embroidery are banished. The future Henry V has the cropped hairstyle and the completely plain houpelande of the new regime, although he retains the ermine lining. The prince has the ducal open sleeve, but the writer wears the humbler bag sleeve as he was not allowed to copy royalty.

only cloth made in English territories might be worn in the kingdom, and no foreign cloth was to be imported. In 1355 he ruled that prostitutes were to wear red or striped clothes inside out, to make them obvious and impossible to confuse with decent women. In 1362 Parliament complained to the king that too many people were dressing above their station, copying the new cotes and short styles, so Edward III issued a detailed statute which is a good example of social regulation. Yeoman and handicraftsmen were forbidden to wear cloth costing over 40s. a piece, and they could have no silk, cloth of silver, chains, jewels or buttons, so they could not copy the cote. Gentlemen and esquires worth under £100 a year were restricted to cloth not over $4\frac{1}{2}$ marks, and no cloth of gold, silver, silk or pearls. The gentleman with 200 marks a year could have cloth at 5 marks a piece, silk, cloth of silver, ribbons, silver girdles and miniver. All knights with incomes in the range 400 marks to £1,000 a

year could wear what they liked except for royal ermine. The wealthy merchant worth £500 a year could wear the same as an esquire on £100, and the merchant worth £1,000 could dress the same as the knight on £200 a year. Thus the commercial class had to be five times richer than a titled person before they could have the same clothes and materials. At the bottom of the heap, carters, ploughmen, oxherds, cowherds, shepherds, swineherds, and dairymen were limited to undyed blanket cloth and russet at 1s. a yard; not that they could afford silks in any case.

The very next year the English Parliament complained that there were too many statutes, so they were all recalled, and the sumptuary ones disappeared in the process.[17] In much of Europe such laws were proclaimed by the town criers and preached about from pulpits, but in the absence of an enormous inspectorate to enforce the regulations, observation was temporary. It was different in small city states where it was possible to keep an eye on the population, but not so in a kingdom. Tuscan sumptuary law forbade *mi-parti*, striped and checked clothes, for the rulers disliked optical fashions, and banned the citizens from wearing such aristocratic items as embossed velvet, brocade, samiate silks, and gold and silver embroidery.[18] In 1343 the Signoria in Florence sent out inspectors to examine people's clothing chests and they did discover many of the forbidden silks, which were obviously being worn indoors, but England and France were too big for this sort of investigation.

The next dress law in England did not occur until 1411. There had evidently been some abuse of the livery system, for Henry IV ruled that no archbishop, bishop, abbot or prior was to give livery to anyone except their own menials and officers. Likewise, knights were not to give livery cloth or hats to anyone other than the staff of their own household, on pain of a 100s. fine and 40s. for the recipient. The Wars of the Roses distracted the Crown from further legislation on dress, and not until Edward IV had defeated the Lancastrians did a new sumptuary law appear in 1463. Declaring that inordinate and excessive apparel was displeasing to God, and impoverished the kingdom while making foreigners rich, Edward IV set out 'what kind of apparel men and women of every vocation and degree are allowed, and what prohibited, to wear'. Nobody below the rank of lord could wear cloth of gold, gold-decked fabrics or sables. No bachelor knights were to wear velvet upon velvet except for Knights of the Garter, fine 20 marks. Nobody below the rank of lord was to wear

6 Pisanello, *The Vision of Saint Eustace, c.* 1420. The hat was elevated into fashion at the turn of the century. The capuchon hat was a hood twisted into a sort of turban, with the end hanging down. This example is lined with fur and there is matching fur round the bottom of the riding tunic, to make a set.

purple silk. No esquires or gentlemen under rank of knight were to wear velvet, satin, counterfeit silk or ermine, fine 10 marks, and they could not wear satin damask unless they were esquires of the royal household, like the sergeants of the King's House and yeomen of the Crown, fine 100s. The steward, chamberlain, treasurer and comptroller of the King's Household were allowed sables and ermine. Mayors, aldermen and sheriffs worth £40 a year might wear the same as esquires and gentlemen. Nobody worth under £40 could have marten's fur, pure grey or miniver, gold or silver belts, or foreign silk coverchiefs costing over 5s., fine 3/4d. Yeomen could not have wool or cotton stuffing in their doublets but only a lining, fine 6/8d. Labourers were not to wear wool worth over 2s. a yard, close hose over 14d., coverchiefs over 1s. or silver belts, fine 3/4d. What was very unusual about this statute was that it sought to restrict that masculine exposure which had been quite common for a good 120 years. No knight below the rank of lord, esquire or gentleman could wear short gowns, jackets or cotes which exposed their privy members and buttocks, fine 40s. The law also attacked the long-toed shoe which was just as old, ruling that knights were not to have shoes more than two inches long in the pike, fine 3/4d., and that shoemakers selling long shoes would be fined 4/4d. The statute excused riches used in church services, and the royal family, the Master of the Rolls, the barons of the Exchequer and the Chancellor of the Exchequer were all exempt. Scholars must obey university statutes over dress. Heralds and pursuivants were excused as they wore livery, and minstrels and actors were also exempt as some finery was needed for their profession.

The long-toed shoe was part of that elongation of the figure beloved in Gothic art, and it was considered very elegant by those who did not have to walk far. Accordingly, those above the rank of knight could keep them along with the exposing cotes and gowns, for the aristocracy was above the moral laws made for the benefit of the vulgar masses. A display of luxury was considered essential to an aristocrat's rank. In Boccaccio's *Decameron* of about 1350 the tale of the misfortunes of the Count of Antwerp ends happily with the king granting him all the clothes, servants and horses that were proper to his rank. He could not be a count and be poor. The French aristocracy even wore its long-toed shoes to war, but when they came to battle at Poitiers in September 1356 they found that Edward III had fortified his position so that the French were forced to attack on only a very narrow front. They were obliged to dismount, but in order to walk and fight they had to chop off the pikes of their shoes. They lost and their king was taken prisoner. After this disaster the Estates General published a sumptuary law banning the wearing of gold, silver, pearls, ornamented clothes and hats, and stopping all entertainment for one year, in token of national mourning. The nobility could not do anything without splendour about them, as was shown in 1386 when the French were preparing an enormous invasion of England to seek revenge. The dukes and counts of the French court spent fortunes on velvet and silk outfits to wear on the other side of the Channel, as well as gilding the prows of the ships, silvering the masts, and striping the sails with cloth of gold. Preparations were not complete until November 1386, when the stormy English Channel persuaded the French to postpone the invasion – indefinitely. All that expenditure had been for nothing, but

the French aristocrat would spend on a gilded surcoat before he would spend on a siege engine.[19]

In 1482 Edward IV introduced another act of apparel, which again ruled that persons below the rank of lord were not to expose their private parts by short doublets. Evidently the effect of the previous law had faded away. This act did make some changes, for cloth of gold and purple silk were now reserved for the royal family alone. Cloth of tissue of gold was allowed to dukes, and plain gold cloth to lords, but the real thing was prohibited. Only those above the rank of knight could wear doublets and gowns of velvet, damask or satin; no yeomen could wear such fabrics. The aristocracy could wear silks, but everyone else had to wear English wool or risk the enormous fine of £10.

The protection of home industries was a constant theme of sumptuary laws, but the restrictions for the labouring class were largely irrelevant because of their extreme poverty. Where the law hit hardest was in its limitations for the middle class and the gentry, the classes most likely to imitate their titled superiors in clothes and manners. This can be seen in the *Canterbury Tales* where the merchant is in *miparti*, the two-colour contrast, as is the physician

7 Jean de Wavrin, *Les Chroniques d'Angleterre*, 1470. King John of Portugal entertains his father-in-law, John of Gaunt. John of Gaunt and the cook at the serving hatch remain loyal to the buttoned cote, but the serving men wear the revived tunic now in a highly pleated form, which is still as short as the shocking cotes had been. The long piked shoes had to have the points pulled up. The musicians are in livery tabards and livery badges.

in purple and blue, a sure sign that they were copying their betters, and a signal that the fashion was now on the wane, for once the second estate started to copy, the first estate changed the style. By the turn of the century buttons were on the way out and the old tunic made a comeback, but in very different form from the peasant's sack shape. The tunic was cut fuller so that it formed deep pleats, held in place by the belt, and the only thing it had in common with the ancient tunic was that it was pulled on over the head. Clothing in general became more voluminous – the only alternative to the narrow line of the fourteenth century. Nevertheless, short hems for men did not disappear and survived alongside calf-length and ground-length hemlines, with the shorter version obviously more appropriate for riding, and the long ones better suited to attendance at court.

Men's fashion in the highest circles of society

8 Follower of Andrea Verrocchio, *Tobias and the Archangel Raphael* (detail). The folds in the tunic were made permanent by being stitched down and padded like sausages. The garment only reached the top of the thigh, so exposure of the privy parts continued. There was a return to longer hair.

became increasingly ornate, because two of the most influential courts were dominated by men who considered themselves great connoisseurs of taste and elegance: Richard II in England, and in France Jean, Duc de Berry, the famous collector of art. Richard II is credited with the invention of the handkerchief, being much too exquisite to blow his nose on to the floor, or on his sleeve. It was usual to blame new fashions on foreigners; the English would blame the Flemish, and the Italians would blame the French, but when Richard II married Anne of Bohemia moralists began to attack that country. Certainly one influence Anne brought with her was the 'crackowe', for Poland was part of her family's realm. This was a vogue for curving the long toe of the shoe upwards, and attaching it by a thin chain to the leg; the name suggests that it began in Cracow. It was quite a practical idea, retaining the length but keeping it out of the way.

Richard II took as his personal device the white hart, wearing it embroidered on his houpelandes and hung on chains about his neck.

The King's closest associates were allowed to wear his device too, and this gave rise to the vogue for embroidered patterns and symbols on sleeves and gowns. The alternative to embroidery was the use of bezants, small metal shapes in gold or silver, representing stars, flowers, or letters, which were sewn all over a houpelande. They were very popular at Jean de Berry's court, where blue strewn with gold bezants was particularly favoured. The block colour was now taking over, and *mi-parti* contrasts were passing over into livery and English legal dress. Occleve stated that these big houpelandes cost £20 each, but the elaborately decorated ones at court plainly exceeded that. Additional decoration was supplied by a taste for rich baldrics worn across the body, with little gold bells or florets hanging from them. Similar attachments hung from the gold collars worn by aristocrats. Elaboration was on the increase and from England to Italy dagging was the latest craze; the cutting of the hem of the sleeve or gown into fluttering finials, like rose leaves or points. These were emphasized by colour contrast, for example a blue velvet houpelande might be lined with white silk, so that the white would flutter against the blue. It was a subtle variation on the *mi-parti* idea. There was an air of fantasy about these masculine styles in the early 1400s. The relative simplicity and discipline of the cote was replaced by a fondness for over-decoration which was the personal taste of Richard II. His portrait in Westminster Abbey shows his houpelande embroidered all over with roses and his own initial, and he was accused of having a costume valued at 30,000 marks, which must have been smothered in jewels. As might be expected, his court was trying to outshine all others, but Richard's warlike uncles felt that he was spending too much time on finery instead of pursuing the war with France. Richard preferred a truce with France and a second marriage to a young French child-wife. The man who deposed Richard II, Henry Duke of Lancaster, is credited with having brought the jacket to England. According to Froissart, quoted by Planché, Henry returned to London in a *court jacques* of cloth of gold '*à la fachon D'Almayne*'. The *court jacques* was a very short garment which in English became the 'little jack', and was probably an adaption of the cote to hip-level.[20]

Fantasy ran riot in the area of men's hats. Whereas ever since Roman times Europeans had been content with hoods, by 1400 there was more variety. First, probably originally inspired by a joke, the hood was worn the wrong way

round, with the face hole around the head, and the hood and its liripipe wrapped around somewhat like a turban crossed with a cock's comb. The next step was to turn this into a permanent assemblage, consisting of a padded roll with the ends of the old hood hanging over one side, which was termed a 'capuchon'. Hats proper now became acceptable in the west, for they already existed in the Byzantine Empire, and peasants had their straw hats for hot weather, but only now did European aristocracy begin to take them up. A functional style can have been around for hundreds of years before high society makes it fashionable. Tall hats, fur hats, felt hats, wool hats, now proliferated, and became a permanent feature of the fashionable man's wardrobe. Indeed they became a mark of distinction, increasing the height, adding an air of dignity, and becoming a symbol of social superiority. This vogue for hats could have sprung from a desire for fun after the high mortalities of the previous century, while the truce between England and France gave leisure for relaxation, until Henry V renewed the English

9 Jean de Wavrin, *Les Chroniques d'Angleterre*, 1470, The Wedding of Edward II to Isabelle of France. The event of 1308 depicted in the style of 1470. Ermine was restricted to royalty, and long gowns were worn on formal occasions, but exposure was still common, as can be seen by the boy's tunic. Everybody is wearing long piked hose and pattens, despite attempts to ban such excess. The musicians are in mi-parti tabards with livery badges. Hats have settled down into simple shapes in fur or felt.

claim to the French throne. The argument had begun when the French concocted a law denying any woman the throne, directly affecting the claim of Edward III's mother, a French princess who would have been in line for the throne in her own right. The code of chivalry required a son to right a mother's wrongs. The martial tone of Henry V's reign can be seen in the new fashion for very short hair. The curls of Richard II's court were replaced by the pudding-basin cut, shaved right up the back of the neck. No doubt it had a practical origin, for short hair is easier to wear under a helmet than long, which would have had to be tied out of the way.

Despite Henry's victories, the lead in men's

10 Joos van Wassenhove, *Music* (detail) *c.* 1476. The lower orders were banned from wearing extremely short tunics but the aristocrat could do as he pleased. This noble youth shows his rank by the brocade tunic lined with fur. The open sleeve seam is the latest style in Italy, allowing the shirt sleeve to protrude. Hair continues to lengthen, and tunics grow even shorter.

was the build-up of the sleevehead to produce the effect of massive shoulders. This was another aspect of that celebration of the male body which was the principal theme of late medieval menswear. The big shoulders could be balanced by long skirts on the houpelande, but the style was less attractive on very short tunics and jackets, for the result was bulk atop two thin legs, which verged on the ridiculous. One thing the men of the day did not worry about was that their garments were shrinking even higher up the leg. Over the years 1420–40 the hemlines of tunics reached the top of the thigh, and the occasional glimpse of the male sexual organs that had caused such an outcry in the fourteenth century, was now replaced by the permanent exposure of that zone.

The next step was sensational, and the look came directly from farmworkers and building labourers. In summer they often removed their tunics and worked in their underwear: the waist-long doublet, and the hose laced to it. In a heat-wave they went even further down to the last level, the shirt and breeches, particularly when harvesting. The increasing trend of exposing the male form took over this working class tradition, discarded tunics and houpelandes and sent young men outdoors in their underwear. The big difference was that these were young men of good family, not workers. For the lower orders to work in their underwear was just another sign of their vulgar ways. For the aristocrat to do the same was astonishing, and it goes without saying that priests and the senior generation condemned this naked look most strongly. It seemed naked because the hose stretched all the way up to the waist with nothing to hide the bulge. The cod-piece or purse had to be invented to fill up that gap between the hose in front, through which the breeches gaped. It is usually suggested that this naked look was the result of the Renaissance period's discovery of the classical nude, particularly the male nude, which was seen as symbolizing the heroic, but this is too simplistic; the trend of exposing the male started back in the Gothic period. The Renaissance may have made possible the last step, the wearing of underwear in the street, but it did not initiate the movement.

The conversion of underwear into outerwear has happened since then, and the translation of a functional form into high fashion is a regular feature of the art. The look became skin-tight and this affected the clothes underneath. The bulky shirt and breeches had to be slimmed down considerably, and the breeches were trans-

fashion passed to the court of Burgundy, which was striving to make itself a power in Europe. Fanciful styles were abandoned and the Burgundian look was more brutal and severe by comparison. Elaborate decorations were replaced by plain velvets and wools, and patterned brocades were not superimposed with more ornamentation. Trailing hemlines were raised to the ankle, belts became plain, baldrics were banished, and the look sobered up considerably. Deep pleats were now applied to tunic and houpelande alike and this was part of the sharp character of Burgundian style, which was very geometric in outline. The most obvious feature of the look

11 Froissart presents his Chronicle to Richard II. The enormous shoulders introduced by the court of Burgundy in the 1440s dominate in northern Europe, but when worn with very short tunics the effect could be comic, as shown by the man in the background. Long gowns accord with the dignity of rank and age, but the young men's tunics are now so short nothing is left to the imagination.

formed into tiny briefs. Indeed some of the hose in Italian paintings look so streamlined that it seems as if the man is not wearing any briefs at all.[21] The idea of *mi-parti* was revived when the hose were made with either leg a different colour as they had been back in 1340, but in 1450 the idea seemed new. By the end of the century it looked as if even the shirt might become an outer garment, for it had begun to seep through the doublet. The doublet sleeve seam was left open at intervals for the sleeve of the shirt to be pulled through, and the shirt also peeped out of the front opening, but it was restrained and not allowed that final leap into complete daylight. The generation gap was even more obvious than it had been back in 1400, for the skin-tight naked look required slender figures to wear it and it did not suit the middle-aged man who had lost his waistline. Perfection of physical proportion was essential; the line was too lean to allow any padding to help a man's deficiencies. It was the celebration of the male body but in an ideal form which all men did not possess. This is a common failing of fashion – to concentrate on a particular type as the perfect look for that age, and exile all those not cast in that special form. The main theme of both the fourteenth and the fifteenth centuries was that a man should be slim, whether he was a knight or a Renaissance statue.

13 Francesco Colonna, *Hypnerotomachia Poliphili*, 1499. Italy, with the help of Greek refugees, took the lead in rediscovering classical art such as Roman armour, columns and architraves. Going about in one's underwear was thought to be a way of looking like a classical statue, but by the end of the century it was felt that things had gone too far, so long gowns gained a new importance.

12 Franco-Burgundian Tapestry, *Peasants hunting Rabbits with Ferrets, c.* 1465. Working in the underwear was a tradition among peasants in warm weather. The men in the foreground are properly dressed in their tunics, but the man on the right and the man in the centre back have both removed their tunics to expose their underwear of doublet and hose, and shirt beneath. The way the hose were laced to the doublet can be clearly seen on the right, and this undress became high fashion from the 1460s with young courtiers daring to appear without tunics in their underwear of doublet and hose only. The peasants' heavy-soled boots will be noted, so very different from the impractical pikes worn by the fashionable.

Chapter Two

Renaissance Man

Fashion follows power. Italy was the leader in art during the Renaissance, but political and economic power was passing to the north of the Alps. The discovery by the Portuguese of a direct sea route to Asia round Africa, which the Dutch and English exploited, cut out all the Mediterranean middlemen. Those spices, jewels and gold which hitherto had been subject to custom charges all the way across the Near East to Venice and thence into Europe, could now be shipped the entire distance without encountering a single customs post. Those ports with ease of access to the Atlantic, like Antwerp and London, were to reap the profits, and this had an impact on menswear. The naked look was all very well in Italian summers, but the weather was less reliable in England, Flanders and Germany, so that gowns often had to be worn on top. The North was going to create a covered-up line. Competition between kings over land now spread to territories abroad, as the English, Dutch, French and Spanish fought to see who would control the Atlantic routes.

A military event could spark off a fashion for men, and the style of a victor was often swiftly taken up by everyone with an interest in that victory. The Swiss defeated attempts by larger countries to end their independence, and as their soldiers' clothes got slashed in the battle, this was taken up by their compatriots as a symbol of national pride. The Swiss gained a reputation for military prowess and accordingly were in demand as mercenaries in France, Germany and Italy, so they took their 'slashed' look with them. It appealed to the Germans above all, who went to extremes, slashing everything that could be slashed: hats, shoes, doublets, sleeves, hose, to such an extent that it became a national characteristic of the Swiss–German region. Other nations copied it, but in a less extravagant manner. The cheerful abandon of this Germanic style was perhaps a celebration of the new political importance of that area, for by dynastic marriages the Hapsburgs of Austria, the rulers of the Holy Roman Empire, were gaining Flanders, Burgundy, and Spain to create the biggest empire seen in Europe since Roman times. Accordingly, what happened at the Hapsburg

14 Moretto da Brescia, *Portrait of a Gentleman*, 1526. This Italian displays the strong influence now coming from the North, where a more covered-up look developed, although oddly enough this did not apply to codpieces. The black gown, brown suit and russet hose accord with the concept of restraint for gentlemen. The elaboration of the upper hose creates the first type of kneebreeches, while the frill on the collar is a forecast of the ruff. As hair was long knights wore hairnets and turbans to tuck it out of the way.

court influenced other courts. One German style which was to have an enormous impact was the frilling of the shirt collar, gathering it at the top, the first hint of which appeared in the 1490s. It was from this little frill that the fashion for ruffs was to develop. Men's hair had grown very long by the turn of the century, for when their sexual organs were on show no one need worry about long hair looking feminine. The Germans took the lead in cutting it all off, and from 1510 the square-cut look came to the fore, with a straight fringe and the hair cut straight on a level with the chin. The Emperor Maximilian I adopted it and that was the signal for the rest of European monarchs to keep up with the Hapsburgs. The 'square' look began to spread.

Gowns became wider, sleeves bigger, and shoes square in the toe. It was certainly a masculine look, only more so, for it made males much broader and bulkier than most of them could be by natural means. The cote made a comeback, but in a very different form, without buttons. It was cut wide at the front, displaying the shirt and subsequently a stomacher, and it gained deeply pleated skirts, an echo of the pleating of the early 1400s. Such skirts skimmed the knee, so a general cover-up was in process, but strangely enough the one area which was not concealed by these skirts was the codpiece. In fact it was padded and made even more obvious than before. All the rest of the torso was concealed beneath swinging gowns and skirts.

The Italians were curious to learn just what was going on among these northern nations, and the reports by Venetian ambassadors are particularly useful. Francesco Capello visited England in 1500 and his secretary reported about these islanders:

I have understood from persons acquainted with these countries that the Scotch are much handsomer, and the English great lovers of themselves and of everything belonging to them; they think there are no other men than themselves, and no other world but England; and whenever they see a handsome foreigner they say that 'he looks like an Englishman', and that 'it is a great pity he should not be an Englishman'.

He was highly critical of the English custom, barbaric to his eyes, of sending children at the tender age of seven to take up apprenticeships in trade, while aristocrats still sent their sons to serve in great houses.[1] Andrea Badoier was Venetian ambassador in 1512. He travelled simply in an English doublet to avoid attention, but when he reached England came up against the problem that when he wanted a new ward-robe England was the country of wool. Silk had to be imported from Lucca, Genoa or Florence, so the ambassador was obliged to have his official gown made in frieze wool which he knew he could not wear back in Venice because it would look too English. The arrogance of the English was put down to their not being used to foreigners, but their insularity did not stop them from following foreign fashions. Unfortunately foreign visitors could not agree as to whom the English copied most. The Greek Nicander Nucius of Corcyra said English dress was French, Girolamo Cardano said their clothes were Italian.[2] It all depended on the visitor's sophistication and breadth of experience. In the opinion of ambassador Sebastiano Giustiniani in 1515 the dress was French and Swiss, which was a good observation, for the Germano–Swiss styles had to reach England through France.

He found a dynasty only 30 years old, and a king who succeeded in 1509 and was very aware that the Tudors were parvenus in the royal world. Henry VIII was determined to dazzle Europe into forgetting this inferior status, and like the *arriviste* that he was, became the showiest king in the West. Giustiniani was impressed:

His Majesty is the handsomest potentate I ever set eyes on; above the usual height, with an extremely fine calf to his leg, his complexion very fair and bright, with auburn hair combed straight and short in the French fashion, and a round face so very beautiful that it would become a pretty woman, his throat is rather long and thick. He was born on the 28th of June 1491, so he will enter his twenty-fifth year the month after next.

On St George's Day April 1515 Giustiniani waited on the King at Richmond Palace. Henry VIII was standing under the most expensive canopy the ambassador had ever seen. It was cloth of gold embroidered in Florence, nor was his attire less striking:

He wore a cap of crimson velvet in the French fashion, and the brim was looped up all round with lacets, which had gold enamelled tags. His doublet was in the Swiss fashion, striped alternately with white and crimson satin, and his hose were scarlet, and all slashed from the knee upwards.

Over this fashionable suit the King was wearing his Garter robe of purple velvet lined with white satin, and a gold collar with a diamond the size of a walnut from which depended an enormous pearl.

15 Hans Holbein, *Henry VIII with his father Henry VII*, 1536–7. North of the Alps the square look dominates, a revival of the Burgundian look of the century before, with the gown as wide as it is long. The King wears the coat now revived in a frock version with deep skirts and no buttons. The front is cut away to display a stomacher decorated with puffs of shirt and jewels. Although Henry VIII brought the Reformation to England, he did not tone down his clothes. The square effect also applied to shoes after two centuries of pikes.

At the end of his embassy in 1519 Giustiniani was still impressed, for he reported to the Venetian senate that Henry VIII was the most handsome sovereign in Christendom, and much handsomer than François I of France, but that as Henry had heard that François had a beard, he had grown one too, which looked gold because his hair was reddish. The King was also a sportsman: 'He is extremely fond of tennis, at which game it is the prettiest thing in the world to see him play, his fair skin glowing through a shirt of the finest texture.'[3] To the sunburnt Italian the possession of a pure white skin was the epitome of noble blood. Peasants were tanned brown, so the upper classes were at pains to ensure that they looked white. This was less easy for the olive-toned Europeans to achieve, so they envied the northerners who could remain white without much trouble.

Henry VIII launched himself with splendour in 1509 when he succeeded to the throne at 18. The Christmas joust at Richmond Palace was followed by a masquerade where Henry appeared as a Turk in a long robe powdered with gold, a crimson velvet hat turbaned with gold cloth, and a rich scimitar hanging from a baldric. The Earl of Wiltshire and Lord Fitzwater came as Russians in long gowns of yellow satin decked with white and crimson satin, and big hats of grey fur. Admiral Sir Edward Howard and Sir Thomas Parr dressed as Prussians in low-necked doublets of crimson velvet laced down the front with silver chains, short cloaks of crimson satin, and hats with pheasant feathers. Their torch-bearers were in crimson and green satin with blackened faces representing Moors. The musicians were in white damask with green hats and hose, and the torchbearers in blue damask. Next Henry VIII and his guests changed into short suits of blue and crimson velvet which had long sleeves slashed and lined with cloth of gold. The bodices were embroidered with castles and sheafs of arrows, and their bonnets were in damask embroidered with gold and silver and topped with plumes.[4]

The youthful King enjoyed dressing up, and played a trick on his minister Cardinal Wolsey, Archbishop of York, by arriving by barge at his house with companions dressed like shepherds in highly unrustic cloth of gold and paned crimson satin with matching caps. The King and his companions were disguised by whole vizards and by hair and beards of fine goldwire silk or black silk. The 16 torchbearers were also in crimson satin to match. The King pretended to be a foreign ambassador, and the Cardinal was taken in until the mask was removed. Wolsey invited the King to dine, but the latter replied that he would change first, so he must have brought his ordinary clothes with him.[5]

The royal jousts were as rich as any which took place in the Middle Ages. In 1510 Henry Guylford attended the joust in russet cloth of gold and cloth of silver, with his mount in russet and white satin. The Marquess of Dorset and Sir Thomas Bulleyn came as pilgrims, in tabards of black velvet covered with gold scallop shells, and their horses in the same. Their servants were dressed in black satin with gold shells on the chest. Henry of Buckingham and his charger were attired in cloth of silver embroidered with a device with a posy of crimson damask, and golden arrows, bordered with roses, and topped by a silver pomegranate tree. Jousts across the Channel were equally fine, and in 1515 the Dauphin invited the leading European knights to a tourney in Paris. He himself and his suite wore a different outfit each day. On the opening day it was cloth of gold and silver, the second day crimson and yellow velvet, lastly green and white velvet and satin with embroidery and gold work. The Duke de Bourbon and his suite were all in tawny velvet and cloth-of-silver. The Count de Sainte Polle and his team were in purple velvet cut over purple satin. The Infante of Aragon appeared in cloth of gold and silver, and the Duke de Vendôme was in cloth of gold and plucket velvet. The English knights all wore the cross of St George on their outfits.

Henry VIII's chance to outshine the Emperor Maximilian himself came in 1514, and he put his whole court into gold. All the noblemen were in tissue of cloth of gold decorated with gold, with gold baldric chains, and golden bells on the horses. The Duke of Buckingham and his mount were both in purple satin decorated with pure gold antelopes and swans, with spangles and little golden bells. The king wore gilded armour and a surcoat of pearls and jewels. His nine henchmen were in embroidered white and crimson gold cloth, and their horses had long gold bells and gold tassels. In the event the weather was foul and the finery got soaked. Moreover the empress had just died, and Maximilian and his entire court were all in mourning black, so that Henry's golden extravagance looked out of place.

Henry VIII's younger sister Mary Rose had been married to the old King of France, much against her will. In 1515 Louis XII died and the now Queen Dowager of France wanted to come home, so Henry sent Charles Brandon, Duke of Suffolk, to fetch her, the very man she had wanted to marry in the first place. A marriage took place at once, just in case Henry should change his mind, and then Mary Rose came home. Henry VIII laid on an entertainment at Shooter's Hill where the royal company encountered Robin Hood and his Merry Men (actually the royal archers, all attired in green), who showed the new duchess the pleasures of the outlaw's life. In the afternoon there was a joust which continued the rustic theme, for the Duke

of Suffolk and his side were all in green velvet and cloth of gold, as were the Marquess of Dorset and the Earl of Essex. Their aides wore the same colours but in silk.

In 1516 Henry's other sister, Margaret, Queen of Scotland, paid him a visit, so he arranged special jousts on 19 and 20 May to honour the present and the former queen. The King, Suffolk and Essex all wore black velvet decorated with branches of honeysuckle in flat gold damask with leaves that actually moved. Dorset, Surrey and Hastings all had frocks of blue velvet fringed with gold. The second day the king and his aides were in purple velvet decked with rose leaves in cloth of gold, with points of damask gold, and letters round the border in gold bullion. His suite consisted of 5 lords and 14 knights in yellow velvet frocks bordered with cloth of gold, and 30 gentlemen and 40 officers in yellow satin edged with cloth of gold. The counterparty were all in white satin traversed with cloth of gold. (The term frock refers to frock coat, the new version with the pleated skirts to the knee.)

One of the most famous examples of court competition for glory came in 1520 at the Field of the Cloth of Gold, when Henry VIII met François I of France (whose beard he had copied). The first day saw Henry in a gown of thickly pleated cloth of silver ribbed with gold, and a doublet of rose velvet. His cap was black velvet encircled with rubies, emeralds and pearls with a white plume. His horse had tissue of cloth of gold over russet velvet, with the gold cut into waves edged with gold to signify the English lordship of the sea. Cardinal Wolsey was present, all in violet velvet. François I met them in a suit of cloth of silver with a cloak of satin decked with pearls and stones, and on his head a coif of damask gold spangled with diamonds. He did not mean to be outshone; nor did the French aristocracy, and it was said that they were beggaring themselves and wearing their mills, forests and meadows on their backs. Symbolism was much employed, and the horse of François I was covered in purple satin embroidered with ravens' feathers in black hatched with gold. This was a pun on the French word *corbeyn*, raven, taken to mean a heart in pain (*un cor en penne*), which was illustrated by a heart surrounded by an endless raven's feather. On Wednesday 13 June François followed this up by wearing a frock of purple satin over a gold doublet, and a gown of purple velvet embroidered with little rolls of white satin with the word *quando* on them, signifying that his heart was in endless pain when (she) ... Henry answered in a costume embroidered with mountains and basil with a legend round the border, 'Breke not these sweet herbs of the mount; doute for damage', meaning that anyone who insulted England could expect trouble. On Thursday 14 the English all turned out in *mi-parti* of white satin and blue velvet, with the blue embroidered with a woman's hand holding a man's burning heart and cooling it with a watering can. François continued his theme of love with a cloak covered with little satin books containing the words *a me*, and with a chain embroidered around the hem. This meant, 'Liberate me from the chains of love.' On Friday 15 June, Henry shone in a *mi-parti* of cloth of gold tissue and cloth of silver, bordered with gold letters in knots, and cyphers in gold and pearls with the device 'God my friend my realm I may'. In the jousts Henry defeated the French champion, and he gave François a sword which that king could hardly lift but which Henry could swing with ease. Henry even challenged François to a personal wrestling match, but being less portly than Henry, François managed to floor him. The difference between the two was clear in their devices, with the French king's stressing love in a diplomatic manner, while Henry's threatened. The wearing of gold, silver, satin and velvet, with jewels and pearls in quantity, continued at the dances and the feasts of this international conference. The Duke of Norfolk put all his suite in crimson satin patterned with golden flames. On the way back to Calais Henry VIII said that as his noblemen had spent so much on their clothes and attendants, they could send half their servants home in advance to save expense, but the lords protested. To suggest that they could not afford such fantastic expenditure stung their pride, even though many of them got into debt over the royal jamboree.[6] The Venetian ambassador to France in 1537, Francisco Giustiniani, estimated that the French crown spent 30,000 *livres* on clothes and furnishings a year.[7]

All this lavish expenditure by the English and French courts benefited the Italian silk industry considerably. France imported as much silk as the Turkish empire and the Levant, but in 1546 ambassador Marino Cavalli reported to Venice that the French Queen Regent was trying to stop this by planting mulberry trees in France, and opening silk mills at Tours, with the help of Venetian, Luccese and Genoese experts. A change of monarch in England did not reduce court finery. When Etienne Perlin visited the court of Mary I in 1558 he found 'gentlemen

16 Bernardino Licinio, *Ottaviano Grimani*, aged 24, 1541. The Procurator of Saint Mark's, Venice, wears the Swiss fashion of slashing which swept all over Europe. The doublet had crossed over from underwear into outer wear, and here forms part of a leather suit with fur on the inside. The Italians preferred a sloping shoulderline to the northern square one. The breeches are in *mi-parti*, with even the codpiece in two tones. No wonder Luther and Calvin said the Catholic Church lacked morality and modesty.

dressed in all kinds of velvets, some in black, others in white, others in violet, others in scarlet, some in satin, others in taffeta, others in damask, of all colours, with a tremendous number of gold buttons'.[8] The size of a courtier's wardrobe in Paris was described by ambassador Lippomano in 1577, who said a wardrobe of 25 to 30 costumes was necessary to be esteemed rich, and a different outfit had to be worn every day. Such changes involved them in considerable sums, especially the young with their fondness for new fashions in wool, silk or cloth of gold.[9] Ambassador Cavalli observed that François I still liked devices on his clothes towards the end of his life, writing that the king liked 'a little research' on his clothes, which were braided and decked with rich stones and ornaments. Even his doublets were worked in tissue of gold, through which the shirt in finest linen appeared through the centre front.[10]

All this magnificence was still reserved for the court by law. Henry VIII repealed existing statutes but issued his own in 1510. Cloth of gold, of silk and purple were for the royal family. Only dukes and above could have tissue of cloth of gold, only earls and above could wear sables, and no one below the rank of baron could wear gold, silver, satin, silk or mixed cloth, although as cloth of gold cost £4 a yard upwards it was beyond most people's means. The fine for wearing imported cloth remained at £10 as in 1482. Crimson and blue velvet were for the Order of the Garter and its superiors, fine 40 shillings and loss of the garment if found on lesser mortals. Only mayors and officials were entitled to velvet gowns and marten's fur, fine 40s. and confiscation. Unlike its predecessors, this law tried to limit the *amounts* of cloth used in garments. Only four yards of broadcloth was allowed in a gown, and three yards in a riding gown, although the clergy, graduates and lawyers were excepted. Serving men could only have $2\frac{1}{2}$ yards of cloth, and no hose over 20d. unless their employer gave them better. Labourers were not to spend more than 2s. a yard on broadcloth, and 10d. on hose. The act was given extra clauses in 1515 ruling that the sons and heirs of barons might be promoted to doublets in tinsel, crimson and black velvet, and gowns and jackets of black damask or camlet cloth in russet or tawny. Officers of the royal household were allowed damask and satin. Another act appeared in 1553, which declared that dukes and marquesses might have tissue of cloth of gold at £5 a yard. The act also covered the Irish in Galway who were instructed to shave off their moustaches, and to give up uncivilized mantles in favour of English cloaks, gowns, doublets and hose. Their shirts were limited to 5 ells of linen. It was reported that the Irish were happy to obey, for the English style did offer better coverage of the body. While most English civic authorities were content to leave it to the central government to make sumptuary laws, in 1532 the city of Coventry issued one of its own insisting that common folk were not to wear fox or lamb fur, and no fine worsted, silk or satin in their doublets and jackets on pain of a fine of £10. This suggests that some citizens had been dressing above their station.

By 1577 there seemed to be such variety in menswear that ambassador Lippomano was perplexed how to describe it. The French aristocracy wore a short habit, for its profession was arms, but it was so varied in colour and form that it was impossible to give a model of it. Sometimes, he explained, they sported very wide hats which overhung the shoulders, and sometimes a tiny beret which hardly covered the top

17 After Holbein, *Prince Edward, later Edward VI, c.* 1542. In the 1540s the width of the square look begins to modify towards more natural dimensions. The Prince has the very short hair-style the Germans introduced, and the simplicity of his clothes shows the modesty that the Protestant Church considered so important, although his hat is as bejewelled as his father's was.

of the head. There were cloaks which descended to the heel or capes and hooded cloaks which scarcely reached the loins. Their boots in the Greek style or in the fashion of Savoy were so big and high that they reached to mid-leg, or else so narrow and so short they resembled tubes. The hose were joined to the breeches which were so tight they faithfully portrayed the natural form beneath. The collars of the shirts, trimmed with lace, were so big they were like ships' sails and over a *quarta* wide. They were either plain at the back or else carefully worked. Novelties in dress succeeded each other day by day, and hour by hour. If the form of their clothes varied, the manner of wearing them was no less bizarre, Lippomano continued. They always had the cloak covering one shoulder and hanging from the other, one sleeve of the doublet wide open and the other buttoned up. On horseback they had sword in hand and rode through the town as if they were pursuing an enemy in the manner of Polish cavalry. The older generation wore more modest attire in silk or fine wool, and donned a long cloak and hat when going out. The tiny beret was only the fashion at court; outside one would find only ten people in a thousand sporting it, because the country was very exposed to winds.[11]

By this date the lead in fashion had passed from the Swiss–German region to Spain because the Emperor Charles V retired there, and divided his vast realm: Spain, Flanders, and the Americas to his son Philip, the Austrian lands to his own brother. Spain was a new creation, formed only when the Moors were expelled and Aragon married Castile, but the discovery of the gold mines of Mexico and Peru gave the new kingdom enormous economic power. This, of course, affected the seat of high fashion. The very covered look of the North was not necessary in Spanish sunshine, so the voluminous gown was discarded in favour of capes worn with doublet and breeches. The skirted frock coats were discarded too and the male silhouette was revealed again. The breeches evolved out of the elaborate slashing of the hose, for a more robust fabric was needed to support the slashes, so that wool or satin were used to construct trunk-hose, the shortest form of padded breeches. Breeches which reached the knee were termed 'canions' (Spanish breeches like the tube of a cannon), and those over the knee long Venetians. Even so, all this creation of breeches did not conceal one vital spot. After two hundred years of being flaunted and padded, the decade of the 1550s saw the codpiece vertical. Spanish pride was boasting of its achievements and its conquests of new worlds, and what could illustrate this better than a phallic exhibition padded into permanent erection? Just as victorious troops would rape the women of a conquered city, the codpiece vertical raped the world. In the 1550s the Spanish male felt triumphant, and to display that and to receive his reward, like generations of men before and since, he turned to sex. Success means prowess.

Strangely enough, however, the Spanish-Hapsburg court which promoted this arrogant look was the very court to bring about its demise. Having reached this extreme upright position in codpieces, the only way to go next was back down again. There was one style above all which was recognized as being particularly Spanish and that was the wide farthingale for women which had existed in Castile and Aragon in the previous century. To emphasize Spanish identity this farthingale was brought back in the sixteenth century, which affected menswear, for when women became very wide the men had to

18 François Clouet, *Charles IX of France*, 1561. The evolution of the collar frill into a ruff is very clear in this portrait. However, the concept of modesty did not appeal to the French court and the King's doublet is richly embroidered with bullion thread and lined with white fur. Very small hats were popular at the French court but not outside, as they blew off.

follow suit to keep in proportion. The new fashion was for width, and that meant for both sexes. A complete reversal took place, from the broad shoulders of the 1520s, down to the wide hips of the 1560s, and since hips are a feminine characteristic there was some muttering among the moralists that men were growing feminine. It was this development which literally swallowed up the codpiece, for as breeches grew wider with ever more padding, the codpiece disappeared into the bulk. The Spanish court was aware of two important women at this date: Catherine de' Medici, the determined Queen Mother in France; and public enemy number one as far as the Spanish were concerned, Elizabeth I of England and her sailors. Accordingly Spanish foreign policy had to take into account the character of both women more than had been necessary before when all rulers had been male. For menswear to become more feminine at this stage was a salute to this difficulty, acknowledging that here were two queens who had to be treated as honorary men because they were heads of state, so perhaps it was a courtesy to them for menswear to adopt certain female characteristics.

The other most significant Spanish contribution to menswear concerned collars. The low-necked German–Swiss look was replaced by the Spanish taking a doublet right up to the neck. This obliged the wearer to hold his head up high and this was precisely what the Spanish were doing in the world. This affected shirts also, for they had to rise at the neck, and so the frilled edge of German origin was now peeping out at the top. The ruff was born, starting as a tiny frill in the 1540s and growing wider and ever wider as it progressed towards the millstone ruffs of the 1580s. Fashion had found a brand new idea, so it exploited it to the full. In time wire supports termed pickadillies became necessary, and one Englishman was to make his fortune from them by becoming royal pickadilly supplier: Robert Baker. The house he built about 1612 on open fields north of Charing Cross was dubbed by the locals Pickadilly Hall and so gave its name to a London street.[12] This development coincided with the introduction of lace. Catherine de' Medici brought it to France from Italy in 1533. Lacemaking was set up in France and Flanders, until Spanish religious persecution drove the Flemish lacemakers to England. The first laces were cut-work, with a pattern cut from the linen, and needlepoint-work, which teased the edge of the fabric into a design. A very expensive business due to the long hours involved in producing a piece of lace, fine lace was to be another monopoly of the upper classes. It was used to edge collars and ruffs, and the wrist frill was designed as another platform for it. The elegant wrist frill was to continue in menswear right into the nineteenth century, as an instant distinguishing mark between a gentleman and a labourer.

Trousers had begun to resurface. Worn by the Celts in antiquity and retained in the East, in the fifteenth century very tight pantaloons, like tights without feet, were being worn by European peasants. By the 1580s English, Dutch and Belgian seamen were wearing wide trousers which could be rolled up when wading ashore. Trousers became the mark of the sailor, for they

19 Sanchez Coello, *Infante Don Carlos*, 1564. The vertical codpiece and the high collar were both symbols of Spanish arrogance and pride. The nation raped South America, so perhaps it was felt that a permanent erection behoved the Spanish male as an invincible hero, until England's Virgin Queen dented that image. Short cloaks and capes were another Spanish contribution to fashion now that Spain was a dominant nation.

protected the legs when sliding down ropes in the rigging. Even so, it took high fashion over two hundred years to grant them sophisticated approval, when the French Revolution made working-class dress the rage. Up till then the mark of the gentleman was that he did not wear trousers, which were a working garment unworthy of his attention. A gentleman, by definition, was not involved in manual labour.

The vogue for padding men's chests seen in the 1360s took on new life in the 1570s and 80s. The doublet was built up in front to give a more robust and solid look, but it was taken to an extreme until the belly overhung the belt. Dubbed the 'peascod belly', this line suited the drinkers, but it was condemned by Philip Stubbes in his *The Anatomie of Abuses* in 1583. He declared that it was not handsome, the padding was as much as 5lb in weight, and the extension was bombasted, quilted, and bedecked with slashes, pricking and cuts. It was a monstrous creation, Stubbes asserted, and delivered a diatribe declaring that pride in dress was an offence against God. The nobility could wear rich attire but reverence was due to virtue, not clothes. Magistrates might dress well, as they represented the law, but it was illegal for private subjects to wear sumptuous raiment. One could tell a gentleman by his virtue, not by silks, satins, velvets, gold or silver, but Stubbes complained there was now such a 'mingle-mangle' that one could not distinguish the aristocrat from the gentleman or officer. Like ambassador Lippomano in Paris, he felt that there was a superfluity of fashions and apparel, so many different styles, so many different hats in silk, velvet, taffeta, and felt, with feathers or bejewelled hatbands. The ruffs were monstrous, great millstones of cambric, holland or lawn, which flapped in the wind, and had to be supported by pickadillys. The fine shirts in cambric or lawn, often decorated with needlework and costing 10s., 20s., or even an incredible £5 or £10, were a disgrace. Such soft clothes on their lily-white bodies made men weak, he asserted, whereas our rugged ancestors in meaner apparel were stronger men. They were happy with frieze coats and hose of the colour of the sheep. He protested that instead of good old woollen stockings the town fops were now sporting silk hose. There were some coats with collars and some without, some fitted, others loose, some buttoned down the front, others under the arm, and some down the back. Cloaks came in far too many colours, for they were white, red, black, green, yellow and purple, or violet, in cloth, velvet, or taffeta,

laced with gold or silver lace. Even the swords and daggers were damasked or gilt.[13]

Stubbes' criticisms reflect the century's discussion on what the ideal man should be like. Old ideas were challenged by Renaissance scholars, and the idea of chivalry came under attack. Petrarch declared that jousts were stupid and wasteful, and Sacchetti claimed that chivalry was only for those who were too stupid to appreciate the finer arts. G. B. Nenna said in his *Nennio, or a Treatise of Nobility* in 1528, that 'while nobility might come through blood or riches, or through virtue, of these virtue is the ornament of the soul and true nobility is of the mind. Do not fall into the common error of thinking that fine clothes make a man, for wise Diogenes went barefoot in a patched cloak.'[14] The aristocratic response came from Count Baldassare Castiglione, whose *The Boke of the Courtyer*, 1528, was to be very influential. He conceded that the nobility ought to be more educated and take a greater interest in the arts, but he said that the ideals of chivalry and knighthood should be combined with scholarship to create an all-rounded man of standing. Where appearance was concerned, he thought colour suitable only for tourneys, masques and theatricals. A gentleman should dress either in black, or in the sombre tones of Spanish taste, for to dress in sundry colours with laces and fringes was to look like a jester. Declaring that 'the garment judgeth the mind', he said clothes for a gentleman should be of modest precision, handsome and clean. The saying, 'The habit maketh not the monk' is a valid one, so the courtier should 'determine with himselfe, what he will appeare to be, and in such sorte as he desireth to be esteemed so to apparaile himselfe, and make his garmentes helpe him to be counted such a one'. The gentleman should have a certain gravity, sense of honour and dignity, good manners, be clean in his person and language, and reflect all this in his clothes.[15] The Spanish sobriety which Castiglione pointed to as the ideal has been said to be responsible for putting all the Europeans into black when the Spanish fashion became dominant, but this is untrue. Spanish taste for dark colours ranged over browns, deep greens, and dark red, and it was not until 1623 that black was made compulsory wear at the Spanish court, by which time the fashion lead had slipped to France.[16] In the event Castiglione's advice was to be followed more in the Protestant countries than in the Catholic, for the French and Italian aristocracy did not abandon their finery, and it was in the Protestant North that greater modesty

characteristics listed by Sir Thomas Elyot in his *The Boke named the Governour* of 1531. The correct accomplishments were music, poetry, law, ancient literature, dancing, archery, and hunting, to which the gentleman should add industry, circumspection and modesty.[19] In his *The Scholemaster* of 1570, Roger Ascham stated that young gentlemen should study Castiglione's *The Booke of the Courtyer* as the best book on manners, but that was the only Italian influence he would allow. In fact he denounced Englishmen who studied Italian culture as a whole, declaring that the country was not Christian with its corrupt church, commonplace adultery the norm and sin occurring on all sides. Ascham listed the correct accomplishments for the courtly gentleman: 'To ride cumlie; to run faire at the tilte or ring: to plaie at all weapons: to

20 Hans Eworth, *The diplomat Anthony Browne, Viscount Montague*, 1569. In the north fur-lined gowns lingered on, and the square silhouette lasted into the 1570s. While the Viscount's doublet is outlined in gold thread, the dark colour and the absence of jewels in his hat reflect the impact of Protestant sobriety.

was slowly instituted. Dr Martin Luther stated that the good Protestant should have as his daily bread 'every thing that belongeth to the want and supply of our life, that is meat, drink, clothes, dwelling, gardens, lands, flocks, money, wealth, happy marriage, virtuous children, faithful servants, upright and just magistrates, peaceful government, wholesome air, quietness, health, modesty, honour, true friends, faithful neighbours'.[17] The concept of modesty was stressed by Calvin in his *The Institutes of the Christian Religion*, 1535. Arguing that nobody who was a Christian could lack a special love for righteousness, he emphasized that the Protestant had to be pure in view of the direct relationship with God. Accordingly self-denial was important, for one should shun worldly lusts and trifles. Sobriety, justice, piety and humility were the path of the reformed church,[18] therefore their clothes had to be sober, pious and humble.

The concept of modesty for gentlemen had reached England already, for it was one of the

21 R. Lockey (attrib.), *James VI of Scotland*, 1574. The feminine silhouette with wide hips comes to the fore, at a time when both England and Scotland were ruled by queens. The expansion of the padded hips was to end the display of the male genitals after 200 years. The kneebreeches have entered the wardrobe on a permanent basis.

shoote faire in bow, or surelie in gon: to vaut lustely: to runne: to leape: to wrestle: to swimme: to daunce cumlie: to sing and playe of instrumentes cunnyngly: to hawke, to hunt, to play at tennes.' He was disgusted that some of the nobility 'count it their shame to be counted learned; and perchance, they count it their shame to be counted honest also, for I heare saie, they medle as little with the one as with the other'. Ascham challenged noble youths to equal the attainments of his most famous pupil, Elizabeth I, who was skilled in Latin, Greek, Italian, French and Spanish. Yet he did not hesitate to blame the court for all the monstrosities of fashion:

'If three or foure greate ones at Courte, will nedes outrage in apparell, in huge hose, in monstrous hattes, in gaurishe colers, let the Prince Proclame, make Lawes, order, punishe, commaunde everie gate in London dailie to be watched, let all good men beside do everie where they can, surelie the misorder of apparell in mean men abrode, shall never be amended except the greatest in Courte will order and amend themselves first.

He recognized, however, that even when there were sumptuary laws the court did not obey them. Some bold fellows would think themselves clever for flaunting the regulations and the court would wink at them.[20]

His star pupil preferred to issue proclamations on dress rather than statutes. In 1571 Elizabeth I ordered the English to wear knitted woollen caps finished by an English capper to help the wool industry, or risk a fine of $3/4d.$ a day. Her attempts to reform dress started in 1559 when the nobility was told to check its servants to ensure they were not wearing prohibited fabrics. A book of unlawful garments was to be kept in the Counting House, and she reminded the country of her father's statutes. In 1563 she proclaimed dress needed to be reformed, and in 1576 stated that excessively long cloaks and huge ruffs were monstrous. The Queen wished 'that all persons in modest and comely sort leave off such fond, disguised and monstrous manner of attyring themselves'.[21] Of course, the Queen did not stop wearing enormous ruffs herself, for the court was allowed its excesses. It was other people who should not imitate her.

The fundamental business of clothes was something not even the century's most famous artist could escape. All men were involved in the obtaining of garments, either as gifts or to satisfy their families' requirements. While Michel-

22 Anon., *Robert Dudley, Earl of Leicester, c.* 1575. Englishmen wore their Queen's colours in honour of her constant virtue, so that Leicester's satin suit is white and his gown black. The codpiece begins to disappear into the expanding trunkhose, as these short breeches were termed. The collar is that of the Order of the Garter.

angelo was still in Florence in 1519 he wrote to Pietro Urbano in Pistoia that he was sending him a jerkin, a pair of hose, and a riding cloak by a man called the Turk. Michelangelo had trouble with his tailor and complained to Ser Giovan Francesco Fattuci, chaplain of Santa Maria delle Fiore in Florence, that the tailor he had recommended would not let him him try on a doublet in the shop and that now it proved to be too tight across the chest. It should have been made to fit, unless the tailor was trying to cheat him over the amount of material used! He asked Ser Giovan to sort the matter out, as he did not want to have to change his tailor when his mind was on painting and sculpture. By 1542 Michelangelo was in Rome and wondering what to give a musician in the Sistine Chapel Choir as he owed him a favour, so he inquired whether a piece of satin for a doublet would be best. It is clear that his family, the Buonarrota Simoni back in Florence, did not think he could get the

23 Anon., *Sir Philip Sidney*, *c.* 1586. The soldier poet honours his Queen with black and white. His leather doublet is pinked and spiked, and the curve in front represents the evolution of the peascod belly. The codpiece is just visible between the enormous hips, so that a man is now as wide across the hips under Queen Elizabeth as he was across the shoulders under Henry VIII.

best quality cloths in Rome, so Lionardo sent him a roll of *rascia*, the most expensive wool-silk mixed cloth made in Florence, and in 1553 Cassandra sent him eight shirts in the very best-quality linen. Michelangelo evidently shared their opinion, for there is evidence of his ordering cloth from Florence. In 1555 he wrote to Lionardo to send him a draft for money to buy 19 *palmi* of dark violet *rascia* for a dress for Urbino's wife, and again in 1556 to ask for seven *braccia* of black cloth, light and good quality, again for Signora Urbino. By April 1556 the black cloth had not reached Rome, so Michelangelo told Lionardo to question the muleteer, get him punished and make him pay for cloth, and send a replacement.[22] It was customary to send the material rather than garments, as it could be made up at the other end, but given such a big traffic in cloth it was important to be on the alert for tricks being played by the muleteers, who could sell the cloth while pretending to have been robbed.

Many hands were involved in the production

of clothes and fabrics, and John Stow included the trades in his survey of London which had:

Armourers, apothecaries, bakers, barber–surgeons, blacksmiths, bottle- and horn-makers, bowyers, brewers, bricklayers and tylers, butchers, carpenters, clerks, clothworkers, cooks and pastriers, coopers, cordwainers, courriers, cutlers, dyers, drapers, farriers, fishmongers, fletchers, founders, fruiterers, girdlers, goldsmiths, grocers, haberdashers, embroiderers, inn-keepers, joyners, ironmongers, leathermen, lorimers, masons and marblers, mercers, merchant taylors, painter–stainers, pavers, pewterers, pinners or plasterers, tallow chandlers, plumbers, poulterers, salters, scriveners, stationers, turners, vintners, upholsterers, watermen, wax chandlers, woodmongers and woolpackers.[23]

24 Anon., *Admiral Sir Francis Drake*, *c.* 1585. During the 1580s the codpiece disappeared, and the peascod belly dominated that region. All the padding involved did make a man look big and strong, but the fashion did not outlast the century. The ruff has reached millstone proportions and has to be supported by pickadillies. Although Drake was a bitter enemy of the Spanish, he does not object to wearing a short cape in the Spanish style.

There was nothing worn that was not made by hand.

London was visited by Frederick, Duke of Wirtemberg in 1592, who found that 'the inhabitants are magnificently apparelled, and are extremely proud and overbearing', as they did not care for foreigners. He approved of the court of Elizabeth I:

The lords and pages of the royal court have a stately, noble air, but dress more after the French fashion, only that they wear short cloaks, and sometimes Spanish capes, and not such broad hats as the French; they keep many retainers, for the most part portly and good-looking men who go without cloaks, but have only jerkins of their lord's colour and bearing his arms rolled up and buckled behind; they likewise have the same arms upon their sleeves, so that they may be distinguished.[24]

That the English should follow French rather than Spanish fashion at the end of the century was also advocated by Polonius in Shakespeare's *Hamlet*, Act I. sc.iii:

Costly thy habit as thy purse can buy,
But not express'd in fancy; rich, not gaudy:
For the apparel oft proclaims the man:
And they in France of the best rank and station
Are most select and generous chief in that.

This, of course, was a tragedy performed for an English audience, not a Danish one. The Dutch consul Emanuel van Meteren wrote in 1599 that the English were more changeable than the Dutch where clothes are concerned:

The English dress in elegant, light and costly garments, but they are very inconstant and desirous of novelties, changing their fashions every year, both men and women. When they go abroad riding or travelling, they don their best clothes, contrary to the practice of other nations. Their garments are usually coloured and of a light stuff, and they have not many of them, like as they have in the Low Countries since they change so easily.[25]

Even so, changing their fashion once a year was less annoying than the number of times the French changed, according to ambassador Lippomano. England was unique in being ruled by the Virgin Queen, in whose honour the court wore a special livery. This was noted in 1598 by the German lawyer Paul Hentzner who observed much wearing of black and white at Greenwich

25 Attrib. to 'H.', *Sir Walter Raleigh*, 1588. At 34 the soldier/sailor poet and historian sports his Queen's colours with an intricately slashed white satin doublet, with large pearl buttons, and a black cloak and black breeches decorated with pearls in abundance. The pearl earrings give a feminine touch which is countered by the fashion for beards to guarantee the masculinity beneath. As ruffs had grown so enormous they began to be left off in favour of collars, but their abolition took decades.

Palace.[26] In colour symbolism, black represented constancy, and white or silver virginity, so this livery honoured the queen's constant virtue. Drake, Raleigh, Leicester, Essex, Sidney, and Hatton honoured their Queen in doublets of white satin or cloth of silver, and black velvet cloaks, throughout her reign. The severity was Protestant although the pearls and decorations were courtly. If the clothes were rather feminine with their wide hips and narrow waists, masculinity was maintained by a fashion for beards, and all the finery did not prevent the wearers from defeating the Spanish Armada. Indeed, if the clothes were rather feminine to honour the sovereign lady, the man inside had to be a special example of virility, excelling in jousts, or sweeping the Spanish Main. The period saw a lot of swagger. The Spanish admired the military bravado, the English and Dutch the bold sea dog. The Renaissance man should be able to translate Italian verse like the Earl of Surrey, write *Arcadia* and die in battle like Sir Philip

Chapter Three

Effeminate and Wanton Age

King James I of England and VI of Scotland was homosexual, and this changed the character of the court considerably. The heroic days of Good Queen Bess became a golden memory, and the court was now under the influence of the posturing favourites of the King. He showered honours upon them, creating one Earl of Somerset, and another Duke of Buckingham, to the disgust of the aristocracy. John Donne in his *Satires* said that a courtier was now 'a silken painted foole . . . a many colour'd Peacock', whose fame rested on his finery:

All repute
For his devices in hansoming a sute,
To judge of lace, pinke, panes, print, cut and plight,
Of all the Court, to have the best conceit.[1]

Above all, a court which had revolved around a strong woman now saw women held in contempt by those who feared their competition. Even the Queen had to take second place to the favourites of the King who, effeminate themselves, resented the presence of women. John Aubrey observed: 'King James' Court was so far from being civill to woemen, that the Ladies, nay the Queen herself, could hardly pass by the King's Apartments without receiving some affront.' The court was now the home of 'fooles, bawds, mimicks and catamites'.[2] In his advice to young noblemen, ΗΡΩ-ΠΑΙΔΕΙΑ of 1607, James Cleland stressed that they should avoid the painted favourites' example, and not employ drugs, balms, ointments, painting and *lac virginale* to try to improve on nature, nor adopt irons, poking sticks and brushes for stroking up moustaches. He expressed a wish that there was a censor in England to force young men into moderate raiment, instead of squandering their rents and possessions on finery: 'In your garments be proper, cleanely, and honest, weareing your cloathes in a carelesse, yet comelie forme.' Even King James recommended that men should 'be neither too superfluous like a deboshed waster, nor over shabby like a miserable wretch, nor artificially trimmed like a courtisan, nor sluggishly clothed like a country clown, or over lightly like a candy soldier, or the vain young courtier'.[3]

The age was aware of a great loss, the glories of the Elizabethan period now replaced by James I's pacifism, which to the old heroes looked like cowardice. This can be seen in the turn-of-the-century vogue for the melancholy man. He began as a sad lover aware that his mistress Queen Elizabeth had to die, as in the portait of John Donne *c.* 1595 which bears the legend *Illumina tenebras nostras domina*: 'Illuminate our shadows, lady'. By the reign of James I it was a craze judged to lead to total madness, and Robert Burton, who surveyed the fashion in his *Anatomy of Melancholy*, sighed 'to see men so empty of all virtuous action'. The melancholic affected a negligent attire, with his collar undone, and a suit usually of mourning black with a wide hat, in which he would stroll solitary by country brooks, musing on his misfortunes. Sir John Davies described the melancholic male:

He thinks not of the warre 'twixt France and Spaine,
But he doth seriously bethinke whether
Of the gull'd people he be the most esteem'd
For his long cloak or for his great black feather,
By which each gull is now a gallant deem'd. . .[4]

The long cloak was another part of mourning costume, emphasizing the delight in depression. The trend was imported from Italy, where it began in the 1580s. There, too, a feeling of decline was in the air after earlier glories.

Black was also official wear at the Jacobean court, for James I adopted the Elizabethan livery, and had himself portrayed in white doublet and black trunkhose and cloak embroidered with pearls, although he was far from being the constant virgin which those shades symbolized. Many felt that he was abusing the colours of the great Queen. James did not dress exclusively in black and white, but it was the image he liked to project in his portraits. Johann Ernsten, Duke of Saxe-Weimar, visited King James at Theobalds in 1613:

He was dressed in a satin robe of an ash colour, thickly covered with gold lace chevronwise, and a rather long cloak of black cloth lined with velvet. In his hat was a magnificent jewel, with a tree of large precious stones one above the other, set in gold.

The following day the king prepared to go hunting, for which activity green was the most popular rustic colour:

He was attired in a green satin dress, and having a grey hat upon his head; he sat down upon a chair near the table, and had a pair of black boots pulled on; on his left leg a blue silk ribbon hung just above the boot, which denotes the Order of the Garter, and the young Prince wore the like. This is not merely confined to the King and Prince, but the lords, who are Knights of the Garter, daily wear on the left leg a remarkably handsome blue garter.[5]

It was customary for the courtiers and royal servants to exchange gifts with the sovereign at New Year. They would present goods or gold, and the monarch would give gilt plate in return. In the exchange of 1605–6, James I's servants gave him a pair of pantofles embroidered with Venetian gold, a pair of mittens embroidered on the cuffs with flowers in silk, a pair of perfumed gloves laced with four bone laces of Venetian gold, and two pairs of undecorated perfumed gloves, a nightcap of tawny velvet embroidered with gold and silk, a shirt of fine holland linen

27 Anon., *Henry Wriothesley, Earl of Southampton*, c. 1600. Shakespeare's patron wears the new tight sleeves and shoulder wings, although his combination trunkhose and knee-breeches are going out of fashion. The long lovelock incensed the moralists for its feminine nature, and hips were still feminine in width. The embroidered gloves remained in fashion down to the Restoration period, and were a popular gift.

with the band (collar) and cuffs of cut-work, a cambric handkerchief edged with gold lace, and from each of the royal musicians one pair of plain perfumed gloves.[6] Scented with orange or rose, which offset the smell of leather and tanning, perfumed gloves with often rich embroidery around the cuff were a luxury that was much in demand, and they occur repeatedly in seventeenth-century wardrobe accounts as one of the most common gifts among the rich.

The showiest person at the English court was James I's favourite George Villiers, Duke of Buckingham, who was allowed to play the statesman and military commander with no experience in either field. On his visits as royal ambassador to France and the Netherlands in 1625–6, the new duke was resolved to outshine all other mortals. A Parisian reported:

It must be confessed that the Duke of Buckingham had the finest outfit one could see in a lifetime. I am moved to describe it. It was of gris-de-lin coloured satin, embroidered with pearls, the embroidery being in bands: the pearls in the middle of the band might be worth ten crowns apiece, those on the edge, twenty at least. The buttons were pearls of twenty crowns in value, the buttonholes of pearl embroidery and the tags were also made of pearls in graduated sizes. He had a chain which went six times round his neck, made of pearls of immense value. His girdle was worth at least thirty thousand crowns. In his hat was a plume of heron's feathers at the base of which was a badge of five very large diamonds and three superb pear-shaped pearls. From his ear hung a large pearl with a great diamond at the ear-clasp, but this scarcely showed because his hair was so long and so much curled as to hide it.[7]

Here was vanity in danger of being incapacitated by its own finery, for the weight of the costume must have been considerable. It was a typical example of a royal favourite trying to outdress royalty itself. Needless to say, this example of extravagant behaviour was condemned by the Puritans, who declared that Buckingham enjoyed great possessions 'upon no meritt but that of his beauty and his prostitution'.[8] His assassination at Portsmouth in 1628 was not to be wondered at. There had been great hopes that the Prince of Wales, Henry, might be a natural heir to the cult of chivalry that had centred around Queen Elizabeth and that he might reform the court, but he died young. It devolved upon the shy and lazy second son, Charles, to bring that about and even his political opponents admitted that he did make the court more moral and chaste when he succeeded to the throne in 1625. James I left debts of £5,891 2s. 10d. to his tailor Robert Erskine, which Charles I paid, and Charles I proved to be just as lavish in his expenditure on clothes. During the years 1630–1 he spent £4,494 13s. 11d. on clothes, the equivalent of about £200,000 today.[9] His tailor Patrick Black produced satin suits by the dozen in pink, sage, scarlet or black, decorated with buttons, braid and gold or silver lace.

The fashion lead had been taken by France, which Cardinal Richelieu was turning into a centralized state with power increasingly concentrated in the hands of an absolute monarchy. As the cardinal was determined to make France supreme, fashion was encouraged at the French court as part of the visual illustration of French cultural superiority. The Spanish were only too well aware that their heyday was over, and in his Capitulos de Reformacion of 1623 Philip IV of Spain banned such French styles as ruffs and long hair, and launched a suit which was made compulsory at the court in Madrid. It was simply a revival of the sixteenth-century Spanish style of doublet and breeches, but it was regarded as a symbol of historical pride, and henceforth it had to be only in solemn black. This remained the official court dress for men in Spain until the country acquired a French king in 1700. Even foreign visitors to the Spanish court were required to wear it, as Charles I of England discovered while still Prince of Wales. By insisting on this old-fashioned style the Spanish court was trying to pretend that recent history had not happened and that it still ruled European dress. It was a sensitive matter and the difference in clothes illustrated the political situation. The French style was guaranteed a fond reception in England because Charles I married the French princess Henriette Marie and not a Spanish Infanta. Austria, being a Hapsburg realm which did intermarry with Spain, adopted the Spanish black court dress for men out of Roman Catholic and family solidarity, and this influenced the Roman Catholic states in southern Germany to adopt it too. It was a case of clothes being used to display loyalty. While France was also mainly Catholic, it wanted to break the Hapsburg ring that enclosed it on two sides, so that French foreign policy was anti-Catholic and pro-Protestant, although its domestic policy was the exact opposite.

Ideas for fashions come from competition at court between rivals, from working dress, from military costume and sometimes from children's clothes. While for most of history children were dressed like young adults, there were brief periods when children were given simpler styles, and one of these occurred at the end of the sixteenth century, which meant that those children who had worn such simple garments clung to them as adults. At the start of the seventeenth century, children's fashion became the adult one. Traditionally, up to the age of five or six a boy was under the control of the distaff side of the house, ranked as a baby in petticoats, but at about five he would be breeched and declared a man, a great day in every family. (Girls, of course, were not so honoured.) The late-Tudor parent in vast ruff, peascod belly and tight canions topped by wide breeches, frequently allowed his sons to forego such a stiff imprisonment in favour of a loose wide collar, a simple doublet, and breeches that were melon-shaped rather than excessively wide at the hips. Not surprisingly, the young generation preferred to keep this model and it was the basic fashion for the early 1600s. At court, however, status demanded that a simple outfit could not be plain, so the suit of clothes was adorned with lavish embroidery and decoration: bands of gold or silver lace, or silken flowers, or patterns in pearls and diamonds. The doublet became much leaner because the late Elizabethan leg-of-mutton sleeve had grown so large that a retreat was inevitable. The young man of fashion after 1600 strove for a lean line above the waist, with narrow sleeves and a tight bodice. As this generation had worn collars in their childhood, it was with them that the demise of ruffs began, but it was a gradual process, and the Calvinist burghers of the Netherlands were still wearing ruffs in the 1660s. At court, however, matters were more advanced and ruffs began to collapse, as shown by the half-ruff which was high at the back but low at the front like a collar, and collars proper made a comeback. They had to be wide because the ruffs had been wide and people had grown accustomed to the head being presented on this white plate of starched linen. Initially the collar was backed by a piccadilly to support it. The vital decade was after 1610 when collars began to dominate, and ruffs were restricted to formal and legal dress, where conservative styles were the tradition. As ruffs often had decorative edges, collars were given the same treatment by being edged with lace or cut-work, which was too costly for ordinary mortals to copy.

Fullness still dominated breeches but it was given a variation, and the melon shape of the 1600s changed to a form of breeches which, while still fairly wide at the top, became much

wider above the knee, an effect produced by deep pleating from the waistline. (See front of jacket.) They were as full as skirts and were another illustration of the effeminacy at court which the Puritans attacked. With Jacobean fops sporting make-up, a tassel in one ear, and curled hair, or the latest idea: a lovelock falling on one side, the Puritan lobby would declare that every outbreak of plague was God's punishment on Sodom, and Bishop Laud would affirm that immodesty in dress caused earthquakes. It was the sin of vanity and should be punished, although divine disasters seemed to affect both the innocent and the guilty.

One way to distinguish the Jacobean fop from the ordinary man was by the walk. For the first time men were wearing heels of one or two inches in height, instead of the usual flat shoe. These new shoes were embroidered and decorated with large shoe roses, matching the silk stockings with their embroidered clocks. In summer the fop shone in a suit of silk, and in winter in a suit of velvet and finest wool, the fabric so covered with lace or braid that it was almost invisible. Among all this richness was one relaxed and casual note which became a tradition down to the 1660s; the leaving of the lower buttons of the doublet undone. For those at the top of the tree a degree of untidiness was allowable, but their servants and inferiors were not allowed to appear in such informal dress before their masters. It was a form of reverse snobbery, with the lord less tidy than his staff.

Ben Jonson in his *Every Man out of his Humor*, 1600, took a look at the type:

CARLO. First (to be an accomplisht gentleman, that is, a gentleman of the time) you must give o'er housekeeping in the countrey, and live altogether in the citie among gallants: where, at your first appearance, 'twere good your turnd foure or five hundred acres of your best land into two or three trunkes of apparell. (I.ii)

The fop would only travel 'As far as Paris, to fetch over a fashion and come back againe', while the cost of an outfit would be:

FUNGOSO. Let me see, the Doublet, say fiftie shillings the Doublet, and betwene three and four pound the Hose; then Bootes, the Hat, and Band: some ten or eleven pound would do it all, and suit me for the heavens. (II.i)

But there was no place for virtue amongst such finery:

MACILENTE.
Be a man ne'er so vile,
If he can purchase but a Silken cover,
He shall not only passe, but passe regarded. . .
That Raiment should be in such high request.
(III.ii)

Another playwright, Thomas Dekker, said that 'Good cloathes are the embrodred trappings of pride,' in his *The Guls Horne Booke* of 1609, but he blamed it all on foreigners. Back in old Adam's day there were 'no Spanish slops, no Swiss blistered codpieces, no Danish sleeves sagging down like a Welsh wallet, no close Italian troussers, or French standing collars, or treble or quadruple Daedalian ruffs and stiff-necked Rebatoes'. (The reference to Daedalus was that he could fly in the ruffs, they were so wide.)[10]

The good Protestant was expected to forego such proud and vulgar show. The Protestant Clothing Ethic demanded modesty and good taste. This was understood by Henry Peacham in his *The Compleat Gentleman* of 1622. Ruling that learning was an essential part of nobility, he advised gentlemen:

Be thriftie also in your apparell and clothing, least you incurre the censure of the most grave and wisest censor for, *Cui magna corporis cura, ei magna virtutis incuria*: and Henry the fourth, last king of France of eternall memory, would oftentimes merily say, By the outside onely, he could sound the depth of a Courtier: saying, who had the least in them made the fairest shew without.

Peacham recommended that gentlemen should follow that 'moderate and middle garb' which even the greatest princes wore. He cited the Protestant leaders Henri IV and the Prince of Orange as examples of princes who would dress plainly in grey or hair colour. They did not seek to outshine the rest of creation like previous rulers, but dressed as ordinary gentry except for state occasions. Peacham also included the Catholic Charles V on his list but in this he was mistaken, for that ruler was just as showy as

28 Anon., *James Hay, Earl of Carlisle*, 1628. There was a transitional fashion for collars as wide as ruffs still supported by pickadillies, because people were so used to white near the face. The Earl's doublet and breeches have the small-scale patterns that were all the rage in the 1620s. A more sloping shoulderline is emerging with the wing set low. The top half of the sleeve was paned, that is, slashed, and in the 1630s the bottom half was paned too. The breeches were now supported by hooks and eyes.

Henry VIII in his younger days and simplified his dress only in old age when he had the gout and could not wear rich and heavy costumes. Peacham felt that it was the military who were in the greatest danger of 'womanish vanity', for they loved display. The Spaniard would enter the field in a cassock and his richest jewels, the French were all in scarlet, gold lace and huge feathers, the Italians prided themselves on Neopolitan coursers, the Dutch and the Germans were 'dawbed with gold and pearls', and the English were too fond of rich arms and good swords.[11] The real gentleman, he suggested, should avoid all this finery, and not strut like a military peacock. He should dress soberly and modestly as befits the servant of God. Of course, it took time for this Protestant ideal to become established at court in England because the next rulers of the Stuart dynasty, Charles I, Charles II and James II, were all pro-Catholic, and none of them abandoned magnificence, but after the Glorious Revolution of 1688 put William and Mary on the throne, the Protestant ideal of modest monarchy began to make an advance. There is, however, a big difference between a king dressing plainly at a court where everybody knows who he is, and a sovereign appearing without an entourage in a strange town where he might be received without due respect. Accordingly, the simply attired leader was rarely without those accessories which established his rank, such as a coach and six, a good number of grooms and pages, and a staff of elaborately clad gentlemen. The monarch who favoured modest attire might allow his close friends to dress the same, but all his staff and servants had to wear uniforms and liveries. This still applies today, where the democratic sovereign may be wearing a simple suit, but the footman is still in his ornate livery. The Protestant Clothing Ethic was inhibited at court by the fact that status must still be exhibited, if not directly by the king then indirectly by his servants.

Men's waistlines moved several times during the unstable and war-torn years of the seventeenth century. Waistlines rose over the period 1615–25, went back down again by 1629, rose once more in the early 1630s, sank to the normal waist in the 1640s, then dropped to the hips in the 1670s. An important characteristic of a high waistline is that it is a youthful style requiring a slim figure to wear it, for a high waist merely emphasizes a portly belly. It was the dominant line of the reign of Charles I, where elegance and taste ousted the gaudy posturing of his father's court. Make-up for men was definitely out of

29 George Harding, *William Prynne*, *c*. 1635. The Puritan lawyer was a ferocious critic of effete court fashions for long hair, lace, silks, satins, and bows. He himself has moderate hair, a plain collar with just a lace trim, and a plain doublet. His pointed beard is copied from the king he criticized.

fashion now, and marital fidelity was the royal rule. The fashions at court depended on the nature of the incumbent ruler and his circle, and Charles I was a man fascinated by art and masques who could apply artistic principles to his attire. While his reign began with heavily braided suits, the trend was to discard ornamentation, and gradually clothes lost their layers of decoration and began to appear with the fabric unadorned. A more relaxed look was created, and stiffness was banished. The favourite fabric was satin in pure colours, apricot, yellow, red, brown or green. Lace, that extremely expensive item, was used in abundance, to form the wide collars, to trim the wrists of shirts, to top the stockings, and to edge garments. The result was an elegant simplicity which could not be imitated by the masses because the satin was expensive and the lace cost hundreds of pounds, often being made of gold and silver thread, or of silk. The simplicity was of the most luxurious sort.

Hair became an area of dispute. Moderate Protestants wore it to below the ear or to the neck, but the court favoured long hair trailing over the shoulders. Zealots in the Protestant camp favoured cutting the hair off completely, but this was a minority view. The Puritan barrister William Prynne went as far as to declare that long hair was against natural law, and damned lovelocks as effeminate. He aroused the fury of the King when he wrote that all actresses were whores, because the queen herself acted in the court masques, and Prynne was fined heavily and had his ears cut off. This obliged him to wear his hair at chin-length to conceal the fact. One question which occupied Prynne and other moralists was why the court should launch fashions at all. Prynne blasted the variety and changeability involved: 'Infinite, and many are the sinfull, strange, and monstrous vanities, which this Unconstant, Vaine, Fantastique, Idle, Proud, Effeminate and wanton age of ours hath hatched and Produced in all the parts and corners of the World: but especially, in this our *English* climate, which like another *Affricke*, is always bringing foorth some *New, some Strange, Mishapen*, or *Prodigious formes* and Fashions every Moment.'[12] John Bulwer was another critic to wonder at the existence of fashion. 'It is a wonderful testimony of the imbecility of our judgements that when we have hit of a convenient Fashion, we cannot keep to it; but we must commend and allow of Fashions for the rarenesse or novelty. . .'[13] Yet the novelty and the variety were one of the ways in which the court maintained its superiority when the middle classes were so eager to copy. Sumptuary laws had proved difficult to police, but the court still had the economic power to monopolize the finest fabrics, so its fashions were always in the costliest materials which only rich merchants could copy. As soon as the city did begin to copy, that was the signal for the court to change the fashion. It was well understood among the aristocracy that fashion was about class competition and group identity. One displayed one's rank by keeping ahead of everybody else in style. To the masses, of course, who could be 200 years behind the court, fashion was a remote area beyond their experience. It was all very well for a duke to wear satin and lace but his annual income exceeded the entire lifetime's earnings of a labourer. In fact the simpler style of the Carolean court was one of the few times when the peasantry could attempt an approximation of the court mode. The plain doublets and breeches without complicated slashings and paning could be copied in rough wool, so gradually working men adopted this new look, retaining it for the next two hundred years, right into the nine-

teenth century, because it proved a practical outfit. The hip-length doublet did not get in the way as the long-skirted coats of subsequent fashions did, so the peasantry stuck to the style of the 1630s.

The Anglo-Scottish court discussed sumptuary laws but Charles I did not issue one until the Civil War had started, when economy suddenly became essential. In June 1643 he forbade 'the wearing of any Lace, Embroidery, Fringe, Riband, Buttons and Clasps or Loops of Gold, Silver, and mixed Gold and Silver, Cloth of Gold or Silver, Bone Lace, or Silk or Linen Thread',[14] but by now it was too late and the royal writ was no longer obeyed throughout the land. The government of his brother-in-law Louis XIII of France took a different view and issued several edicts and proclamations banning lavish finery in 1617 and 1623, and in 1633–4 the ordonnance which caused the greatest shock, for it increased the fine from 500 livres to 15,000 livres! In Paris ornamentation vanished from clothes overnight. The 'Déclaration du Roy, portant règlement général sur la reformation des Habits' aimed at restricting the importation of Italian brocades and cloth of gold and silver in order to assist French-made silks and velvets. Decoration was restricted to the seams of garments and could only be a finger wide, to end the application of lace and braid all over an outfit. The wearing of gold and silver fabrics was, as always, restricted to the royal family. As France was about to enter the Thirty Years' War against the Hapsburgs, some economies were required to keep money in the country. The fact that much of Europe was involved in wars during the period 1618–48 was an important influence in limiting court luxury, and the French and English civil wars of the 1640s made simple clothes a necessity. Out went wide lace collars in favour of narrower, plain ones, and in England the cavaliers invented a craze for knotting a scarf around the neck, which was to be the origin of the cravat. Plain woollen cloth and buff leather jerkins replaced satin and silk. Although Carolean fashions had been damned as effete, there had been one masculine element in the wearing of boots and spurs indoors instead of shoes. This vogue began in the 1620s, and led to boots being elaborated into the bucket-top boot with a very wide top and fanciful butterfly leathers. This was seen as yet another aspect of the degenerate court converting a practical article into an impractical toy. This was usual, however, for when fashion adopts an article from the active world it will elaborate it, decorate it

30 Pieter Nason, *Chief Justice Oliver St John*, 1651. Although this member of the Commonwealth regime is dressed with appropriate simplicity, his hair follows the fashion for even longer locks, and he sports the bucket-top boots with wide leathers beloved of the Cavaliers. His small collar and black breeches would please the Puritans, but not the striped ribbons on his breeches and hat. The breeches are now simple tubes to below the knee and they are growing wider.

and render it more stylish. This could be seen very clearly with lacing. The medieval tradition of lacing the hose to the doublet was carried over to breeches, which were laced to the doublet in the same way, now that hose no longer had to reach to the waist. Lesser orders made do with belts, or else the waistband of the breeches was made tight enough to hold them up, but in fashionable circles a degree of impractical elaboration could not be avoided, for it was part of the flourish of superiority. Consequently the laces were not left as simple knots, but had to be elongated and tipped with gleaming metal, like modern shoe laces, and tied into fanciful bows. This fashion required a manservant to set the bows every time his lord and master went to stool. The complication was part of the class distinction, for the costume could not be managed single-handed. With the simplification of the silhouette in the 1630s these bows and knots were

discarded, as they spoilt the line, and John Aubrey says that thereafter breeches were held up by hooks and eyes.[15]

For all the elegance of the Carolean court, it was not very considerate to others. At the start of the civil war the king moved to the college of Christ Church at Oxford University, but the scholar Anthony Wood was shocked at the behaviour. 'To give a further character of the court, though they were very neat and gay in their apparell, yet they were very nasty and beastly, leaving at their departure their excrements in every corner, in chimneys, studies, cole-houses, cellars. Rude, rough, whore-mongers; vaine, empty, careless.'[16]

By now, of course, the military were flocking to the court, with the aristocracy playing its traditional role of warrior, so perhaps it was not surprising that their manners left something to be desired. Courtesy was a quality the aristocracy exercised only within its own class, and those modern people who regard the cavaliers as intensely romantic would not have enjoyed the arrogance and contempt which the Royalist aristocrats displayed to all their inferiors. The idea of being polite to all classes was introduced when Charles II came to the throne. Thoroughly immoral though he was, he would raise his hat to every woman, whether she be duchess or maid-servant, probably because he favoured all women!

The Royalists were defeated in the Civil War because not all the aristocracy supported the king, and because Cromwell forged a superior army for Parliament. The Puritan Commonwealth was established, and Charles I lost his head. As it was a cold morning he went to the block wearing two shirts; the royal martyr did not want to shiver and give the impression of fear. The ensuing régime was not a republic in the modern sense of the term, for Cromwell was ranked as a prince, his children were given the precedence of dukes, and he was empowered to create peers himself. The Puritans did ban ancient pagan festivals, and closed all the theatres and the brothels, but oddly enough they did not pass any sumptuary laws for clothes. Parliament did discuss the problem of dress and suggest some new laws, but the members' wives advised them to drop the idea. After all, a commonwealth was supposed to be for the common good, so it should not restrict what materials citizens could wear. Accordingly it was left to the parsons, with church attendance being compulsory, to give stern directions in their sermons reminding the populace to be plain and modest in their attire, and to single out immodest dressers for public condemnation. Adultery was made a capital offence, and the rule for sex within holy matrimony was 'never on Sunday'. Although the whole population did not take to wearing black, it was very widespread; the gentry and nobility still wore colours, although not of a garish tone. Sobriety was supposed to reign, but town guards could be bribed. Suits remained simple, but this could not last, because of the influence of France. In 1658 Louis XIV came of age, and was determined to outshine all other monarchs. Simplicity would not suffice to give the correct image of his reign. Splendour and fantastic decoration were the new ideas for menswear. France had had a civil war too, and now it was time to celebrate. A similar feeling broke out in England when the monarchy was restored in 1660. After Puritan repression it was time for abandon.

Firstly exposure increased, and that slight revelation of the shirt seen at the start of the century was taken to an extreme, with the doublet being shortened until it was simply a bolero, displaying inches of shirt around the waist. Sleeve seams were left open and here too the shirt was pulled out. The actual sleeve was made a good foot longer than the arm so that it could be pushed back to swell out of the openings. Petticoat breeches reached England in 1658, according to Randle Holme, who wrote that a suit now consisted of: 'a short-waisted doublet and petticoat-breeches, the lining being lower than the breeches ... tied above the knees; the breeches are ornamented with ribands up to the pocket, and half their breadth upon the thigh; the waistband is set about with ribands, and the shirt hanging out over them'.[17] The 'ribands' were ribbons, now used in abundance by the score of yards. There were ribbons on the hats, round the doublet, round the breeches, on the sword knot, on the garters and on the shoes. It was due to French influence, since Louis XIV would not wear anything plain. The points worn in his father's day were not enough; now there had to be ribbons everywhere. John Evelyn was moved to write a complaint, *Tyrannus* or *The Mode*, in 1661:

It was a fine silken thing which I spied walking th'other day through *Westminster-Hall*, that had as much Ribbon on him as would have plundered six shops, and set up twenty Country Pedlers: All his Body was dres't like a May-pole, or a *Tom-a-Bedlam's* Cap. A Fregat newly rigg'd kept not half such a clatter in a storme, as this Puppets Streamers did when the

31 Ter Borch, *Portrait of a Man*. Triangular man, from his sugarloaf hat down to the voluminous petticoat breeches which had grown so wide they became skirts. A matching flared frill decorates the knees, and there are ribbons round the waist, on the hat, round the skirt and on the shoes. The doublet is shrinking and sleeves have opened up, so that more shirt is on display. The hair reaches below the shoulders and will soon require some false assistance if it is to be even longer. In all, the fanciful costume celebrates peace after civil wars across Europe.

53

Wind was in his Shroud's; the Motion was Wonderfull to behold, and the Colours were Red, Orange, and Blew, of well gum'd Sattin, which argu'd a happy fancy: but so was our Gallant over charg'd, *Indutunme an onustum hominem, habere vestem, an bajulare*, that whether he were clad with this Garment, or (as a Porter) only carried it, was not to be resolv'd.[18]

A French tailor, he maintained, was like the sorceress Circe, changing people's shapes, sometimes into loose clothes, and sometimes into tight, like a malefactor in a sack. Evelyn argued, 'There is a certain *honestas in observatione decori*, which if men could once light on, would be of infinite more Reputation to us, then this slavish defference of ours to other Nations.' He appealed to Charles II to reform menswear and to ban French fantasies, but the king did not respond. After the poverty of exile Charles II was delighted to have money to spend on fanciful clothes, and as Louis XIV was his cousin he did not wish to be put in the shade by the Bourbon branch of the family. What effeminacy, declared the Puritans, men in petticoats like babies!

High heels were back in favour because Louis XIV's brother the Duke of Orléans was short and needed some assistance. Consequently, the fashionable man was now a tottering triangle, wide at the knee in voluminous petticoat breeches and tapering towards a tall pointed hat at the top, resembling the cone-shaped sugar loaf. In fact the petticoat breeches were a logical development; during the 1650s on the Continent breeches had been growing wider and wider until they were like culottes, so putting a skirt over the division was the next step. These skirts would swing as the wearer walked, and they represented the new spirit of levity that was in the air after the gloomy Commonwealth and the Thirty Years' War. There was much to celebrate. Austrian Catholic imperialism had been defeated and the clock was not turned back to before the Reformation. The Netherlands gained their independence from Spain in 1648. The French and the English monarchies had survived, so a mood of celebration was general.

There was a vogue for folly, hence all the ribbons, and hence the new periwigs. The word was not a new one and in the earlier part of the century had meant various types of hairpiece. The long hair worn by cavaliers had grown as much as most men could achieve, but for extra length and volume some artificial aids were necessary. Whole-head wigs were available in France in 1656 with blond a favourite colour, for yellows were in vogue as part of the cheerful mood of the day. A gallant could now parade in a blond wig and a yellow satin suit trimmed with yards of ribbon. The early periwigs were very curly around 1660, but those of the 1670s had ringlets. Their introduction was gradual. The naval administrator Samuel Pepys took the plunge in 1663, James Duke of York did so in February 1664 and Charles II not until April when he was growing grey. Louis XIV, for once, took even longer, sporting his own abundant locks, of which he was very proud, into the next decade. Wigs proved an excellent illustration of rank, for they cost several pounds, so the peasantry could not copy them, and right down to the Napoleonic period the wig was an instant method of distinguishing the gentleman from the artisan. Anybody who wore his own hair was obviously a mean fellow of low standing. William Prynne, now keeper of records at the Tower of London (the military rule of the 1650s had turned him into a Royalist) must have been astounded that all his campaigning against lovelocks should end in periwigs! Even the Governor of the Tower was sporting one in 1663, as can be seen by his portrait there. Pepys did worry somewhat over whose hair he was wearing, whether it might have come from a corpse or a diseased old woman, but then one had to keep up with the town. He took as his bible for clothes Francis Osborne's *Advice to a Son* of 1658 which recommended, 'Weare your Cloaths neat, exceeding, rather than comming short of others of like Fortune.' The son of a poor tailor who had enjoyed a university education, Pepys was very self-conscious about his wardrobe as he rose through the ranks at the Admiralty Board, and tried to keep up with gentlemanly fashion until friends told him in 1669 that he had gone too far. A civil servant should not sport gold lace.[19]

The male suit underwent a considerable change at the Restoration. The overcoat, which existed as a fur-lined hunting coat in the 1620s and as the loose cloak-coat, started to become an article of indoor wear. Some men, instead of wearing the overcoat over the doublet, preferred to wear it directly on top of the shirt. This started a vogue and Samuel Pepys took to it in February 1661: '*Lordsday*. This day I first

32 Romain de Hooghe, *The Mode*. In the 1660s the coat begins to replace the doublet. Worn as an outer garment before, the coat now became an indoor component of the suit, but it fitted badly over petticoat breeches and had to be pinned up. By 1666 the cravat was taking the place of collars. Ostrich feathers were a prized item of adornment.

begun to go forth in my coate and sword, as the manner now among gentlemen is.' He wore the new style on 29 October: 'my new Coate of the fashion, which pleases me well; and with my beaver [hat] I was . . . ready to go my Lord Mayors feast'. The idea probably came from the military, who could wear their long buff coat on top of the shirt without the doublet in between, particularly in summer. A problem developed in wearing these coats over petticoat breeches, because the length of the coat made the skirts bunch forwards, so for a few years it was usual to pin the flaps of the coat back at the sides to keep them out of the way. Notwithstanding this difficulty, the coat as a replacement for the doublet gained considerable ground, for it pleased those men who felt that the court's fondness for ribbons and puffed shirts had gone too far. A long coat cut out the short doublet and the masses of ribbon down the side of the breeches. It made for a better line without these breaks in the middle, had a simple shape and made a man look taller, so the popularity increased, and it was to be greatly assisted by two disasters. The Great Plague hit London in 1665, and in 1666 the Great Fire of London demolished much of the old city, including Saint Paul's. Clergymen were quick to point out that this was God's punishment upon a sinful town and court. The contempt for Puritan principles displayed by Charles II and his cronies, like the drunken second Duke of Buckingham, their whoring and trips to the brothels, their affairs with actresses, their blatant adultery, had brought God's judgement on the land. Worse would follow if the court did not mend its ways. It was a good moment for John Evelyn to remind the King about his little book pleading for the reform of menswear. This time Charles II paid attention and agreed to launch a reformed costume. Doubtless some discussion took place between the King, Evelyn, the Earl of Sandwich, Master of the Wardrobe, and the King's tailors, John Allen and William Watts. On 7 October 1666 Charles II informed his council of his resolution of setting a fashion for clothes which he would never alter. It would be a vest, and Pepys wondered what that was, for the term was often applied to eastern garments.

Now Evelyn and Pepys were both admirers of Persian dress, which Evelyn first saw in Italy in 1645, and the playhouses showed examples of Turkish dress in Davenant's drama *The Siege of Rhodes* of 1656, where the celebrated actor Betterton appeared in a turban and Turkish vest. This garment was as long as a coat to the knee,

33 Gerard Soest, *Henry Howard, Duke of Norfolk*, *c.* 1666. Enter the English three-piece suit with the coat and vest of equal length, worn over narrow breeches, as introduced by Charles II in October 1666. This vest of blue brocade smothered with gold lace was probably worn to the Queen's Birthday Ball when such garments cost £100. The Duke sports the new periwig which the English court adopted in 1663–4. The concept of the three-piece suit is still with us.

but made of richer materials like silks and brocades. In addition there were the new artistic vests as well, for artists were complaining that fashion made their paintings go out of date, and they asked sitters to wear a plain silk coat instead of beribboned foppery, in the vain hope that this would give the portrait a timeless look. Thus vests were not completely unknown when Charles II began to wonder how to improve men's clothes.[20]

It was winter at the time, when wearing a coat over the shirt would not be warm enough, so one needed a doublet underneath, but what if the doublet were elongated to the knee so that it was the same length as the coat, like a Persian or Turkish or artistic vest? It would level things up, be moral in covering up the shirt (which was underwear), and produce a more stately line. All that beribboned abandon had to go, so the result would be a sober suit which ought to keep the clergy quiet. Charles II decided that black pinked over white would be sober enough, indicating mourning for national disasters and virtuous intentions for the future. It was decided to make these new suits with long coats and long vests in the one material, and so the three-piece suit was born. Obviously petticoat breeches would be invisible under such garments, so they were replaced by narrow breeches. Allen and Watts worked away, as did other tailors, for when Charles II appeared in his vest on 15 October 1666, so did some lords and members of Parliament, too. Two days later the king felt the black over white made him look like a magpie, so he ordered his vest to be plain velvet, as Lord St Albans had his in plain black. Such sobriety must have pleased many a bishop, but it proved short-lived. The Queen's birthday ball fell on 15 November, and Charles II wore a vest of silk trimmed with silver; others had cloth-of-silver vests, and Pepys estimated they must have cost £100 each, while those embroidered with jewels were worth thousands. In the Baroque period courts had to look glorious, and the English courtiers did not want to look like a collection of parsons and become the laughing-stock of European nobility. So splendid did vests become that the coat was cut back in front to display them better, which Pepys found chilly: '*4 November 1666*: it being very cold, to White-hall, and was mighty fearful of an ague (my vest being new and thin, and the coate cut not to meet before upon my breast).' Notwithstanding these teething problems, the English three-piece suit had been born, and is still in being 320 years later, the most durable combination of clothes (apart from shirts and drawers) in modern history. It was the start of the British tradition of tailoring, the creation of the best menswear in the world.

The French court did not like it. While rumours that Louis XIV had put his servants into English vests as a deliberate insult proved to be unfounded, there was no doubt that the French would do their level best to undermine this British attempt to seize the lead in high fashion for men. The fact that it annoyed the French court ensured the success of the vest (waistcoat) in Britain where it quickly became a gesture of national defiance; vests were anti-French and anti-Catholic. The two courts did not meet until 1670 when Charles II's favourite sister Minette (Henriette, Duchess of Orléans) headed a visit to Dover. The real purpose of the meeting was to offer Charles II a secret subsidy from Louis XIV, so that he could rule without

Parliament's controlling the purse-strings: a French bid to force Britain back under Catholic control. This agreement was signed, although it broke the treaty with the Netherlands, Britain's Protestant ally. As far as the public was concerned the family reunion was aimed at laughing the English court out of its vests, and Charles II is supposed to have succumbed to his sister's request and returned to the French style of coats without vests. Yet Elkanah Settle in the epilogue to *Pastor Fido*, 1676, refers to vests having lasted seven years, and by 1678 French opposition had collapsed, for that year the engraver Jean de St Jean was issuing fashion-plates in Paris which showed the latest style for gentlemen: namely the English suit with its long coat and long vest. It would not do for the British to publicize the fashion, but the French were happy to do so and to pretend that it was theirs. The vest put down very firm roots in Britain because it was more respectable than the French modes of the early 1660s. Who wanted to incur the condemnation that had befallen the beribboned buffoons whom Anthony Wood had damned in 1663?

'A strange, effeminate age, when men strive to imitate women in their apparell, viz. long periwigs, patches in their faces, painting, short wide breeches like petticotes, muffs and their clothes highly scented, bedecked with ribbons of all colours. And this apparell was not only used by gentlemen and others of inferior quality, but by souldiers especial those of the Life Gard to the King, who would have spanners hanging on one side and a muff on the other, and when dirty weather some of them would relieve their gards in pattens'.[21]

Surely the vest was an improvement on that, and was the new look not more manly and mature? To some extent, but the periwigs and the lace frills continued – and continued to be criticized as effete.

There was only one sumptuary law under Charles II which was enforced with any thoroughness, and that concerned the deceased. There was actually a trade war going on with France. Hitherto grey English cloth had clothed the French army, but now Louis XIV's minister Colbert was insisting that French troops wore French cloth, the *serge de Berry*, and imposed high taxes on English cloth, which had been a major French import. However, French raw wool was of inferior quality to English, so the French still needed to import English wool. England, of course, wanted to keep the work of weaving cloth in England, so it was opposed to

34 J. D. de St Jean, *Homme de Qualité en Habit Garny de Rubans*, 1689. After a lot of fuss the French adopted the English type of suit and pretended it was their idea. Henceforth menswear became variations on a set number of garments. In the 1680s four vertical pockets on the coat were the mode, but in the 1690s two horizontal pockets with flaps were sufficient. Stripes were the rage, and the vogue for ribbons persists. There are even bows of satin ribbon behind the cravat. Fringed gloves now oust embroidered ones. High-heeled shoes with tiny buckles complete the ensemble, and with the high periwig make a man several inches taller.

the export of raw wool. There were repeated appeals to Charles II to retaliate by banning the importation of French silks and brocades. Foreign lace and trimmings were banned in 1662, but nothing was done about the fabrics. To quieten the wool trade, an act for burying in wool shrouds was issued in 1666, and reinforced in 1677 and 1680. It stopped the import of linen for shrouds, and ruled that every person in the

British realm should have the coffin lined with wool, and the shift, shroud or winding sheet or shirt made of wool. The chief reason why Charles II could not ban French silks was because he was in the pay of the French government. The Weavers' Company appealed to him in 1673 and 1674, and in 1675 and 1677 Parliament wanted a ban on French silks and linen because Louis XIV had placed an impost of 25–50% on English cloth. As the royal family was so pro-Catholic it was a vain request, even more so when the openly Catholic James II succeeded. It was only when he was deposed in 1688, and the Protestant William and Mary assumed joint rule, that the desired ban came into force, forbidding the import of all French commodities from 1688. Even this could not stop the trade completely because Romney Marsh was a hotbed of smuggling, some customs officers could be bribed, and the French were willing to pay a high price for English wool to improve their own cloth.[22]

The character of the joint monarchs had a big impact. William III was a soldier with no great interest in clothes, while Mary II was deeply religious. The next sovereign, Queen Anne, was too often ill with the gout and with pregnancies to be a fashion-setter, while her heir was George I, another soldier without any interest in fashion or the elaborate dressing so beloved of Louis XIV. Thus the English court became very sober compared to the French, with the Protestant ideal of modest attire much in evidence. This affected the nobility who did not have to dress up in finery except for royal birthdays. They were not required to live at court, unlike the French, so they could spend more time on their estates in country clothes. An enormous difference grew up between the two kingdoms, with the French court still lavish, and the British one restrained. By the time the Swiss César de Saussure visited London in 1725, the difference had become an institution:

[Englishmen] do not trouble themselves about dress but leave that to their womenfolk. When the people see a well-dressed person in the streets, especially if he is wearing a braided coat, a plume in his hat, or his hair tied in a bow, he will, without doubt, be called a 'French dog' twenty times before he reaches his destination.

Leopold Mozart was to encounter the same problem. If one looked too smart and Continental, the mob would shout 'French burgher' – at least, that was how Mozart interpreted their abuse. Saussure was surprised at the total absence of display:

Englishmen are usually very plainly dressed, they scarcely ever wear gold on their clothes; they wear little coats called 'frocks' without facings, and without pleats, with a short cape above. Almost all wear small round wigs, plain hats and carry canes in their hands but no swords. Their cloth and linen are of the best and finest. You will see rich merchants and gentlemen thus dressed, and sometimes even noblemen of high rank, especially in the morning, walking through the filthy and muddy streets. Englishmen, however, are very lavish in other ways. They have splendid equipages and costly apparel when required. Peers and other persons of rank are richly dressed when they go to Court, especially on gala days.[23]

Of course, gala days were infrequent, so that modest attire for which some men had been calling for centuries was at last established, from the merchant to the duke. Such dressing down could lead to social misunderstandings on occasion. One day the Duke of Bolton, attired in plain coat and wig, was pushed off the pavement by a footman in the Duke of Somerset's livery. When Bolton protested the footman threatened to punch him on the nose. Next day, now arrayed in ducal splendour, Bolton called on Somerset to complain. Somerset obliged by giving all his servants a lecture, but afterwards he told Bolton it was his own fault for going about dressed like a common gentleman. Nevertheless, it became a British characteristic for persons of station and authority to dress plainly, with finery reserved for special occasions. This was the opposite of the rule at Versailles, where the French nobility were expected to reside and wear full gala dress at all times. This cost them a lot of money, and represented the French crown's attempt to weaken their power, whereas the British nobility could afford to improve their estates which led to British agriculture being regarded as the best in eighteenth-century Europe. It was considered social death for a French aristocrat to reside on his estates. They still regarded themselves in the light of knights dedicated to military service, who could not touch agriculture or trade without total loss of honour.

Now that the British court seemed to have lost all interest in high fashion, the French considered that the lead had returned to them as their natural prerogative, notwithstanding the fact that French ladies had adopted two British fashions for women: the low commode headdress

35 J. Closterman, attrib., *James Craggs the Elder*, c. 1710. The English suit is plain with only the vest allowed to be in a rich material. Here it is a blue brocade worn with a plain velvet coat and breeches. The periwig reaches its greatest extent in the early 1700s, almost reaching the elbow. The first vests had long sleeves so that the cuff overlaps the coat cuff. The French fondness for ribbons is banished.

and the hooped skirt. The Duke of Saint-Simon was most indignant at these British introductions, but at least menswear was not affected – or was it? Hoops began to appear in London in 1708, which meant a new accent on width, whereas coats, periwigs and high heels had all sought to make men taller. If width was coming in, would not men have to shrink?

There are four basic ways fashion can go. It can be wide or narrow, and tall or short. A lot of variations can be played on those four themes, but they are the only alternatives. Having worked the tall theme for 50 years, the only way to go was down again. Accordingly heels were reduced, and wigs grew flat on top, while coat skirts began to be flared out to increase the horizontal look. The inevitable happened. Having resolved on width and lowness, fashion took it to the extreme point, pushing width as far as ingenuity could take it. If women had hoops men had an equivalent, for wires were inserted into coat skirts to make them stand out. The extreme point was reached in the 1740s when a man's skirts could be five feet wide. Once again the voice of criticism was heard, and the complaint was the same as in the seventeenth century: menswear was too effete. The artistic third Earl of Shaftesbury conceded that the age was a feminine one: 'Whilst we look on Paintings with the same eye, as we view commonly the rich Stuffs and colour'd Silks worn by our Ladys, and admir'd in Dress, Equipage, or Furniture, we must of necessity be effeminate in our Taste'.[24] In England such French extremes could be seen on gala occasions, for notwithstanding the general mood against such fancies there were still some young men who considered it good taste to imitate things French. After one such party in 1722 Sarah Byng Osborn reported: 'I believe the gentlemen will wear petticoats very soon for many of their coats were like our mantuas. Lord Essex has a silver tissue coat, and pink color lutestring waistcoat, and several had pink color and pale blue paduasoy coats, which looks prodigiously effeminate.'[25]

The eighteenth century was determined to tidy up society. It has been called the age of encyclopaedists which sought to classify every-

thing from men o' war to grasses. Dictionaries tried to regulate spelling, and this regulation affected many areas. It can be seen in the streets of Georgian houses all built to a regular pattern, and it can be seen in the way the period treated hats. In the years 1670–1700 a man was free to cock his hat any way he pleased, up at one side or the other, up at the back, or up in the front which was a style popular among the military. After 1690 the mathematical cock was introduced, which was turned up on three sides in equal proportion. The new Age of Reason said that this geometric triangle was the only hat a man should wear and it became the only hat the fashionable would wear in town. Regulation also affected periwigs. When they first came out they could be blond, black or brown, but by the 1690s they were being powdered white and the new age insisted that white or grey should be the only colours for wigs. This obliged the young man in a wig to look older than his years, but the Age of Reason favoured the mature and senior male, and expected the young to conform to this uniform white wig. Men could be forgiven for feeling that women were taking over. Austria was ruled by the Empress Maria Theresa, a strong believer in good behaviour, while Russia had four empresses regnant, Catherine I, Anna, Elizabeth I, and Catherine the Great. In France taste was under the control of Louis XV's mistress-in-chief, Antoinette, Marquise de Pompadour, while Paris saw several famous salons run by ladies. The Age of Reason came under strong feminine influence. Queen Elizabeth and

36 Studio of William Hogarth, *The Fleet Prison Committy*, 1729. The advent of eighteenth-century uniformity with all wigs powdered grey or white. Rococo taste was for a short figure and small scale, so men are shrinking, with flat-topped wigs and low-heeled shoes. The plainness of English suits astounded foreign visitors, but they represented the Protestant Clothing Ethic. Cuffs grew very large in the 1720s and 30s, stretching up to the elbow. The Members of Parliament were investigating cruelty at the prison, and their wigs denote that they are gentlemen, while the gaoler and prisoner show their humble rank with their own hair.

Queen Anne could both say, did not a queen regnant drive men to win their greatest victories?

At the city of Bath good taste came under the rule of the master of ceremonies, the beau Richard Nash, 'Beau Nash', as he became known. Born in 1674, he read law at Oxford and moved to Bath in 1705. Firstly he ruled that no gentleman should appear before ladies in the morning in his cap and gown when going to take the waters. This referred to undress, the nightgown, as dressing gowns were then termed, and the nightcap, in which men would relax of an evening with just their shirts and knee-breeches on underneath, and which they would don in the morning before dressing fully. The wearing of periwigs had caused several men to shave off their own hair, so a cap or turban or the Spanish *montero* fur-lined cap was used to keep the scalp warm when the wig was taken off. Nash ordered that this costume should stay indoors. He was also very annoyed at country squires who would wear their riding boots at all times. To display his disapproval he arranged a performance of Punch and Judy where booted Punch refuses to remove his boots even to go to bed, at which his mistress throws him out. If Nash did spy a booted squire in the assembly rooms Nash would approach and say 'Sir, you have forgot your horse.' He himself always sported a white three-corned hat in the mathematical cock, and explained such singularity by saying that this prevented it from being stolen, when most hats were black. According to Oliver Goldsmith, Nash was large and somewhat clumsy but dressed very well, albeit as a beau of several generations, because he would keep some of the old style while donning some of the new, with a cautious approach to avant-garde novelties. It was not good taste to look too fashionable. He used to say that 'wit, flattery and fine cloaths were enough to debauch a nunnery', and this illustrates what the Bath season was all about. Apart from taking the medicinal waters or gambling, it was a suitable venue for parents to offer daughters to the highest bidder, and a good hunting ground for younger sons looking for an heiress. It was important to be noticed, and what mattered was the individual's skill to achieve this result without going too far or looking too fantastic. An outfit that was smart and restrained would impress a father more than one which was all French ruffles and silver embroidery. Marital fate could hang on the outcome. Nash observed that he was old enough to have seen three generations making love. During the Restoration the

approach had been very formal and majestic; under Queen Anne it was all *billets-doux* and witty repartee; under George II it was the vogue to pretend not to be interested, which was supposed to intrigue the lady more than anything.[26]

Nash's regulations did not apply at other watering places. When the Scot John Macky visited Tunbridge Wells in 1722 he found both men and women outdoors in the mornings in dishabille, and at Epsom men were walking about in their nightgowns. While formal suits had to be worn in London, in the country standards could be relaxed. In Henry Fielding's novel *The History of Tom Jones A Foundling*, 1749, the respectable woman servant Deborah Wilkins always allows a decent time to elapse before answering her master's bedroom bell so that he can make himself decent. When her master Allworthy discovers the baby in his bed, he forgets about decency, and rings for Mrs Wilkins, who nearly swoons with horror on finding him in only his shirt. She declares that she has never seen a man without a coat in her life. She was surely speaking about gentlemen, for as she was living in the country she must have seen farm labourers working without their coats hundreds of times. Nevertheless, it illustrates the gulf between respectable society and the fast behaviour at Epsom and Tunbridge Wells which would no doubt have given Mrs Wilkins the vapours.

Macky was very impressed by what he saw at Newmarket Races, where the Protestant Clothing Ethic was much in evidence: 'All Mankind are here upon an equal Level from the Duke to the Country-Peasant: No body wears Swords, but without Distinction are cloathed suitable to the Humor and Design of the Place for Horse-Sports'.[27] The trouble was that the British aristocracy and gentry were so used to wearing modest country clothes that they wanted to wear them in town too; hence Nash's battle with squires. As Saussure pointed out, this was most obvious in the morning, but in December 1738 the London *Evening Post* reported with horror that in the evening persons seen wearing great-coats, dirty boots and whips at the theatre were not servants sent to keep a seat, but gentlemen who could afford a box. It was the end of the world, for the theatre required correct dress as it was part of the social round. The gradual intrusion of country styles into high society was to prove a battleground for decades to come. By 1754 this English conduct was creeping into France, where the first signs of Anglomania affecting French menswear were detected.

Young Parisian males were strolling about *à l'anglaise*, discussing English horseflesh, which they could not ride, and wearing imitation English frock coats, although the waist was not as low as it should be.[28] No doubt it gave their parents and grandparents apoplexy. Was it not bad enough that the English should have given the French their formal three-piece suit, without their introducing informal attire too?

The institution of the suit made an enormous change. Instead of menswear undergoing significant changes in number and types of garments worn, the composition was now fixed at three pieces. Changes were matters of detail, rather than the adoption or abandonment of garments. The pattern established in 1666 is still with us today – alterations can be seen in the silhouette but the garments are standard. Accordingly the eighteenth century varied the suit but did not add to it. Coat sleeves were very full in 1700, grew enormous cuffs in the 1720s and 30s, and then shrank to a narrow shape in the 1750s and 60s, but they were still coat sleeves. Coat skirts flared out in the 1740s, but subsided in the 1750s, yet were still coat skirts. Knee-breeches grew narrower, so that they had to be opened up at the knee to get them on, and a row of buttons and a buckle were inserted, but they were still breeches. Menswear was now variations on a theme, a subtler art than it had been before.

The periwig did not face a serious challenge until 1715, and once again the modification came from the military. During the War of the Spanish Succession cavalry officers found that full periwigs could be blown across their eyes, so they took to tying them back. This proved such a practical idea that it was applied to all the cavalry, and at the Battle of Ramillies in 1706 both the French cavalry and the Allied troops under Marlborough wore tied-back hair or wigs with the ends neatly gathered into a black purse. This became known as the bag-wig and by the 1720s some bold civilians were sporting bag-wigs. One of the first civilians to do so was Lord Bolingbroke, who arrived at an emergency cabinet meeting in a tie-back wig. Queen Anne was not amused and said he would be coming to court in his nightcap next. In her reign it was too

informal, but gradually opinion relaxed and in the 1730s tie-back wigs gained considerable acceptance. The part over the ears was frizzed out into a style called 'pigeons' wings'. In his narrative poem about Bath, C. Anstey recorded in 1766 that a Mr Marmozet's pigeons' wings had taken the barber a whole afternoon to achieve. A single black ribbon, the 'solitaire', was worn around the throat over the cravat to anchor the bag at the back. Thus equipped a man was a beau:

For I ride in a Chair with my Hands in a Muff,
And have bought a Silk Coat and embroidered the Cuff,
But the weather was Cold, and the Coat it was thin,
So the Taylor advis'd me to line it with Skin:
But what with my Nivernois' Hat can compare,
Bag-Wig, and lac'd Ruffles, and black Solitaire?
And what can a Man of true fashion denote,
Like an ell of good Ribbon ty'd under the Throat?[29]

By 1761, when Hogarth published his print *Five Orders of Periwigs*, the full-bottomed wig had retreated into formal and official wear for clergymen, aldermen, and judges. The pigeon's-wing type with a long tail he dubbed half-natural or composite, while the type which disciplined the wings into two sausage-like rolls on either side of the face he called Queerinthian. Nevertheless this kind accorded with the neatness and regulation beloved of the period, so it became very popular. A preference for small scale was one of the chief methods by which the Rococo style distinguished itself from its grandiose Baroque predecessor. From a towering gallant of the 1690s wearing a soaring periwig with a torrent of curls and high-heeled shoes, man had shrunk into a small-headed, neat-wigged, low-heeled being. It was bad luck for the fellow who was naturally on the lofty side, for he could not be in the fashion. At least the Baroque period had provided the short man with some assistance by adding inches, but it was not so easy to take them off under Rococo rules.

The vest, which Charles II had made the gaudiest part of the suit, continued to be the most splendid part of the ensemble. It was the only piece of brilliance the British male was allowed in high society, but the royal precedent for drowning it in silver lace was not applied. Richness was limited to satin or brocade, which sufficed in themselves. The Continentals would smother the vest with lace, tassels, raised embroidery, sequins, and gems; English finery was more restrained and less garish. Moderation,

37 Philip Mercier, *Frederick, Prince of Wales*, c. 1736. The idea of tying wigs back came from the Army, and they were termed bag-wigs from the black silk bag at the back to hold the ends of the wig. The Prince has allowed himself some embroidery but his outfit is still much simpler than Continental princes wore. It was correct form to carry the hat under the left arm with the hand in the pocket, and the period was very fussy about polite behaviour.

as Peacham had said, was the principle, and it could still produce a dramatic effect. The coat and breeches of deep-red velvet, brown or darkest blue, made a superb background for vests of brocade, or satin embroidered with small-scale flowers and tendrils, which were the rage in the 1760s. All the original vests had sleeves and this continued for 100 years. At first the sleeves were in the same material as the body, but by the first decade of the eighteenth century the invisible parts hidden by the coat, the sleeves and the back, were being made in cheaper material. The sleeveless alternative saw light in the 1720s, and a red corded-silk gala suit in the Museum of London (cat. no. 4) has both a sleeved and a sleeveless vest to go with the coat. There was a slight modification in the length of vests, from on the knee in the seventeenth century, to just above the knee by 1720, where it remained into the 1760s. It was only on royal birthdays or receptions and society weddings that the British aristocrat was expected to have an entire outfit in figured silk. 'Looking rich' was for special occasions, not the everyday requirement of foreign courts. The difference was noted by Henrietta Louisa, Countess of Pomfret, on her tour of France and Italy in 1739–40.

Paris: receptions have an air of magnificence not common in our country. The dress of the company makes a great shew; and I have been to several balls, where, in this respect, they far out-shone some of our latter birth-days. The different coloured furs with which they trim their clothes in winter, have a nobler appearance than one can imagine without seeing them.[30]

In Siena she was surprised to see Italian society ladies attired in the gala costume for religious festivals, where at home such clothes were obligatory only for royal birthdays. Similarly in Florence she witnessed the race of Il Corso, with big prizes of gold brocade and velvets. Before the event the court drove through the streets which formed the course, all dressed up in their finery. Such Catholic display was the exact opposite to Protestant England, where races were held out of town in the country, and where everyone dressed down in rural informality. On his inspection of England in 1748 the horticulturalist Pehr Kalm of the Swedish Academy of Sciences observed Englishmen actually wearing riding boots in the centre of London, although they always carried a whip to signify that they were riding.[31] Doubtless the shouts of urchins

38 B. Dandridge eng. L. Boitard, '*How to Salute a Lady*', from Nivelon's *The Rudiments of Genteel Behaviour*, 1737. First remove the right glove, then doff the tricorne hat and make a deep bow. Genteel conduct was the mark of the gentleman, and the Age of Reason loved making rules. The long cuff has endured, and long wigs are required for formal receptions.

would have been less polite than Nash's remark. 'Where's yer 'orse?' was a common reaction, but the breach of polite rules grew apace, and the country was coming to the town with a vengeance. Kalm was surprised at the number of men wearing short white wigs, which even some of the labourers managed to afford. Poor ones cost one guinea, and a better quality cost two guineas. This was half the price Samuel Pepys had had to pay back in 1663, but wigs by 1748 used a lot less hair. An advertisement in the *Daily Post* for 18 December 1731 gives the price of suits: 'Next door to Brown's Coffee House Spring Gardens Charing Cross. Men's suits of superfine cloth 6 guineas, for large men 6½ guineas. Suits lined with silk 8 guineas.' Those social events when the nobility had to dress up were recorded by Mrs Mary Delany, inventor of the flower mosaic. In March 1728/9 she witnessed a reception given by George II: 'The King was in blue velvet with diamond buttons. The hat was buttoned up with prodigious fine

39 Francis Hayman, *Dr Maurice Greene, Composer to the King, and Dr John Hoadly, dramatist and chaplain to the Prince of Wales*, 1747. Ever since the Restoration in 1660 it had been correct for gentlemen to receive their equals and inferiors when undressed in their nightgowns (dressing gowns), but not their superiors, when they should be fully dressed. Thus the composer can write music in his study in his nightgown and receive the clergyman, his friend. When the wig was left off turbans or fur caps were worn to keep the scalp warm.

diamonds. The Prince of Wales was in mouse-colour velvet, turned up with scarlet, and very richly embroidered with silver.' On March 14 1733 she attended the tremendous crush at the wedding of Princess Anne to William Prince of Orange, an occasion when richness was obligatory. 'The Prince of Orange was in a gold stuff embroidered with silver; it looked rich but not showy. The King was in a gold stuff, which made much more show, with diamond buttons to his coat, his star and George shone most gloriously. The Prince of Wales was fine, as you may suppose but I hardly ever remember men's clothes.' She was too much concerned with what her female rivals were wearing. Nevertheless she did notice Lord Crawford's outfit at the state ball, for he was in white damask laced with gold.

Mrs Delany attended the Prince's birthdays in January 1738–9, and again in January 1739–40. At the first she was not impressed: 'Nothing extraordinary among the men; much finery, chiefly brown with gold or silver embroidery, and rich waistcoats.' She found an improvement next year, however: 'The men were as fine as the ladies ... My Lord Baltimore was in light brown and silver, his coat lined *quite throughout* with ermine.' (It was usual only to trim the coat.) The fondness of brown and mouse will be observed tones of suitable Protestant sobriety, contrasting nicely with the splendour of waistcoats.[32]

After one of George II's drawing rooms in 1742 Horace Walpole criticized ladies who had been absent from the court for a long time, but it applied equally to elderly men: 'Out they come, in all the accoutrements of Queen Anne's days.'[33] The older generation always sticks to the respectable styles of its youth, so aged peers at court kept to periwigs and full-skirted coats but rejected the enormous spread of coat skirts which were reinforced with wire, canvas or buckram, as being too effete.

The coronation of George III at Westminster Abbey in 1761 attracted many foreign visitors, and was an occasion for the ultimate in splendour. Count Frederick Kielmansegge of Hanover was most impressed. 'The dress of the fashionable world was nothing but velvet and cloth of gold, very little cloth of silver.' He loved the robes and the Knights of the Bath in their plumed hats. Horace Walpole did not share his opinion.[34] He declared that the aristocracy had overdone the diamonds and decorations. In his view only the Countess of Pembroke was 'the picture of majestic modesty,' so he must have expected Protestant restraint to apply even at this most magnificent event. The Protestant ideal was the exact opposite to the attitude in Catholic countries where *fa figura, faire figure* was all-important for Latin males. Count Kielmansegge encountered an example of a peer dressing his servants more grandly than himself when he dined with the Duke of Newcastle. The servants in long wigs and gold lace he mistook for guests, so he thought he could not offer them the normal tip of one shilling, and felt obliged to increase it to half-a-crown.[35]

The country had to observe only one sumptuary law at the time. Following Bonnie Prince

40 After W. Hoare, *Richard 'Beau' Nash, c.* 1761. The arbiter of dress and conduct at Bath, who banned nightgowns from appearing in public. He wears his distinctive white three-cornered hat, the 'mathematical cock'. His plain coat and the simple line of embroidery on his waistcoat reflect his disapproval of extreme styles.

Charlie's invasion in 1745, the Act of Dress banned Highland plaids, trews and kilts, except for Scots serving in the Scottish regiments of the British Army. The nobility, of course, considered itself to be above the law, so it continued wearing kilts and trews in a mixture of tartans, not as clan types. It was another area where a form of trousers was in being long before high fashion condescended to notice.

In the opinion of Philip, Earl of Chesterfield, fashion was a folly, but even he had to concede that where making a good impression was concerned, clothes were important:

Here invoke the assistance of the Graces: even that silly article of dress is no trifle upon these occasions. Never be first nor last in the fashion. Wear as fine cloaths as men of your rank commonly do, and rather better than worse; and when you are well dressed once a day, do not seem to know that you have any cloaths on at all, but let your motions be as easy as they could be in your nightgown. A fop values himself upon his dress: but a man of sense will not neglect it, in his youth at least. The greatest fop I ever saw, was at the same time the greatest sloven: for it is an affected singularity of dress, be it of what sort it will, that constitutes a fop, and everybody will prefer an over-dressed fop to a slovenly one. Let your addresse, when you first come into company, be modest.[36]

This was the advice he gave to his nephew, the next Earl. It echoes Beau Nash in not rushing into a new fashion, but adopting new styles slowly while still keeping something of the old. The stress on modesty would have pleased Calvin.

The problem with dressing the aristocracy was that some of them were reluctant to pay the bills. In 1740 Lord Tylney paid his tailor, but then with Lord Castelmain dressed up as highwaymen and robbed the poor tailor of his earnings. Subsequently they encountered the tailor at an inn who denounced their lordships as robbers, but nobody believed him. In the end their lordships relented, said it was all a prank, and paid the tailor back. He then demanded an extra £50 in compensation for the fright, and to keep his mouth shut about the incident, which did nothing for their lordships' reputations. Whether he got it was not reported.[37] Nevertheless, the incident illustrates just how equivocal the nobility could be about its debts. The problem persisted into the next period. Dressing up as highwaymen was part of the country look and equine passion. Lord Chesterfield opined that young men followed two types, swaggering would-be heroes and country oafs:

Most our young fellows here, display some character or other by their dress; some affect the tremendous, and wear a great and fiercely cocked hat, an enormous sword, a short waistcoat, and a black cravat. Others go in brown frocks, leather breeches, great oaken cudgels in their hands, their hats uncocked, and their hair unpowdered; and imitate grooms, stage coachmen and country bumkins.[37]

Despite his displeasure, the latter was going to win over the former.

Chapter Four

NEO-CLASSICAL NUDES & DANDIES

The signs of a revolt against the regimentation of the Age of Reason began in the 1760s, when young men expressed a dislike of wigs, and started wearing their own hair. By 1765 the royal periwig makers were so worried that they petitioned George III to stop it, but as Walpole remarked, this was an impossible request. How could a government stop it? The rejection caught on, and in his diary for 7 May 1767 Sylas Neville noted: 'Had my hair clipped off for the last time, being resolved to let it grow, as it is much more natural and agreeable than a wig, except in some extraordinary cases.'[1] Needless to say, it shocked the older generations who had been wearing wigs since boyhood, so they maintained wigs for as long as they could. At the time of the Gordon Riots on 3 June 1780 Lord Willoughby lost his wig, and Lord Bathurst had his torn off by the mob. On the other hand, Lords Hilborough, Stormont and Townshend had been wearing their own hair tied back in a bag, but in the chaos the bags had come off so their hair was all around their ears.[2] The fashionable subjects were now nature, sentiment, and enthusiasm, the precise opposites to reason, and one of the ways to declare one's loyalty to the new ideals was to sport one's own hair in natural manner. From the anonymity of the common white or grey wig, there was a swing to individuality of hair colour. The rationalists had a strong suspicion of things natural, which was illustrated by the French scholar J. P. Grosley when he described the paintings of William Hogarth in 1772; 'pure nature, but too naked and too true'.[3] He preferred the art of Chardin and Greuze which employed charm and sentiment to disguise the crudities of life, a type of nicety now challenged by the new age. The Rococo style was damned as too frivolous, immoral, domestic, and feminine.

The rediscovery of antiquity had an important impact on attitudes toward art and clothes. A serious campaign of archaeological investigation was undertaken to hunt for Roman treasures. In 1738 King Charles of Naples ordered tunnelling to begin at Herculaneum, and in 1748 at Pompeii. In 1760 Duke Philip of Parma founded a museum of antiquities and ordered the excavation of Velleia to stock it. Collecting ancient statuary became a craze among the wealthy, with European aristocrats competing to build up celebrated ensembles of marble. Antique art was the only true art, declared the critics, the only correct form, so it should be followed by contemporary artists instead of continuing with Rococo trivialities. Ancient art was nature: an eternal ideal unaffected by fashions and imperfections. When the sculptor Canova saw the Elgin marbles for the first time he exclaimed, 'The truth of nature!' because they seemed perfect.[4] They were not, of course, true to nature in showing such genuine human physical imperfections as warts, varicose veins or flabby flesh. They were a Greek interpretation of the human body into an impossible perfection, but after 2,000 years they seemed endowed with eternal qualities. The new interest in statuary had an impact on menswear, for it meant that bodies were back in fashion. Consequently clothes were made more revealing. Coats were cut right back with only two flaps in the skirts. The vests or waistcoats which for a hundred years during the effete Baroque and Rococo eras had modestly concealed the male sexual organs completely, were now shortened and rose at a rapid rate until they only reached the hips or lower waist. The breeches and the flies were revealed, and given the admiration for classical limbs, breeches became tighter and ever tighter, moulding the male thighs and making the sexual bulge an unavoidable presence. Masculinity at its most blatant was making a comeback. And what style of clothes could best dress this natural man if not the British country look? The English cutaway riding coat and simple frock with its collar, the buckskin breeches for riding, and the riding boots, all became town wear at last, even finding their way into court receptions. So well did the British country look satisfy the new quest for nature that it spread all over Europe, with Russian and Italian princes sporting riding boots for everything except court balls, where of course shoes must be worn. An unadorned simplicity was now important, for it showed the perfection of the natural look, so that velvet coats were replaced by honest woollen cloth, while skin colour became the tone for waistcoats and breeches. This did give an impression of nakedness at a distance. Taste now required ladies not to blush but to admire the perfect sculpture of the male limbs.

When Horace Walpole was in Paris in September 1765 he observed that the British influence was growing stronger. Not only did the salons discuss the English novel, but 'In their dress and equipages they are grown very simple.' He was less pleased that his hostess insisted on his obtaining a French wardrobe, for Lady Herford 'has cut me to pieces, and thrown me into a caldron with tailors, periwig-makers, snuff-box-wrights, milliners, etc., which really took up but little time; and I am come out quite new, with everything but youth'. Like other

41 Sir Joshua Reynolds, *Warren Hastings*, Governor General of India, 1766–8. The first signs of a revolt against wigs, as young gentlemen start to keep their own hair as part of the back-to-nature movement. Hastings' suit is of dark-blue wool with a velvet collar and gold buttonholes. The coat is the simple English frock coat with narrow skirts. The waistcoat is beige with the small floral pattern showing the new awareness of nature. Waistcoats are beginning to shorten as the idea of the natural figure being shown gains impact. A Continental governor would not have been seen dead in anything so common as wool, but in England modesty counted.

English and German visitors before him, Walpole concluded that the French were quite mad. They did not wear hats when it was raining but hid under umbrellas or drove all exposed in open carriages. They put a hat on when it was dry, contrary to the English, who used hats for protection from the weather. The court at Versailles he found a mixture of grandiose parade with evident poverty. The Duke of Praslins had put his servants into red neckerchieves. This was surely intended as a deliberate insult against all those English dukes and gentlemen who had the affrontery to visit Paris dressed like country people, for the red neckpiece was the dress of ostlers, but given the British aristocracy's love affair with horses, they were proud to sport such accessories. On his way home Walpole lost half his linen at Chantilly when a portmanteau was mislaid, and was later robbed of a new frock coat, waistcoat and breeches laced with gold, and

a white and silver waistcoat with black velvet kneebreeches, garments he had worn to the French court. The fact that he wore a black velvet suit there underlines his fidelity to the Protestant Clothing Ethic.[5] On his return home he found that London tailors were trying to promote clothes edged with Brussels point lace and buttons trimmed with fur, as being the latest French novelties, but he had not seen any such thing in Paris. 'Singularities grow here, and are not exotic'. Walpole was back in Paris in 1775 to see the new Queen, Marie Antoinette, and judged her 'a statue of beauty'. Note the word *statue*, for now everybody was being appraised according to their resemblance to a work of classical art. The clothes at the court ball he found lacked taste, given the French fondness for excessive decoration.[6]

In Spain ever since the Bourbon dynasty took over in 1700 there had been a struggle to impose French fashions on the country. First Philip V banned the black male court costume and plain collar, but met such opposition from the Spanish aristocracy that he said all grandees who did not adopt French clothes would lose their estates. In 1766 the royal government had another go. The Spanish fondness for long cloaks with capes and slouch hats was condemned as a masquerade costume contributing to assassinations, as weapons could be concealed underneath. Spaniards were ordered to wear French cocked hats, and short cloaks without capes. They obeyed for one day, but next day riots broke out, and yet another French attempt was worsted by national resistance. Walpole could only wonder that the Spanish would riot against cocked hats but not against the Inquisition.[7]

The French still liked to claim that they dominated fashion in London. On his visit in 1772 Grosley waxed eloquent on the insults to French visitors from porters and watermen, and cited the example of an English surgeon who got his face slapped by ruffians for wearing a French coat in London, but he insisted the English did not invent fashions of their own to distinguish themselves from the French. On the contrary, they copied everything:

A mode begins to be out of date in Paris, just when it has been introduced at London by some English nobleman. The court and the first-rate nobility immediately take it up; it is next introduced about St James's by those who ape the manners of the court; and, by the time it has reached the city, a contrary mode already prevails in Paris, where the English bringing with them the obsolete mode, appear like people from another world. The little hats, for example, at present so fashionable in France, begin to be worn by the nobility who borrowed the mode from Paris; by degrees the English will come at the diminutive size, but the great hats will then be resumed in Paris.[8]

The little hats were the Nivernois, associated with the French ambassador to London, the Duke of Nivernois, and the brim was attached to the crown at the sides. Yet Grosley allowed himself to be confused by all the seasonal fashions that were about, the plethora of temporary vogues which were forgotten by the end of summer. What he could not detect, although Walpole could, was the main-stream development, the increasing submission of all of Europe to the British natural country look.

The alternative to the Nivernois was the Kevenhuller, a very wide cocked hat from Germany. The polite beaux of St James's would carry their hats under one arm, which led to the development of a special *chapeau bras* for receptions and assemblies. Characters who wore their tricornes on the back of their heads with one end sticking up in the air were dubbed Gawkies, as they were so inelegant. Wearing the tricorne over one eye was enough to condemn a man as coming from Moorfields, for the correct method as defined by the rationalists was straight on, but dangerous indications of individual fancy were creeping in. Hats decorated with gold braid denoted an officer or a member of the horsey set. The tiny Nivernois hat was adopted by one set in particular. A number of young beaux in London, led by the dissolute Charles James Fox, who considered themselves more 'arty' than any working artist, complained that the British look in country clothes was far too dull. They favoured decoration and began to ornament their suits with braid, tassels and frogging, and adopted fobs and seals with which to crowd the waistline. They revived high-heeled shoes, with the old red heel of the time of Louis XIV, and some of them carried reticules (handbags) hanging from their wrists. Not surprisingly they were damned as feminine absurdities. These Macaroni, as they became known, had a horror of the sturdy simplicity of the rural mode, and liked very long skirts on their coats until mud and insults about their petticoats showing persuaded them to chop them off. Thereafter they wore extremely short coat skirts, and had the waistcoat reduced to the ribs. They liked their clothes very tight, which was in keeping with the new classical taste, but their weakness for deco-

42 Carington Bowles, '*How D'ye like me?*' c. 1770. A Macaroni displays his enormous wig and his tiny Nivernois hat under his arm. The waistcoat has shot up to the waist, exposing all the breeches which the effete Baroque period had concealed under vests. Exposing the figure reflects the neo-classical taste for antiquity, but the wig and the ribbons are retrogressive.

ration lacked the noble simplicity of ancient art. The Macaroni fought a rearguard action to retain wigs, insisting that the artificial was good taste, and regarding unpowdered hair as vulgar in the extreme. Their wigs became notorious for their height, soaring up over the forehead into a puffball, topped by the tiny Nivernois hat. By 1773 they were newsworthy enough for the printshops to be issuing cartoons, but the Macaronis were not an important movement, for they changed nothing in the long run. They were a mixture of the new slim line combined with decoration which was definitely out of date, a confusion of old and new.

Mrs Elizabeth Montagu encountered the breed at Bath in 1780, but felt that the watering spa had gone downhill being frequented by 'the Maccaronies who trip in pumps with Parasols over their head . . . I met a young man who I took for one of the Cherokee Kings lately arrived, but was assured he was an Irish beau

43 Johan Zoffany, *Four Grandchildren of Empress Maria Theresa*, 1778. The humble but ancient trouser receives imperial promotion. At the age of five Prince Louis of Parma is breeched, not into kneebreeches, but trousers, so he will have a favourable attitude to trousers as an adult. His sisters are, from the left, Carolina Maria Theresa, baby Charlotte Maria and Maria Antonia, who wears a head protector, which the English called pudding as it resembled a black pudding. Both sexes wore them when young.

who was to begin the Ball.'[9] She was equally displeased that the masculine wearing of riding clothes in town was now being copied by young ladies who ought to know better than imitate the casual wear of men. The use of parasols and reticules by the Macaroni was a childish desire to shock.

Far more important than the Macaronis was a development in children's clothes which was going to affect menswear for the next two hundred years and beyond. In 1778 no less a person than Louis of Parma, future King of Etruria and grandson of the Empress Maria Theresa, was breeched, not into kneebreeches like a gentleman, but into silk trousers, as depicted by Zoffany. The significance of this was that he would want to wear trousers as an adult and so would the rest of his generation. His grandmother allowed it because of the new feelings about nature. With classical simplicity being promoted by Winckelmann and Goethe as the ultimate in taste, and the most natural art, it behoved their followers to seek a more natural costume. Peasants wore trousers, therefore trousers were natural and rural, possessed of an

honest simplicity without any Rococo trimmings, and consequently imperial grandsons could be allowed to give trousers the accolade of imperial approbation. After centuries of being held in contempt, the humble trouser at last received the blessing of high society, because the country was in fashion. The vogue was international, with Marie Antoinette playing at shepherdesses at Versailles, and King George III of Great Britain being hailed as 'Farmer George' – an appellation that preceding monarchs would not have allowed, but now a term of affection and approval. Even so, the trouser did not have an easy ride ahead, for there were clubs and courts which would ban it, while in the 1790s trousers were to be a hot political potato. But the start was made in the 1770s, although ultimate triumph lay in the next century.

Every gentleman visiting the metropolis was still likely to be given long lists of demands by his family and friends for clothes, fabrics, jewels or prints of the latest look, but the great improvements in English mail coaches, so much admired by foreign visitors like Count Kielmansegge, were to shorten those lists. The coach service meant that a family in the country could now appoint an agent in the city, such as their solicitor, tradesman or innkeeper, to carry out errands for them, and send back purchases on the mail. The nobility could still send servants to town for them, but for the family with a smaller staff, the mail coach was a very useful way of ordering clothes at a distance. The English industrial revolution had begun, and the new mills were to mean more fabrics at a lower price, but an industrial system for making clothes took much longer to arrive. Therefore there were no definite rules laid down for making clothes. In the major centres most of the tailors would follow similar methods, but outside the cities one would find tailors with their own way of doing things. This explains why not every print or later every photograph of a man shows him with his coat buttoned the same way. A lot of men did button coats with the left side over the right, but there were some who buttoned right over left. They may have been left-handed, or perhaps their local tailor made all his coats like that. Before the introduction of an industrial system which said that all coats must be made the same way, there was room for such individual methods. Not until the twentieth century did the industry rule that the sexes must button their clothes on opposite sides without exception. When everything was made by hand things could be different.

In 1782 the Duke of Montrose persuaded parliament to repeal the Act of Dress, the last attempt to regulate dress in the period. Highland wear was now in order for all Scots, and the German visitor Sophie von La Roche saw her first Scotsman near Buckingham House in 1784 but did not know what his garments were called: 'There we saw a Scotsman in highland costume; his blue and white cloak slung round him; his apron and bare knees were new to us.'[10] The neo-classical movement was going to affect kilts. Given the admiration for a sculptural limb, kilts began to inch their way up the thigh. No doubt cartoonists exaggerated when they showed kilts reduced to a brief fringe, but nevertheless more thigh was on show, and on a windy day, more than that, given the absence of drawers. It got bad enough for the War Office in 1804 to consider putting its Scottish regiments into trews. This incurred the wrath of Scottish generals and colonels, who insisted that the hardiness of their men was due above all to short kilts worn in all weathers. Kilts stayed, although the modest Victorians would drop the length to the knee as part of their general cover-up.

In 1784 François Armand, future Duke of La Rochefoucauld, visited England, as his father was a very unusual French aristocrat who took an interest in agricultural improvements. The young man was impressed:

The London shops are indeed worthy of remark; surely there can be no other city which has any thing so magnificent to show. Everything the merchant possesses is displayed behind windows which are always beautifully clean.[11]

London was a port as well as a capital city, the emporium of the world. As part of his education in things English, the young explorer visited some public balls, and there found the absolute simplicity of menswear now well established:

The men's dress is very simple – black breeches and silk stockings. Such is the correct dress for occasions like these. In order to be something quite out of the common, a man may go wearing his cravat and hair in a pigtail with his ordinary clothes. The well-dressed men wear a new coat every time, but a plain coat of cloth with nothing sumptuous about it.[12]

An Englishman who positively loathed dressing up was John, Viscount Torrington. He liked wearing riding clothes and touring round the country, living out of his saddlebags, but when he joined his wife at Weymouth in 1781 he had to dress for society: 'Being obliged to embark in the great world, the grand attention must be to dress, so I labour'd thro' the business; and then was introduced to Miss *That* and Capt. *T'Other*'.[13] He would have been happier in buckskin than fine wool. That the English were so relaxed astounded François Armand, for even assemblies were casual in comparison to France: 'It would be impossible to be more easy-going in good society than one is in England. Formality counts for nothing and for the greater part of the time one pays no attention to it'.[14] Young Englishmen were allowed to whistle, hum, sit where they liked, put their feet up, and occupy any table they pleased, which all counted as bad manners in France, where things were very precise, even when they claimed to be imitating the English. It was this English informality which allowed its young men to wear plain coats at balls in natural wool, a fabric held in absolute contempt by the nobility in the past, but the new ideal of nature had changed all that.

Expressing contempt for the attitudes of the recent past was fuelled greatly by Britain's loss of the American colonies, which declared their independence in 1776. France, seeking revenge for Britain's conquest of Canada, allied itself to the new republic in 1778, and in 1783 Britain was obliged to recognize the new state. Only six years later the liberal ideas France had supported in North America came home to roost; the royal government which had aided the infant American republic was ousted itself by the First Republic in 1789, and Louis XVI was executed in 1793. The *ancien régime* throughout Europe was coming under attack, as the ideals of liberalism and republicanism spread. The past had failed. The advanced should reject it lock, stock and barrel, and of course this included its clothes and its manners. The Age of Reason's fondness for laying down rules about everything, typified by Nivelon's *Rudiments of Genteel Behaviour*,

44 J. R. Smith, *The Promenade at Carlisle House*, 1781. English riding dress dares to appear at a town reception. The young man on the left has the round English riding hat, riding breeches and riding boots indoors! The man on the right is correctly dressed for town in his frock coat, waistcoat, breeches, tricorne, and shoes. The battle between undress and full dress is on, as often occurs between the generations.

1737 (figs 37 and 38), with all its instructions on how to stand, how to walk, how to raise the hat to a lady, and how to bow, led inevitably to a counter-reaction against such detailed discipline. It now became the fashion to break those rules, so here too the English country style was the ideal method to display one's contempt for the neat past by being informal, muddy, untidy, wearing riding boots indoors, and smelling of the stables. It was the deliberate opposite to French fashion with its ornate styles. The strength of the British country look's invasion of French culture is illustrated by the English words entering the French language: the frock coat became the *fraque*, the riding coat the *redingote*, and the jockey hat the *chapeau jockei*. The French beau of the 1780s would express his admiration for Britannia with striped stockings, and by wearing boots and spurs in the middle of Paris, while the ladies fell for *robes à l'anglaise* and *coiffures anglomane*. If it appears rather illogical for the French to be adopting English clothes at the same time as they were fighting against Britain in America and India, it may be explained by the fact that British clothes expressed the liberal approach to life. As they also expressed the new admiration for nature, their impact was twofold, and not to be resisted by any man wishing to be up to date in his attitudes, imperial competition apart. The trickle of the 1750s became a flood 30 years later. The British look appealed to democrats.

Needless to say, the British aristocracy had not been thinking about democracy when it donned country clothes but about its own convenience. Given that court life did not require their constant attendance, they could have homes in the country, and only houses in London. Yet it was the fact that the nobility wore its country clothes in town which established a fashion for the rest of Europe and the colonies to follow. Examples of the upper classes who did this included Lord Shelburne, whom the judge Samuel Curwen from New England saw in St James's Park, 'his dress a brown frock and boots, with a whip in his hand'.[15] The judge was an empire loyalist opposed to the American rebellion, who escaped to Britain in 1775. Other loyalists fled north to Canada, which wished to remain British, a situation paralleled in Ireland in the twentieth century. Another firm follower of rural dress was Sir Charles Turner of York, a hunting man who always wore the same green frock coat with its tallyho buttons representing horses and hounds in 1782, by which time such buttons were 40 years out of fashion. There was Charles, Elev-

45 Wright of Derby, *Muslin manufacturer Samuel Oldknow*, *c*. 1790. The naked look of the neo-classical ideal, with the waistcoat and the breeches in skin-coloured tones, showing the figure. At a distance, a man looked unclothed. The male body is on display again now that the period regards itself as more masculine than the Baroque and Rococo eras. The collar on the English frock coat was becoming a fashionable feature and starting to grow higher. Some men continued to powder the hair.

enth Duke of Norfolk, the Protestant in a Catholic dynasty, whom Sir Nathaniel Wraxall said 'might indeed have been mistaken for a grazier or a butcher by his dress and appearance', in 1784. The Duke was one of the first men to cut his hair short and to dispense with the pigtail at the back. He disliked hair powder and in 1785 proposed that the government should tax it, an idea they later adopted.[16] Sheridan's sister Betsy met the Duke in October 1788 and found his manners as modest as his dress: 'The Duke in appearance gives one the idea of a good honest Gentleman Farmer, dress'd in a plain Grey frock and brown curly head, his face is hansome [sic], but his Person

very large and unwieldy. He is very civil, very good humour'd seemingly, and perfectly unaffected.'[17] A perfect Protestant gentleman, in fact.

There was one small decoration Knights of the Garter and Bath would wear with their simple frock coats, which was to have the star of their order embroidered over the heart. A Prussian visitor in 1782, Carl Philip Moritz, noticed this custom when he went to Ranelagh pleasure gardens and surveyed the crowd from the gallery, a good vantage point to see the generation gap in hair styles. He could 'easily distinguish several stars and other orders of knighthood; French queues and bags contrasted with plain English heads of hair, or professional wigs'.[18] In France wigs remained compulsory at court up to the Revolution, and Lord Thurlow was refused admission to Louis XVI because he did not wear a bob wig, the longer version of wig still required as an echo of periwigs. Moritz was very surprised by the English informality to be seen at Parliament: 'The Members of the House of Commons have nothing particular in their dress; they come into the house in their greatcoats and with boots and spurs. It is not uncommon to see a member lying stretched out on one of the benches while others are debating. Some crack nuts, others eat oranges.'[19] The Whig Charles James Fox, from being a Macaroni, had gone to slovenly extremes, and Moritz considered him very badly dressed. Wraxall was more scathing and said negligence in dress was not excusable in a leading politician who was likely to be copied. Fox annoyed the government by wearing a blue coat and a buff waistcoat, the colours of the American rebels, but on 8 April 1782 there came a major change. Lord North and the Tories were dismissed for losing America, and the Whigs came in. Wraxall reported, 'Never was a more total change of costume beheld than the House of Commons presented to the eye when that assembly met after the Easter recess.' Lord North and his party moved into the opposition seats with their frock coats, greatcoats, boots and spurs, but the new Whig administration entered in full court dress with velvet suits, silk waistcoats, lace frills, swords, and powdered hair. The sight of Fox

and Edmund Burke in court dress caused considerable merriment, and the idea of Fox trying to look tidy was a joke in itself. Evidently, having joined the establishment the Whigs wanted to show it.[20]

The continuing impact of British clothes on the French was examined in 1785 by Dr John Andrews. 'People of rank in France are prodigiously fond of exterior marks of grandeur. From this motive they seldom stir abroad without their equipage, and would, till within these few years, have been ashamed to be seen walking in the streets.' The peace with Britain, however, had allowed the French to visit England, and, 'they have in consequence begun to adopt customs which were peculiar to ourselves; people of fashion are now walking in undress on a morning in the streets of Paris, who formerly would have thought it beneath their dignity'. Even so, the French had not forsaken finery completely. 'Swords and full dresses, the wearing of which, unless on particular occasions, is so uncustomary in England, were, until very lately, almost always worn in France; nor is it uncommon to see numbers of people sauntering in the streets of Paris, as completely and magnificently apparelled as if they were going to court.' Dr Andrews blamed Cardinal Richelieu for involving the French aristocracy so deeply in fashion, taste, good manners and pretty compliments, but it was a clever plan to keep them out of politics. In Britain the nobility had a great deal to do with politics, and so cared less about fashion.[21]

The existence of modes and vogues in dress worried another German visitor, Dr Frederick Augustus Wenderborn, in 1791, because it made such demands on the wardrobe.

In former times, people of some consequence and fortune thought themselves to appear very decently, if they had every year a new suit of cloaths but at present three or more are annually required by a man in the middling station of life, who wishes to make what is called only a decent appearance. Besides the fashions alter in these days so much, that a man can hardly wear a coat two months before it is out of fashion. No wonder, therefore, that the clothiers find that the demand of their manufactures has increased, and they can even raise the price of them without exciting murmur ... These frequent changes of fashion, in regard to dress and furniture, are a great support of British manufactures.[22]

The doctor had put his finger on the commercial reason for fashion where seasonal variations kept

46 J. Gillray, *A Voluptuary under the Horrors of Digestion*, 1793. George, Prince of Wales, whose extravagant tastes were a national scandal. The naked or natural look was less suitable to those without the figure to support it. The details of how a man fastened his flies are now clearly to be seen. Beau Brummell had an impossible task in trying to reform a Prince who did not know what self-discipline was.

47 Peter Vandyke, *Robert Southey*, 1795. The revolutionary young sport long hair devoid of powder as the most natural gesture. Under the impact of the French Revolution, and the scruffy dressing of the Whig party, youth rejected the concept of genteel behaviour.

48 Peter Vandyke, *Samuel Taylor Coleridge*, 1795. Fanciful cravats became the pride of the rebellious young, and as they needed to be supported waistcoats sprouted collars and the frock-coat collar was made larger. Fashion had found a new item to develop towards its extreme.

the trade going, but the changes he complained of were details and not tremendous revolutions. The basic man's wardrobe remained constant; it was the buttons and the cloth, or the neckpiece, which underwent variations every year to keep the market lively. The doctor felt that British design was now equal to French, citing the example of a snuffbox which had been made in Birmingham and sold to France, where it was purchased for 4 louis, by an English tourist. The tourist came home complaining that it was impossible to find such a box in England, only to be informed that it could be had in Birmingham for 10/6.

In France snuffboxes and bob wigs met their dénouement in 1789. Everything smacking of the *ancien régime* was despised. It was termed the fight of the *culottes* against the *sans-culottes*, the class identified by kneebreeches against the peasants and labourers who lacked the garment. Trousers were the identity badge of the revolutionary. The new National Guard and the revolutionary tribunals wore striped trousers. Tricornes were out of fashion, and the uncocked round hat or the red bonnet or cap of liberty were virtually compulsory wear. It was a period

of confusion, so there were several types of dress as a result during the 1790s. At the start of the decade the *muscadins* appeared, the sons of good family who wore their hair long and plaited on either side of the head in dogs' ears, favoured grey coats with black collars, a black or green cravat, and large round hats. They styled themselves the Club de Clichy and spoke with a drawl, dropping their 'r's. Consequently they had to carry cudgels to defend themselves against attack. By 1794 they had been replaced by the Incroyables who wore their hair long but loose, a short coat, and wide pantaloons. They were denoted in particular by their cravats and collars. The English frocks and riding coats had modest collars which were now exaggerated and expanded right up to the ears, as were the shirt collars which sprouted muslin wings. It was said that the Incroyables were buried in their cravats, as half the face seemed to disappear. Such radical styles were quickly imitated in England by progressive poets like Southey and Coleridge, who wore their hair down to the shoulder, and flaunted fantastic cravats. By 1795 one Napoleon Bonaparte was a regular caller at the home of the Corsican Madame Permon, whose daughter

Laure was to marry Napoleon's aide General Junot, Duke d'Abrantès, in 1800. Laure recorded that Napoleon was very scruffy in his early days. He despised the *muscadins*, with their long hair, but he was no example of military neatness. His hair was always badly combed and badly powdered. He wore a round hat down over his eyes, from which two badly powdered dog-ears of hair escaped, a grey greatcoat, no gloves, and ill-made boots. If it was wet and he had to dry the boots before the fire, the smell was so awful that Madame Permon made her maidservant clean them whenever Bonaparte appeared. Laure was not impressed when Napoleon became a general, for his uniform was drab, and there was only one piece of gold braid on his hat, although it was topped by a gigantic tricolour plume. It was to take an older, more sophisticated lady, Josephine, Vicomtesse de Beauharnais, to teach young General Bonaparte how to dress.

During the Directoire period society began to recover from the shocks of the Terror. Many artists and men of letters adopted white togas with red borders, designed by the artist David, and cut their hair very short in the Titus crop, named from the Roman emperor in antiquity. The togas were to display their support for a republic in the Roman manner, and the ideals of neo-classical art were now applied to politics. Society should be a work of classical art, and this was reflected in the extremely tight breeches and trousers worn in Directoire Paris. It was hard luck on the man with skinny legs, unless he used a bit of padding, because a perfect limb was *de rigueur*. When Napoleon became First Consul Paris was smartened up, with regular military parades, while his wars were to sweep many a fop off the streets and into the army. Laure sighed to think that foreigners believed all Frenchmen were wearing moustaches, red bonnets and trousers, but at court, kneebreeches were making a comeback because the consul was about to translate himself into an emperor.

There was a brief peace between France and Britain in 1802, when several English visitors, including Charles James Fox, crossed the Channel to inspect the imperial enemy. Laure, now a duchess, was very disappointed. The famous orator was dressed like a farmer from Devonshire with a dark grey coat, but she invited him to dinner and was soon impressed by his conversation. She had made the French mistake of assuming that if a person did not look magnificent they were not brilliant on the inside. The British proclaimed the opposite. The French fondness for splendour burst forth when

49 Ingres (attrib.), *Louis Charles Mercier Dupaty*, c. 1805. Under neo-classical influence the hair is cropped to resemble the Roman emperor Titus, and the extremes of the 1790s are abandoned. Thanks to Beau Brummell, starching the linen becomes a dominant ideal, with the emphasis on a crisp sharpness that is completely new. Dupaty is dressed completely in the English fashion, with a dark-green frock coat with the enlarged collar, gray doeskin riding breeches, and gleaming white linen.

the Empire was created in 1804. The new dynasty of Bonapartes were *nouveaux venus*, and they behaved much as the new Tudor dynasty had done under Henry VIII, with lavish expenditure on clothes. When the court was at Fontainebleau men had to wear a hunting habit of green cloth faced with crimson velvet, and fastened with Brandenburgs in gold or silver. It was very showy, but Laure, Duchess d'Abrantès, preferred the simple shooting dress of the British pattern. In Paris court wear for men was as ornate as could be imagined, for the new emperor wanted to impress the world. All his court were required to dress magnificently, and Laure wrote 'We lived truly in a whirlwind. Every day balls, every day fêtes.' Her husband had an income of 1,500,000 francs, with over 200,000 francs going on clothes, besides the gold plate and gilded furniture.[23] The amount of embroidery was prodigious, with velvet coats being decorated with oak leaves, laurel leaves, palm fronds or sunbursts, down the front, round the cuffs and down the tails, in shining gold and

silver. A keen observation of developments at court was made by Claire, Countess de Rémusat, who became a lady-in-waiting to the Madame Bonaparte, soon to be created the Empress Josephine. The count was Keeper of the Wardrobe, and therefore responsible for the imperial finery, which was often designed by Garnerey and tailored by Leroy of the rue de la Loi. The countess wrote of Napoleon: 'He liked display, providing it did not interfere with his own particular habits, therefore he laid the weight of ceremonial on those who surrounded him. He believed also that the French are attracted by the glitter of external pomp. He was very simple in his own attire, but he required his officers to wear magnificent uniforms.' Napoleon had a strong dislike of constricting clothes, and having been a soldier all his career, liked to wear a uniform. He did not dress simply for ascetic reasons, but because uniforms were relatively simple. His staff had to conspire how to catch him when dressing him up for a ceremony was necessary. He now had frequent baths, under the influence of Josephine, having been persuaded that they were good for his health. Like the Duchess d'Abrantès, the Countess de Rémusat did not approve of all Napoleon's innovations in dress. When he was one of the three consuls he decreed for himself a long red coat in velvet for winter and a lighter stuff for summer. With it he wore a black cravat and a shirt frilled down the front, but he refused to wear any wrist ruffles. With the coat went a silver waistcoat or else a uniform, and he wore his own hair unpowdered. The other consuls, Lebrun and Cambacérès, being elderly, insisted on hair powder and all the ruffles and swords, which made them resemble courtiers of royal days. In 1804 the Empire was declared, and titles showered on marshals, inspectors, engineers, colonels, naval commanders, and civilian administrators. The revolutionary address, 'Citizen', was ousted by imperial and serene highnesses, graces and monsigneurs. The new courtiers proved to be more sensitive about precedence than the royal court had been, for many of them came from unsophisticated backgrounds and there was a lot of squabbling over place. The coronation cost 4,000,000 francs (£160,000), and court uniforms

50 Gatine after Horace Vernet, *Un Incroyable*. The Incroyables adopted the English country look by 1800, after earlier excesses with long hair and pantaloons. This one wears the English riding breeches and gaiters in skin-coloured leather with matching waistcoat, and plain frock coat with the new high collar. The riding hat developed into the top hat.

were devised at the same time. Men had to wear coats embroidered with silver, with the colour depending on the office they held, which was amethyst for marshals, red for chamberlains, and dark blue for equerries. Princes had to wear white coats embroidered with gold. Over the coats went a velvet cloak lined with satin, a sash; and a hat completed the ensemble, with the front turned up and adorned by a white plume. The sixteenth-century ruff was revived, but it was combined with the cravat hanging down in front, a curious mixture when both articles were supposed to go round the neck.

After a visit to the Bavarian court Napoleon decided to introduce some of its royal ceremonial at his own court, although he would find that such long engagements required more patience than he possessed. As the social graces were sadly lacking among his motley nobility, the old dancing master Depréaux, who had worked for Queen Marie Antoinette, was summoned to teach marshals how to bow and their women how to curtsey. Survivors from the royal court who attended the new imperial one found their social charms and graces unemployed, for Napoleon ran his palaces with military precision. Madame de Rémusat declared that being on constant duty at court was boring amidst all the splendour, for it operated like clockwork and one was simply a cog in the wheel.

The emperor allotted himself a clothing allowance of 40,000 francs a year, and his wife 600,000 francs, on the grounds that those about him should be smothered in heavy splendour. When he was off on campaign the Wardrobe sent fresh sets of linen and clothing to different places, in order to catch him somewhere. While he maintained that he only wished to dress as simply as a guardsman, in fact he expected his clothes to be always of the very best quality, and would throw any unsatisfactory garment in the fire. His impatience was a sore trial for his valet. The new emperor could now afford to smell nice and got through 60 bottles of eau-de-Cologne a month.[24] Despite all the money lavished by his marshals and princes on magnificent attire, no important fashion for men emerged from the Napoleonic court. It was brash and bright with gaudy uniforms. In 1804 the Duke d'Abrantès abolished the use of hair powder and the wearing of pigtails in his regiment, which the emperor approved for the rest of the army, but this was a case of catching up with fashion, not starting it. By now armies were wearing trousers and tight pantaloons, but that had started back in the 1790s. Naval officers still kept to kneebreeches, being more conservative than landlubbers, and because trousers were associated with their sailors. The British Royal Navy in particular was the last place to look for any egalitarianism. The image Napoleon created for himself was a simple one: the figure in the grey greatcoat and white uniform with a bicorne hat, seated on an imperial white horse, in contrast to the golden-embroidered velvet and brocades he had worn for his ceremonies, and the Marshals of France in their plumed hats, gold-smothered coats and stiff collars. However, it proved a durable image where imperial myth-making was concerned. Not every leader believed in simplicity: not the marshals, and not Admiral Viscount Nelson, whose fondness for wearing decorations cost him his life at Trafalgar. On the other hand, Field Marshal the Duke of Wellington went further than Bonaparte in martial simplicity, for at Waterloo he wore a black coat, an open shirt and no cravat, an astounding example of undress in public. He too, however, had his accessories to

support his rank, his staff officers all in full uniform and feathers. It was Wellington who made the first step in reducing military splendour when he created the Royal Green Jackets in Spain, their dark uniform designed for camouflage and night work – a highly original concept in a period of martial pomp. The Napoleonic régime was a military one which did not know how to launch fashions in the way that royal courts had done, being more concerned with richness than novelty.

The most important innovations continued to come from the other side of the Channel, Britain, that inveterate enemy of expansionism in Europe. There could be some confusion of terms when the French adopted a British garment. The jockey hat was not the peaked jockey cap worn during races, which jockeys had borrowed from postillions in the seventeenth century, but the English round hat with a hard crown worn during hunting and rough riding as a safety measure, the ancestor of the top hat. It became very popular, for it increased a man's height even when in civilian dress, and it was also adopted by the British army for some regiments. It was an age when the nation's men could feel very proud of the country's performance, the defeat of Napoleon by land and sea compensating for the shameful defeat over the American colonies. Britons had proved their

51 Martinet, *Promenade de Longchamp*, year X of the Revolution, 1802. The way the riding hat with wide brim changed into a top hat can be seen very clearly here. It should be observed that some of the men's coats are fastened right-over-left, and others left-over-right. Before the advent of industrial mass production there were no absolute rules for making clothes, with room for personal whim. The French are here at their most English in dress for men.

manhood, so a tall hat was their due. If the top hat was six inches high in 1795, by 1805 it was a foot high, and it became the most important hat in the nineteenth century where status was concerned.

The English insistence on wearing riding boots in town transformed kneebreeches into pantalons. The breeches were lengthened to close the gap between the top of the boot and the knee, and stretched as far as the calf, thereby ceasing to be kneebreeches. To achieve the very tight fit they were made from stockinette or doeskin, but a man needed good legs to wear them, as was made clear in an exchange between two famous dandies of the day. The celebrated *horizontale* Harriette Wilson described how Beau Brummell called on her when she was entertaining Lord Frederick Bentinck of the Guards:

'How very apropos you are arrived,' I remarked. 'Lord Frederick wants your opinion on his new leather breeches.'

'My dear fellow, take them off directly!' said Brummell.

'I beg I may hear of no such thing,' said I hastily – 'else where would he go to, I wonder, without his small-clothes?'

Fred Bentinck put himself into attitudes, looking anxiously and very innocently from George Brummell to his leather breeches, and from his leather breeches to the looking-glass.

'They only came home this morning,' proceeded Fred, 'and I thought they were rather neat.'

'Bad knees, my good fellow! Bad knees!' said Brummell.[25]

Alas, that was a knobbly feature that could not be improved on.

Each age produces its own term for the highly fashionable man: the gallant, the beau, the fop, and now the dandy, someone obsessed with looking smart. Beau Brummell was the son of Lord North's private secretary, and was sent to Eton, which put him on terms of familiarity with the nobility and even royalty, although he lacked a fortune. In May 1794 he became a cornet in the Prince of Wales's regiment, the 10th Light Dragoons. Prinny, the Prince of Wales, was notorious for his extravagance over clothes, and in the 1780s had been something of a Macaroni with gaudy striped coats, and an overabundance of spangles. In 1784 he was one of the first to go in for higher cravats, as he developed swollen neck glands which he wished to conceal. He was the complete contrast to his next brother Frederick, Duke of York, and Commander-in-Chief of the army. Frederick declared, 'When not on duty, I wear a brown coat,' which modesty gave considerable satisfaction to their father George III, whereas he made no secret of his displeasure at Prinny's ostentatious ways. The young officer like Brummell could adopt either the sleazy look of the Whigs under Fox, or follow the horsey clothes of the Tories, but Brummell considered both to be too extreme. His feeling was for a more moderate position in dress, and he laid great stress on cleanliness, where the fashionable types smelled either of dirt or horseflesh. Brummell would spend at least two hours a day washing himself, scrubbing his skin with a pig's bristle brush, cleaning his teeth, plucking his eyebrows and whiskers, before he got round to the matter of donning clothes. It was said he spent more time before his mirror than with his troops, but George Brummell was to be the one to reform Prinny's way of dressing. He frequented the same tailors as the Prince, Schweitzer & Davidson, Guthrie, and Weston & Meyer. He left his regiment in 1797 and set himself up as a man of fashion with £2,000 a year from his father's estate. The sensible man could have managed very well on that, but Brummell liked mixing with dukes who had £40,000 a year. He was possessed of an even-natured character and got on well with both the Duke of York and with the Prince of Wales, who developed the habit of dropping in to see Brummell dress.

The horsey set took the wearing of country clothes to an extreme by aping coachmen. The Four-in-Hand Club delighted in driving stage coaches and wearing greatcoats with numerous capes. Jane Austen wrote in *Northanger Abbey* in 1797, a work not published till 1818, of Henry Tilney in his curricle, who drove much better than other gentlemen-coachmen: 'And then his hat sat so well, and the innumerable capes of his great coat looked so becomingly important',[26] but Beau Brummell did not approve. Too many capes, he said, and the Prince took heed, and what the Prince of Wales obeyed the rest of male high society would take note of. Once again the court set the style, but with the assistance of an arbiter of taste who set severe standards of purity very much in keeping with neo-classical ideals. The noble simplicity of the antique should be applied to menswear with even greater determination than before. From being casual the country look was being turned into something smart.

For undress to become full dress it had to be disciplined, so the crumpled effect was out; wrinkled trousers and creased cravats would not do. In *Northanger Abbey* Mr Tilney, as the son of a general, states, 'I always buy my own cravats, and am allowed to be an excellent judge', but in the humbler household of the Reverend Moorland his daughter had to make her brother's muslin cravats as part of her training in needlework. Such soft cravats did not satisfy Brummell, who became famous for insisting on starched cravats. A degree of discomfort now became necessary to achieve the fashionable look, a regular occurrence in women's dress but less frequent in menswear. A heavily starched cravat was like a slave's iron collar, and forced young men to hold their heads very high, while to turn round required the revolution of the whole body. While reports that ears had been chopped off and throats cut by stiff cravats were exaggerations, there is little doubt that they could cause weals. It was necessary to study Brummell's own approach, so his dressing-room became a place of pilgrimage, to see the shirt collar as high as his head and the dazzling white cravats which were a foot wide. Once wound on, Brummell would work it down with his chin until it attained the correct number of folds. His example inspired a pamphlet, *Necklothitania, or Tietania: Being an Essay on Starches*, which declared that the Oriental cravat in very stiff cloth should have no folds, the Mathematical cravat three, the Ballroom should have two collateral dents and two horizontal ones, while the Mail-Coach so beloved of the swells had one end brought over the knot and falling down into the waistcoat.

Men-only clubs were flourishing. Since women were denied the same education as men, men would complain that one could not discuss serious matters with females and so one had to go to the club to find decent company. Brummell frequented Wattier's, owned by the Prince of Wales's former chef, who provided celebrated food. The company would sing glees and catches, but gambling took over with cards and dice. Brummell was elected perpetual president and ruled over dress, manners and snuffboxes. It was Lord Byron who dubbed the establishment the Dandy Club. With his club foot Byron rather envied Brummell's perfect appearance, which Brummell maintained by bathing in milk to keep his skin as white as a classical statue. The period did not realize that the ancients had coloured their works of art. The perfection of line was also seen in Brummell's trousers, for he wore a strap under the instep to keep the trousers taut without a wrinkle anywhere. There was a severity about the Brummell look, streamlined, sharp,

52 Henry Edridge, *Robert Southey*, 1804. The future Poet Laureate has cut off his revolutionary locks in favour of the Titus crop. He has also adopted the trousers, for such peasant garments are in harmony with the Romantic feeling for nature. These ones are so narrow that a slit is left at the bottom in order to put them on. The simplicity of his attire would be acceptable on the street today.

and stiff, daunting those less disciplined fellows who could not equal the result. It was guaranteed to keep copiers in their place no matter what their rank. Brummell was the severest critic of menswear in London society, and the aristocracy were more in awe of him than of HRH the Prince of Wales.

It was Brummell who asked John, sixth Duke of Bedford, 'Bedford, do you call this thing a coat?', and it was Brummell who told the Prince to stop wearing gaudy coats and to honour that well-established British tradition that waistcoats may be decorative but suits must be absolutely plain. He put the Prince into dark blue or black coats for evening, and as kneebreeches for balls were usually black this resulted in the black evening suit. At the very moment that the Napoleonic court was all glitter and gold, London high society adopted black, and over the next twenty years all the rest of Europe copied. Even Beethoven, one thousand miles away in Vienna, in the midst of organizing the first performance of his mighty Ninth Symphony in 1824, felt that he ought to wear a black coat on the night. Unfortunately, he did not own one and had to wear what he had. Even a Catholic capital had fallen for a Protestant style. In the long run Brummell's influence on the Prince could not endure, because the Prince was a voluptuary who resisted discipline, and because he grew jealous of Brummell's dominant position in fashionable society. Nevertheless, his influence was established over menswear and continues so long as evening wear is black.

Napoleon gave riding boots a bad reputation. Many a print showed the Monster bestriding Europe in thigh-length boots, displaying his ambition to ride over the continent. It was Brummell who gave his approval to an alternative, the shorter Hessian boot with a tassel at the top. It was worn by Hessian troops, and the fact that it was German was in its favour, for many of the German states were Britain's allies against Napoleon. The Hessian was particularly suited for wearing with pantalons, as it only reached the calf, and could also be worn under trousers. Where hair was concerned Brummell avoided powder, and wore it curled and to the neck. In his young days he wore sideburns, but by 1815 he had shaved them off and did not grow them again, as their absence produced a cleaner face. He did not go to the extremes over hair which Jane Austen criticized in *Emma*, 1814–15: 'Emma's very good opinion of Frank Churchill was a little shaken the following day, by hearing that he was gone off to London, merely to have his hair cut.'[27] This was a round trip of 32 miles, which took all day by horse and chaise. Many a young dandy was a creature of whim, but some of Brummell's look he had to have, a suit from Weston's in Conduit Street, boots from Hoby of St James's, and snuff from Fribourg & Treyer in the Haymarket. Many of them did not marry until late in life when their dandying was over, for one could not buy the most expensive wardrobe and keep a family at the same time. Economy over clothes and gambling were unthinkable. As Mrs Jennings complained in Jane Austen's *Sense and Sensibility*, 'Nothing in the way of pleasure can ever be given up by the young men of this age'. Not surprisingly they got into debt, including Brummell himself, who in 1816 was forced to flee to France to escape his creditors. He was not the typical blood of the period, for Brummell had no interest in the sports so beloved of the aristocracy, the hunting, shooting, racing and boxing. He was very much a town animal and that is why he converted casual country clothes into superbly smart town wear. The dandy was the sort of gentleman who

53 Anon., *George Brummell*, during his French exile, *c.* 1816. Brummell smartened up trousers by putting a strap under the instep to keep them taut. He believed in a severity of perfection which required a very disciplined approach by those who would follow in his footsteps. He turned the country look into super-smart town wear.

considered himself perfect unto himself. Brummell never married, for as Lucy exclaimed in *Sense and Sensibility*: 'Oh! dear! one never thinks of married men's being beaux – they have something else to do.' For his clique sex was reduced to a mechanical operation at establishments like Harriette Wilson's. It must not be allowed to interfere with the art of dressing.

While the dandies patronized trousers and pantalons, kneebreeches refused to die out. The young might sport trousers, but their fathers continued to wear kneebreeches well into the Victorian period. Moreover, trousers were not allowed at balls or at court. Full evening dress meant kneebreeches, and still does at the British court where they were termed levée dress, which is also worn by the Speaker of the House of Commons and by judges on state occasions. Kneebreeches have had a very long run indeed. There was also an overlap in styles, with the naked version co-existing alongside the new black form. Thus *Ackermann's Repository* for April 1810 illustrated full dress for gentlemen as either a dark blue coat with gilt buttons, a white single-breasted marcella waistcoat, and the skin-coloured kneebreeches in cream kerseymere suggesting statuesque nudity, or else the new black superfine cloth coat and black kneebreeches in florentine silk, which were going to terminate that naked effect. As fashion follows power the black evening dress for men was given a tremendous boost by the British victories over Napoleon. If black was what the British heroes were wearing for evenings then all the capitals allied to Britain followed suit; Madrid, The Hague, Berlin, Vienna, and St Petersburg. Even defeated Paris and Munich adopted the style, and while the military remained reluctant to abandon their finery for decades to come, for civilians British black was the only attire for formal occasions requiring full dress. It was a monumental alteration from previous practice, with all Europe and the Americas, whether Protestant, Catholic or Orthodox, adopting British black, which of course came from Protestant modesty.

Sobriety in menswear became the ideal for the new century, and it was goodbye to the coach drivers' style so beloved of some. When Lord William Lennox was at Westminster School in 1811 he got a chance to ride with the Driving Club where the costume was:

A light drab-coloured cloth coat made full, single-breasted with three tiers of pockets, the skirts reaching to the ancles, a mother-of-pearl button the size of a crown-piece; a waistcoat blue and yellow stripes, each stripe an inch wide; small clothes, corded silk plush made to button over the calf of the leg, with sixteen strings and rosettes to each knee; the boots very short, and finished with very broad straps, which hung over the tops, and down to the ancle; a hat three inches and a half deep in the crown only, and the same depth in the brim. Each driver wore a large bouquet at the breast, thus resembling the coachmen on a drawing-room or levee day.[28]

Brummell's dictum was opposed to such exhibitionism: 'If John Bull turns round to look after you, you are not well dressed; but either too stiff, too tight, or too fashionable', and what he said mattered. Somebody once asked his tailors, Schweitzer and Davidson in Cork Street, which cloth they would recommend for a coat. The answer was that the Prince of Wales favoured superfine, but Mr Brummell wore Bath coating, and 'I think Mr Brummell has a trifle the preference' over the Prince.[29] His biographer Captain Jesse estimated that the Prince's wardrobe had cost £100,000, as it included such gar-

ments as a greatcoat lined with sables price £800, but luxury and lavishness had not resulted in good taste. Brummell stated that to be stylish was simply a matter of looking clean and neat, with no perfumes, but plenty of fine linen, country-washed to avoid city soot. The amount of linen used by a dandy per week in summer was investigated by Prince Ludwig of Pueckler-Muskau from Germany, who visited London in 1826–9. He got the information from his washerwoman, who did for several such gentleman. A dandy used 20 fresh shirts, 24 handkerchiefs, 9 or 10 pairs of summer trousers, 30 neckerchiefs unless he wore black ones, one dozen waistcoats, and stockings à discretion. The dandy changed four times a day, starting with his breakfast toilette of a chintz dressing gown and Turkish slippers, then into morning dress with frock coat, boots and spurs. Dinner meant changing into a dress coat and shoes, while a ball meant pumps. When the prince attended an English ball he found 'the numerous company raven black from head to foot'. He liked the customs at balls: 'There is a delightful custom for the men at English balls. After the conclusion of a dance, each takes his partner on his arm and walks about with her till the next begins.'

However, Prince Ludwig disliked English informality, finding Parliament a dirty coffee shop with the members sprawled on benches, and was astounded by a military parade of Hussars and Lancers at Richmond where 50 or 60 officers turned up in undress jackets or frock coats and coloured cravats. Only the inspecting general and the troops were in uniform, showing that the officers preferred to be men of fashion first and foremost. But the prince did find signs of an end to such informality coming to the fore: 'A strong marble-cold spirit of caste and fashion rules all classes'. Manners were hardening because of the fear of revolution, and because of the challenge from the industrial middle classes. Thus at the very moment when the aristocracy adopted the modest black clothes of professional and commercial man, it became even more snobbish about their existence, as it tried to erect barriers against change.

The fact that British clergymen were still wearing wigs struck Prince Ludwig as worthy of a masquerade, and he was witness to an amusing scene at court on 5 December 1826 when a clergyman was to be knighted. George IV, the former Prinny, was feeling feeble so sat throughout, but when he asked for a sword the Field Marshal had a great struggle to draw it from its scabbard. This made the king impatient, so he

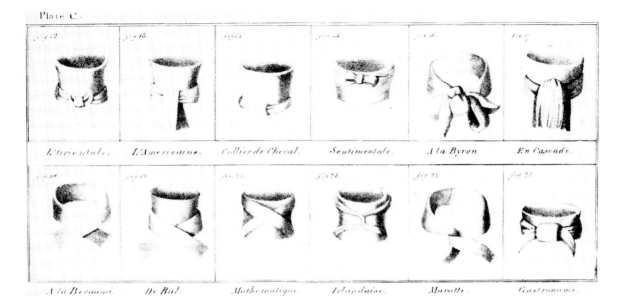

Plate C.

L'Orientale.   L'Américaine.   Collier de Cheval.   Sentimentale.   A la Byron.   En Cascade.

A la Bergami.   De Bal.   Mathématique.   Irlandaise.   Maratte.   Gastronome.

whacked the clergyman on his wig instead of dubbing his shoulders, enveloping them both in a cloud of hair powder.[30] Lord William Lennox observed another incident with wigs when an elderly admirer bowed to present a bouquet to an actress after a performance. His wig got caught in her spangles and when she walked off, his bald pate was exposed to the whole audience.[31] To the young, wigs were an absurdity, but the elderly clung to them until they died. They were part of their generation's identity.

Brummell did allow some colour in day wear, of a subdued kind. In exile he wore a snuff-coloured greatcoat, with a velvet collar, a cashmere waistcoat, which must have cost 100 guineas as it was made from a shawl, dark blue trousers, boots, a large black hat, and primrose gloves. Prince Pueckler-Muskau considered himself very British in his London boots, stiff cravat and tight frock coat, but when he visited the Lebanon in 1838 to see Lady Hester Stanhope her physician found his costume highly picturesque, consisting of an immense Leghorn

54 H. Le Blanc, *The Art of Tying the Cravat*, 1828. Brummell was famous for his cravats, which led to many variations on that theme, some named after celebrated people. Here we see the oriental, the American, the horsey, the sentimental, the Byronic, the cascade, the Bergami, the Ball, the mathematical, the Irish, the Maratte, and the gastronomic. They all required a lot of practice in front of the mirror, which made them exclusive to the leisured class.

hat lined with green taffeta to protect his fair German complexion, an Arab keffiyeh worn over his shoulders like a scarf, Parisian boots, and voluminous blue pantalons which aped the size of Turkish trousers.[32] The policy of many Europeans in hot climes was to be 'When in Rome, do as the Romans do.'

Napoleonic exhibition had been defeated. British black was established for full dress, while day dress became dark too, in blues and browns. It was the Protestant Clothing Ethic at work, but it was also practical, for the new industrial age was making cities extremely dirty and light clothes had to be washed frequently. Fashion was obeying British power.

Chapter Five

Romantic Chivalry to Muscular Christianity

The 1820s and 30s were to see a serious attempt to undermine the establishment of British black. Not surprisingly, it was led by a Frenchman, Alfred, Count d'Orsay. Standing six foot three inches with brown hair and blue eyes, the count could not be overlooked, but he evidently felt his size was insufficient and drew attention to himself by an insistence on colour. Lady Holland reported that Paris 'laughed at his dress, which is composed of sky blue pantaloons of silk and other strange mixtures. He wears his shirt without a neckcloth, fastened by diamonds and coloured stones – in short, a costume that *men* disapprove of as effeminate.' The definition of masculinity had changed completely. The eighteenth century had not objected to men wearing jewellery, but the nineteenth century did. The example had been set by Beau Brummell, who wore one ring and a gold watch chain. The count sought to turn the clock backwards, based himself in London to show the British how they ought to dress, and was regarded as a leader of fashion from 1821. For a drive down to Richmond the count would wear a blue coat with gilt buttons, a buff waistcoat, a vast expanse of white shirtfront, very tight leather trousers, gleaming boots and a glossy top hat much curled at the brim. The humble villagers of Brompton and Kensington stared. As cravats were *de rigueur* in England the count adopted them but favoured black or blue. He promoted tight waists, immensely wide lapels, extremely tight trousers, towering top hats, tasseled canes, beards and whiskers. Jane Carlyle first encountered the count in 1839 in his summer dress:

at first sight his beauty is of that rather disgusting sort which seems to be, like genius, 'of no sex'. And this impression is greatly helped by the fantastical finery of his dress; sky-blue satin cravat, yards of gold chain, white French gloves, light drab greatcoat, lined with velvet of the same colour, invisible inexpressibles skin-coloured and fitting like a glove . . . but his manners are manly.[1]

D'Orsay was sticking to the naked look of neo-classical taste at the very moment when the Victorian age had begun and anything below the waist was 'inexpressible'. He was an amateur artist and sculptor and on 16 July 1839 he called on my great-great-great-great-great uncle, the artist B. R. Haydon, when he was busy with his portrait of Copenhagen, the charger Wellington rode at Waterloo. The count seized a brush and

55 Anon., *The Round Pond, Kensington Gardens*, 1832. The frock coat continues as the most formal garment for town, but the riding tail coat worn by the man with riding boots and a whip was also being adopted for town as an alternative to the frock coat. Trousers continue to have Brummell's straps at the instep, but the silhouette is growing more feminine with wide skirts now that a young princess is heir to the throne, with a long female rule ahead. The boys wear the new tunic and trousers which replaced skeleton suits.

touched up the sky and a flank which uncle modified after he left. Uncle found the outfit astonishing: 'Such a dress – white greatcoat, blue satin cravat, hair oiled and curling, hat of primest curve and purest water, gloves scented with eau de Cologne or eau de jasmine, primrose in tint, skin in tightness.' It was amazing that such gloves would even touch a dirty old paintbrush.

The count had some successes. Caught riding in the rain without a greatcoat, he spotted a sailor in his loose coat, bought it off him for 10 guineas, and launched it as the fashionable *paletot*. His stress on colour even found its way down to building labourers, as Charles Dickens observed in 1839:

Pass through St Giles's in the evening of a week-day, there they are in their fustian dresses, spotted with brick-dust and whitewash, leaning against posts. Walk through Seven Dials on Sunday morning, there they are again, drab or light corduroy trousers, Blucher boots, blue coats and great yellow waistcoats, leaning against posts. The idea of a man dressing himself in his best clothes to lean against a post all day![2]

Yet the count's campaign led nowhere in the end. The British did not rush to follow his example in large numbers. The famous names of the day even started to wear black suits by day: Charles Dickens, the Duke of Beaufort, and the Poet Laureate, William Wordsworth, were all portrayed in daytime black. By 1845 d'Orsay had admitted defeat, and started wearing black himself. He called on Jane Carlyle on April 13:

To-day, oddly enough, while I was engaged in re-reading Carlyle's *Philosophy of Clothes*, Count d'Orsay walked in. I have not seen him for four or five years. Last time he was as gay in his colours as a humming-bird . . . To-day in compliment to his five more years, he was all in black and brown – a black satin cravat, a brown velvet waistcoat, a brown coat, some shades darker than the waistcoat, lined with velvet of its own shade, and almost black trousers, one breast-pin, a large pear-shaped pearl set into a little cup of diamonds, and only one fold of gold chain round his neck, tucked together right on the centre of his spacious chest with one magnificent turquoise. Well! that man understands his trade; if it be but that of a dandy, nobody can deny that he is a perfect master of it, that he dresses with consummate skill.[3]

She did also wonder if he ever thought of anything except clothes. However, it was not just his age which had sobered up his suits; it was the fact that the black suit was now fashionable for day. For a man to stick to colour was now judged to be effete among the young. Of course, the elderly stuck to skin-coloured trousers because they had grown up with them, the Duke of Wellington being one such, but the rising generations scorned them. In any case cream trousers in the industrial age were the height of impractical attire, so only those who did not have to worry about laundry bills, and who could afford dozens of pairs could wear them: namely a few aristocrats. Gradually, as cities grew dirtier and blacker with soot-coated buildings, cream trousers were limited to country events like holidays and the races. In the city black suits were the rule, and some of d'Orsay's compatriots even claimed that it was he who taught the British to wear dramatic black suits with white linen.[4] This was quite without foundation in fact. What happened to black in the early nineteenth century was that it was elevated to the dominant tone

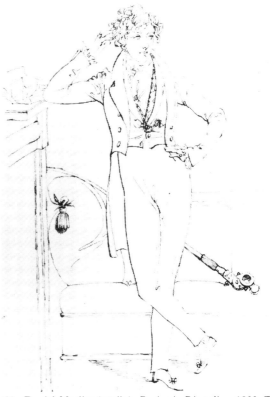

56 Daniel Maclise (attrib.), *Benjamin Disraeli*, c. 1833. The dandy novelist favours the tail coat with brass buttons, and very curled hair. Waistcoats are now the shortest they have ever been and have a special little pocket for watches on a chain. The frill at the wrist is very much the mark of the dandy, but cravats are becoming simpler after their complicated vogue. The instep straps are still considered necessary for smartness.

throughout the whole of society, with the aristocracy copying the middle classes, where professional black was worn by clerks, teachers, doctors, and lawyers. By 1867 Thomas Wright reported that black was being worn by the urban working class, where it constituted their Sunday best, the black suit. Saturday nights had a compromise costume, with the jacket and waistcoat of the black Sunday suit worn with the clean pair of moleskin or corduroy trousers which would be donned for work in the coming week. The only item of any colour was the woollen muffler.[5] The whole country had grown darker in costume and d'Orsay would have been a solitary butterfly if he had not given up his campaign. There were perhaps three reasons for his conduct. Firstly, it was well known that his wife had run off with a French royal duke so a proud front was necessary. Secondly, the count considered himself an artist so his clothes should be an artistic composition. Thirdly, he was a romantic trying to keep the past alive and trying to bring the jewellery and colour back into menswear from the previous century.

The adjective 'Romantic' was on many lips in the 1820s. On the Continent it had meant 'pertaining to novels and stories', but the English had given it the meaning of 'wild and fantastic'. Neo-classicism had grown stale, and was too preoccupied with purity and nobility. In any case, it had republican overtones, since it admired the works of republican Rome, and following the defeat of Napoleon European governments stamped on all signs of liberalism. The aristocracy had received a terrible shock from the French Revolution and sought to return to the old world, where serfs were kept in their place. Politically and artistically, neo-classical ideals were condemned. No longer should a lord build his country house like a Roman temple; it should be a medieval fortress, armed against the masses. A siege mentality occupied many an aristocratic mind, as they begin to see the size of the industrial competition. The son of a farm labourer could end up the inventor of steam processes and machinery, with as much money in his pocket as the tenth Duke of Ditchwater. He could send his sons to Eton and his daughters to finishing-school. The pragmatic British aristocracy condecended to marry those daughters if they had large dowries, but the Continental nobility was less adaptable and grew poorer as a result. According to the Prince of Lampedusa's novel *The Leopard*, not until after 1860 did the Prince of Salina agree to his ducal nephew marrying the daughter of a wealthy but vulgar

57 George Hayter, *Alfred Count D'Orsay*, 1839. The defeat of the French count's attempt to undermine British black by bringing back strong colour. D'Orsay submits to the British look of Protestant modesty with a black stock, black tail coat and waistcoat, and brown trousers, with the watch chain as his only piece of jewellery. His colour campaign had failed to deflect the capital of menswear from its policy of sobriety in dress.

mayor in Sicily, after the revolution had forced him to swallow his pride. By that date Queen Victoria and Napoleon III were granting titles to the new industrial rich, and the railway magnate with no ancestors could become an earl. This was strongly disliked by the old aristocracy. Little wonder that they sought to recall the past, to emphasize their ancient lineage, and to crenellate their stately homes. There were many strands in Romanticism, ranging from artistic to political and social.

Nature was redefined. Where the eighteenth century had tried to tame it into a picturesque composition, the Romantic took the opposite view and declared nature to be untameable, a tremendous force, an overwhelming magnificence before which humankind was helpless. The proportion of neo-classical taste was ousted by contrast, the irregular, the wild, the exotic. The Age of Reason was replaced by the age of untamed emotions. It was very much a mascu-

58 Benjamin Robert Haydon, portrait of his old friend William Wordsworth, 1842. While the poet was pro-revolutionary in his youth, he now dresses with the humility of true genius, in a black frock coat and trousers and a black cravat. His talent could be seen in his verse so there was no need to attract attention through his clothes; this approach has affected Britons ever since.

line movement in its own opinion, heroic, valliant, fervent, fierce and energetic. Lord Byron wrote poetic dramas where the hero battles against towering fates, but women were reduced to simple-minded creatures who had to be rescued by the heroes, an attitude which has endured well into the twentieth century. Neatness and order were feminine qualities, therefore the new movement celebrated masculine drive and irrationality. Romanticism liked to break the rules of decency, so Romantic heroes like Byron looked windswept, wore their collars wide open without a cravat, and wore trousers, not courtly kneebreeches. They declared that brigands were the only free souls in modern society, and liked

to think of themselves as artistic outlaws. Above all, they popularized history and the novels of Sir Walter Scott were extremely important in introducing the reading public to stories of the Middle Ages. His poem *The Field of Waterloo* saw the battle as an act of chivalry, and his novel *Ivanhoe*, 1820, brought the age of knighthood back into fashion. Ideas can take a century to catch on, and research into the Middle Ages had really begun in the previous century, with its fondness for making order out of the past. Studies of medieval chivalry were written in 1759 and 1762, but not until the Romantic era were such histories turned into historical romances.

George IV was an enthusiast for the historical look, and with no Beau Brummell to restrain him now, planned his coronation in July 1821 as the most lavish, expensive and historical event Westminster Abbey had seen. The men's clothes were doublets and trunkhose of (roughly) late sixteenth-century pattern, in silk for the majority, and in cloth of silver and velvet for the King. The spectacle included such historical traditions as the royal herbwoman scattering flowers, and the King's Champion in full armour riding into Westminster Hall to throw down the gauntlet against any challenger. It brought the past alive, and now young men were inspired to become knights too.

It was a very theatrical event, and it was the English theatre which gave the French their first sight of the new Romantic zeal in drama. The French academies had damned Shakespeare as lacking classical rules, but the Romantics adored Shakespeare because he mixed tragedy and comedy. When Charles Kemble took his Covent Garden company to Paris in 1827, his productions of *Hamlet* and *Romeo and Juliet* caused a tremendous sensation, and inspired French writers to break their rules. Both tragedies had medieval settings which appealed to historical tastes, but they were acted in the new style where the frenzy of Edmund Kean had ousted the stateliness of John Philip Kemble. His brother Charles Kemble also presented the first performance of *King John* in 1823 in medieval armour, designed by James Robinson Planché, the Somerset herald, antiquarian, playwright, costume designer and historian, who undertook a tremendous amount of research into medieval tombs and manuscripts. Not only should the Romantic age turn society back into a feudal society, but it should look medieval too.[6]

The idea of a rigid society was promoted by Kenelm Digby in his *The Broad Stone of*

Honour, or, Rules for the Gentlemen of England of 1822, which decreed: 'Let then every class of men be satisfied with the station of life to which they have been appointed. Every station has its advantages; and with regard to happiness, its equal portion'.[7] Many a peasant and labourer might have retorted, 'What advantages?' for the postwar period saw a severe depression, and happiness is a luxury only possible after the basic needs of food, clothes and shelter have been met. Yet Digby took a very Romantic view. He had to concede that feudalism had been brutal but claimed that chivalry had softened it. A convert to Roman Catholicism, he was terrified of science and denied that scientists could have a morality. A similar dislike of the rising middle classes and modernity was shown by John, Duke of Rutland, who wrote:

Let wealth and commerce, laws and learning die,
But leave us still our old Nobility.[8]

This contempt for the very commerce and industry upon which the survival of the country depended was instituted at the public schools, which educated the sons of the nobility and rising gentry to despise trade, an attitude which has crippled Britain ever since. The most famous demonstration of the back-to-chivalry movement came in 1839. Queen Victoria's coronation had been a modest production, because George IV's had been too costly, but the young Earl of Eglinton decided this was an insult to the Crown and mounted a great tournament on his Scottish estates on 28 August. It drew huge crowds, travelling by train, rather than by any medieval form of slow progress. First there was a procession with men-at-arms in costume with demi-suits of armour, musicians in silks on caparisoned horses, trumpeters in tabards emblazoned with the arms of the Lord of the Tournament, banner-bearers, heralds in tabards and pursuivants in surcoats, then the Earl of Eglinton in gilded brass armour topped with yellow and blue plumes, his charger caparisoned in blue satin and cloth of gold, the Knight Marshal in gilded and embossed armour with an embroidered surcoat, the Earl of Craven in a Milanese armour engraved and inlaid with gold, his caparison of scarlet, white and gold, and the Knight of the Dragon in a Richard II period armour of fluted German type. Viscounts Alford and Glenlyon wore polished steel armour, the Earl of Cassilis was in engraved steel inlaid with gold, his mount adorned with scarlet, black and white, Mr Gilmour as the Black Knight had black armour,

horse and trappings, Captain Fairlie as the Knight of the Golden Lion had gilded armour with a caparison of crimson and blue, and Charles Lamb was the Knight of the White Rose in polished steel, his caparison of blue with gold lozenges. It poured with rain, the armour got rusty, the pavilion collapsed, the stands were flooded, and the Marquess of Londonderry grabbed an umbrella, which shattered the image of an ancient knight. Modernity could not be excluded. A defence of the aristocratic jamboree was published by Peter Buchan the following year:

The attempt to revive, at the present day, the chivalrous pastime of 'the Tournament' has been derided by the cold 'philosophy' of a money-getting utilitarian age. Yet let me ask are the mass of the people happier because the 'age of chivalry has past', and, in what was once 'merry England', the sordid, heartless, sensual doctrines of utilitarianism have triumphed over sentiment, and nearly extinguished the fine impulses and generous instincts of man's nature.[9]

Noble sentiments belonged to chivalrous gentlemen, and he claimed that generosity, elevating emotions and heroism were the attributes of the hereditary aristocracy, denying that any industrialist could be noble. It annoyed him considerably that the rising directors and managers of commercial and industrial business could afford to dress like the nobility.

The title of Gentleman is now commonly given to all those that distinguish themselves from the common sort of people, by a good suit of clothes . . . Indeed, almost at all times, among the vulgar a suit of fine clothes never fail of having the desired effect of bestowing on its wearer the name of Gentleman, without any other qualification whatsoever. . . . Deprive them of their fine clothes, their watch-chains and seals, their rings, canes, snuff-boxes, and gloves &c., and you will find, instead of the fine Gentleman, a skeleton of presumption, ignorance, impudence and misery, without a single grain of common sense, prudence or probity. To the tailor and the barber alone, hundreds are indebted for the title of Gentleman.[10]

In fact, the qualities of commonsense, prudence and probity were essential industrial attributes, particularly if the company director were hoping for a title to crown his career, but the Romantic medievalists were sadly lacking in knowledge of the real world. The very suits the aristocratic gentlemen wore were taken from the modest middle classes, and the concepts of sobriety and

customer. In 1849 the Prince became President of France, so Creed followed him and opened a branch in Paris in 1850 near the Opéra. In 1852 Louis Napoleon proclaimed the Second Napoleonic Empire with himself as Napoleon III, and with Henry Creed as the imperial tailor. This obliged the men of the new court to get their suits from Creed too, and so the French court, which for centuries had tried to exclude any British fashion for men, now succumbed completely. The British three-piece suit launched by Charles II and sobered down by middle-class modesty now dominated French high society and the Parisian man-about-town was nothing if he did not obtain a suit of British cut and cloth from Creed. While Napoleon III fell in 1870, Maison Creed went on to even greater strengths, and Henry's heir, another Henry, became tailor to Emperor Franz Joseph of Austria-Hungary, to Czar Nicholas of Russia, and the kings of Italy and Spain.[11] The British suit had conquered the whole of Europe, right to the top.

To a Socialist like Robert Dale Owen the sight of the upper classes dressing with greater modesty was welcome:

The gallants of Queen Elizabeth's day sought distinction by the help of rich velvets slashed with satin, costly laces, trussed points, coats heavy with embroidery. It would have been vain in those days to take them to task about their finery. It has now disappeared, even to its last lingering remnant, the lace ruffle at the wrist; but common sense had to work for centuries, ere men were satisfied to trust for distinction, something better than gaudy apparel.

The aristocracy, the gentry, the bourgeoisie and labourers on Sunday were all attired in decent black, except on holidays when cream trousers might appear. Of course, allowance must be made for the eccentric exception like the character Page whom Owen had met in New York in 1825. He insisted he was the reincarnation of King David's page and a servant of nature and wore a green broadcloth coat to the ankles, a plain Quaker collar, a green cloth cap, green boots, and green kid gloves, while his long hair was parted in the middle. On that side of the Atlantic metropolitan standards and court etiquette did not apply so firmly, and away from civilization people could please themselves, like Professor Joseph Neef at the New Harmony colony on Warbash River, whose summer attire was a linen shirt, trousers and braces, and no hat or shoes.[12] Back in Europe clothes had undergone a similar degree of relaxation for boys. The

59 David Octavius Hill and Robert Adamson, *Calotype of Dr George Buist*, 25 November 1845. The black suit becomes the dominant style for the professions where it had often featured before at middle-class level since the Reformation. Collars are receding and cravats are reducing towards the tie. Sleeves are so tight at the wrist they have to be buttoned. Dr Buist was editor of the *Bombay Times*, Inspector of the Bombay Observatories and founder of the Bombay Reformatory School of Industry. He represented the sort of talented commoner who unnerved the aristocracy.

responsibility had also risen from that level, whereas the nobility had long been notorious for drunkenness, whoring and gambling. Though they resisted as far as they could, the feudalists were gradually pushed back by the class they so despised. In 1832 the electoral system was reformed for the first time, increasing the franchise, while in 1833 slavery in the British colonies was abolished and the Factory Act reduced working hours to 12 a day. The liberals of the middle class were preventing a return to the Middle Ages, and confining it to the pages of Sir Walter Scott.

The British suit achieved an astounding success in the 1850s. Count d'Orsay's London tailor was Henry Creed, whose family firm was founded in 1710. The count introduced him to other French aristocrats, including Napoleon I's nephew Prince Louis Napoleon, who became a

Regency period had imprisoned them in the skeleton suit, an extremely tight outfit where the trousers came very high, being buttoned on at armpit level. Dickens came across a second-hand one in 1839: 'a patched and much soiled skeleton suit; one of those straight blue cloth cases in which small boys used to be confined, before belts and tunics came in'.[13] By the 1830s they were disappearing in favour of the looser knee-length tunic worn over trousers, with the belt, and an open collar. This was a reaction against the skintight clothes of neo-classical taste.

The male form had had another good run since the 1760s with skin-coloured kneebreeches of a tightness that left nothing to the imagina-tion, but from the 1820s there was a return to width and fuller skirts. With modesty being so important the naked look had to go, and an age which termed trousers 'inexpressibles' could not countenance the outline of the limbs beneath. The frock coat expanded to conceal such regions, swelling out from the waist into full skirts to the knee, while overcoats almost

60 Three scholars, c. 1850. Of course there is always an overlap in styles, and the Regency look lasted well into the Victorian era. The man on the right in the tail coat with brass buttons and high black stock could pass for 1820, but the man on the left is more up-to-date with his black frock coat and lower collar. The instep strap had disappeared. The Victorians did not mind if their trousers looked crumpled.

61 Men's fashions for 1853. The black frock coat was most correct dress, but in summer versions in brown or grey were not unacceptable. The man on the right has the brand-new turn-down collar on his shirt, but the others still have the standing collar. The double-breasted waistcoat is the newest trend. The tartan trousers reflect the Scottish craze. After its wide-hipped look in the 1830s to honour the young Queen Victoria, menswear is becoming slimmer and simpler, in which trend the influence of Prince Albert can be detected.

reached the ankles. Combined with d'Orsay's wide lapels and tight waists the effect was very feminine again, but there was another queen regnant in the making, namely young Victoria. Exactly the same thing happened as had under Queen Elizabeth, for as the male silhouette became more curvaceous, beards and moustaches sprouted to guarantee the masculinity of the wearer. Hair grew longer to the neck and was curled on to the face. There were curves everywhere, in the brim of the top hat, in the shape of the collar and lapels like a pigeon breast, in the coat skirts, and in the whiskers and curls. The definition of the male had changed again, and after the frenzied Romantic hero who regarded himself as triumphantly male above all, a period of recovery was needed, so the look softened into more 'feminine' lines. Yet at the very moment when men were looking more womanly, modesty was to require more segregation of the sexes. While the Regency period had allowed girls to play billiards and use libraries, the new Victorian age created exclusive male zones in stately houses, with the billiard room, the smoking room, the gun room and the library all out of bounds to ladies. The house John Walter of *The Times* built at Bear Wood, Berkshire, even had separate staircases for bachelors and maidens, reproduced in the servants' quarters which also had a men's corridor and a women servants' corridor, so that never the twain might meet alone. The adult sexes could only meet in polite society in the drawing room, the music room and the dining room.[14] This segregation was to restrict men's understanding of women even further. The image of woman as a domestic angel, which Queen Victoria seemed to promote, caused the Establishment to denigrate female aspirations toward higher education. With hindsight, it appears that the repression of women during this period deprived it of a good deal of unrecognized talent.

For a while it looked as if the Scots were going to upset the sobriety of menswear. Thanks to Scott, the country became highly fashionable, George IV visited Edinburgh in a kilt, Queen Victoria built a castle there, Mendelssohn wrote a Scottish symphony and Berlioz a *Rob Roy* overture. This resulted in a craze for tartans, and the vogue for giving them names. In 1794 the tartan weavers Wilson had only 3 named tartans, and 22 known only by number. As public demand increased more names were introduced, those of Scottish towns like Aberdeen tartan, Perth tartan, and Glasgow tartan, but with the passion for historical romances so prevalent, the names of clans were substituted.[15] Queen Victoria put her sons into kilts of Royal Stuart, but town fops started sporting tartan trousers and broad checks. It proved a last fling at gaudy apparel for young males and was not adopted at court, as Prince Albert condemned such showy attire. While he had to admit that exact rules over correct dress were not easy to determine, he drew up a list for his eldest son Albert Edward, Prince of Wales, probably written in the 1850s when the son was about to go to Oxford.

The appearance, deportment and dress of a gentleman consists perhaps more in the absence of certain offences against good taste, and in careful avoidance of vulgarities and exaggerations of any kind, however generally they may be the fashion of the day, than in the adherence to any rules which can be exactly laid down. A gentleman does not indulge in careless, self-indulgent, lounging ways, such as lolling in armchairs or on sofas, slouching in his gait, or placing himself in unbecoming attitudes, with his hands in his pockets, or in any position in which he appears to consult more the idle ease of the moment, than the maintenance of the decorum which is characteristic of a polished gentleman. In dress, with scrumptious attention to neatness and good taste, he will never give in to the unfortunately loose and slang style which predominates at the present day. He will borrow nothing from the fashions of the groom or the gamekeeper, and whilst avoiding the frivolity and foolish vanity of Dandyism, will take care that his clothes are of the best quality, well-made and suitable to his rank and position.

To all these particulars, the Prince of Wales must necessarily pay more attention than anyone else.[16]

The 'slang style' of tartan trousers and big checks was of course only worn by a flashy minority, who also flaunted huge bow ties and exaggerated whiskers, satirized by Cruickshank. Prince Albert had grown up when the sporting look of grooms was all the rage among the young bloods, and did not wish to see the heir to the throne adopting such loud styles, but the very clothes he expected his son to wear, the trousers and the tail coat, had both come from the peasantry and from the hunting dress of farmers and gentry. Prince Albert was evidently unaware that a lot of fashions rise from below, from practical and sporting garments. Beau Brummell had turned them into ultra-smart town wear a mere 40 years before.

In the event Albert Edward, Prince of Wales (Bertie to the family), went further than his father wished. Queen Victoria refused to give him an occupation of any kind so he concentrated on pleasure, and loved dressing up and introducing a degree of informality when off duty, although he was also a stickler for correct dress on formal occasions. Prince Albert's tailor was Edward Peacock of 12 Upper Eaton Street, but Bertie determined to go elsewhere. After seeing the actor Fechter in *Robert Macaire* wear a patched and ragged coat where the underlying cut was of obvious quality, the Prince asked who made it. The answer was Henry Poole, his mother's military tailor of 4 Old Burlington Street and 33 Savile Row, with the livery department at 21 Clifford Street. It was usual for

men's tailors to make ladies' riding habits and Queen Victoria got hers from Poole and from Henry Creed who also supplied Empress Eugénie's *amazone* habits. As the Prince Consort died in 1861 at the age of 42, Bertie went his own way and in his holiday wear showed a liking for loud patterns and bold checked tweeds. For shooting he favoured baggy tweed knickerbockers, brightly patterned stockings, high spats, and a voluminous Inverness tweed cape, which he also introduced in an evening version of black cloth lined with silk as an extra-large opera cloak. On holiday in Germany he was reported to wear a green cap with a brown overcoat, knee-breeches, grey shoes and white gloves. English tailors prayed he would leave the outfit behind. Yet these were youthful follies, and Bertie was to have his greatest impact on menswear when he was king, although his fondness for gargantuan meals meant that his styles were created for the portly figure and not for the usual slim ideal.

In the cities dark clothes were now the norm. Prince Albert wore a black suit and black top hat in London and would only appear hatless and in

62 L. Caldesi, *The Royal Family on holiday at Osborne House*, Isle of Wight 1857. Enter the informal lounge suit worn at first by boys. Prince Alfred, Duke of Edinburgh, far left, wears it in a one-colour version, and Albert Edward, Prince of Wales, far right, has a two-tone version. Both boys have soft turn-down collars, but their father Prince Albert sticks to the starched standing shirt collar, and a tail coat. The others present are Princess Helena and Princess Alice with Prince Arthur, Duke of Connaught, in a kilt; Queen Victoria holding Princess Beatrice; Victoria, the Princess Royal; Princess Louise; and Prince Leopold, Duke of Albany, still in his baby petticoats.

light-coloured trousers at Osborne on the Isle of Wight when on holiday. Gradually these dark looks moved outwards from the urban poor to the country labourers, and Thomas Hardy mourned the change he saw in the Dorset farm worker between the 1850s and the 1880s:

The hiring fair of recent years presents an appearance unlike that of former times. A glance up the high street of the town on a Candlemas fair-day twenty or thirty years ago revealed a crowd whose general colour was whity-brown flecked with white. Black was almost absent, the few farmers who wore that shade, being hardly discernible. Now the crowd is as dark as a London crowd. The change is owing to the rage for cloth clothes which possesses the labourers of to-day. Formerly they came in smock-frocks and gaiters, the shepherds with their crooks, the carters with a zone of whipcord round their hats, the thatchers with a straw tucked into the brim, and so on. Now, with the exception of the crook in the hands of an occasional old shepherd, there is no mark of speciality in the groups who might be tailors or undertakers, for what they exhibit externally. Out of a group of eight, for example, who talk together in the middle of the road, one only wears corduroy trousers. Two wear cloth pilot coats and black trousers, two patterned tweed suits with black canvas overalls, the remaining four suits being of faded broadcloth. To a great extent these are their Sunday suits; but the genuine white smock frock of Russian duck and the whity-brown one of drabbet, are rarely seen now afield, except on the shoulders of old men. Where smocks are worn by the young and middle-aged, they are of a blue material. The mechanic's 'slop' had also been adopted, but a mangy coat is preferred, so that often a group of these honest fellows on the arable has the aspect of a body of

63 A farmer with his shepherds at shearing time, *c.* 1880. The lounge suit in black was taken up by workers in town as their Sunday best, and by superior artisans as a working uniform. Thomas Hardy disliked its appearance in the country by 1880 where this farmer could pass for an urban office worker. The shepherds wear their traditional corduroy. The bowler hat started life in the country before the 1860s as a riding hat. The round crown was very similar to the riding hat of 1780, but the brim was much narrower. High society did not approve of bowler hats in town.

tramps up to some mischief in the field, rather than its natural tillers at work.[17]

Clearly Dorset farm labourers wanted to go to work in suits just like the middle classes and wealthy farmers. While most country people had never travelled further than they could go in half a day, with half a day to get back again, the increasing spread of railways to almost every country town, and the subsequent introduction of bicycles, made it possible for adventurous country folk to venture further afield, and see what the rest of society was wearing. Industry was coming to the country in the form of traction engines and mechanical harvesters, so country wear began to reflect industrial wear, which was overalls and suits. Old corduroy, which since its invention in the late eighteenth century had been the fabric of agricultural labourers, distinguishing them from cloth-suited gentry, began to face a new challenge to its monopoly, although it was still around in the 1930s as a recognized form of agricultural dress. It was the smock which vanished first, and that had been around since the seventeenth century when it was termed a cassock/casaque. The fact that the British industrial and now agricultural poor copied the dress of the middle and upper classes was ridiculed by Hippolyte Taine when he visited England in the 1860s. On the Continent regional styles were well established, but France was a large country whereas England was tighter, so that urban influences could spread much sooner. Communication was speeding up, and the fact that country folk could be 200 years behind metropolitan styles was breaking down, as a result. Hardy and Taine might sigh to see the disappearance of traditional styles, but the labourer could reply that all Britons were supposed to be equal before the law, so why shouldn't they have working suits just like other men, even if they sometimes had to buy them second-hand?

The rising tradesmen could infuriate the aristocracy with deliberate gestures. Hoby of St James's Street, the bootmaker to George III, George IV, Wellington, Byron and all the dandies, who employed 300 hands, was the first man in town to drive a tilbury straight from the inventor, Mr Tilbury.[18] That was calculated to make the sporting gentry grind their teeth. In 1856 the Frenchman Francis Wey came across a millionaire butcher who rode about London in a barouche with two bays and a black-coated coachman, while the butcher reclined in his apron with his sleeves rolled up. It was plebian

ostentation by one still running his family firm, but who was richer than many a lord.[19] It was because of this challenge that society tried to close its ranks. Francis Wey conceded that the English dressed more simply than the French but he felt the society was more complicated: 'They may not share our love of uniforms, epaulets, embroidered garments and medals; their buttonholes, often adorned with a flower, are never decorated with ribbons or rosettes; but the rules of etiquette, regarding the titles, which mark the degrees of hierarchy between the social classes, are so rigid and intolerant as to be inconceivable.'[20]

Even so, the industrialist, the bankers, the shipbuilders, the railway magnates, the factory owners, were gaining on the aristocracy of land. Accordingly the Victorian era saw more books on etiquette and correct dressing being published than ever before. The regulations were complicated in order to deter climbers. An aristocrat wrote that no gentleman should remove his hat in the hall, but should carry it into the drawing room to greet the hostess and then place the hat on a table or chair. Only members of the family could leave hats in the hall. When the visitor left, the hat could be put on only in the hall. Gloves might be worn when shaking hands, but some removed the right-hand glove when doing so. The new rich should understand that levees at court were for men, and drawing rooms for ladies. The court reception was elastic in that the aristocracy and gentry now had to share it with the church, the services, the professions, merchants, stockbrokers, and owners of large-scale commercial organizations, but tradespeople were excluded. It was strange that the nation Napoleon I called a nation of shopkeepers should hold that class so much in contempt. For a daytime levee correct dress was claret or brown coat, claret trousers with a gold stripe, a white waistcoat, white tie and gloves, a cocked hat and a sword. Evening dress at court was the full dress of black velvet coat and knee-breeches with black silk stockings, buckled shoes, white waistcoat, and the cocked hat and sword. Elderly men who liked the old court style of bag wig, lace ruffles and silk waistcoats were allowed to appear in it.[21] A whole vocabulary of nuances was constructed, which the man-about-town should have at his finger-tips, from the language of calling cards, to the correct tie pin to wear when the court was in half-mourning.

There was a gradual increase in the number of coats a man might wear. The familiar frock coat and tail coat were joined in the late 1830s by the

64 Napoleon Sarony, *Oscar Wilde*, 1882. A leading campaigner for the return of kneebreeches for daytime, Wilde claimed that trousers were boring tubes, while Dr Jaeger said trousers were unhealthy. Wearing kneebreeches became the mark of the intellectual and Wilde has teamed them with the new smoking jacket, which appeared when houses began to have smoking rooms as exclusive male zones. Wilde's long hair was much condemned as effete.

tailless coat or jacket. It reached to mid-thigh, decently covering up the unmentionable zone, and was the same length all round. It had the same small waist, large lapels and fullness in the skirt as other coats, but it was shorter and became very popular as an informal, holiday, country coat, to wear when boating, fishing, walking, or riding. When these jackets had been around for 20 years a modification took place, for they were shortened to the top of the thigh, and the waist disappeared. The result was the lounge suit, in which Prince Alfred was photographed in 1857. This was very much a country outfit which could never be worn in town, but Bertie, the Prince of Wales, liked it a great deal and wore it frequently when in the country or on a foreign holiday, which made the lounge suit very fashionable. It took adoption at court to make a garment generally acceptable. The early examples could have a dark jacket and light trousers, echoing the usual wear for informal occasions, but the matching jacket and trousers was in existence in 1857 and this became the dominant version. Boys were often dressed in the lounge suit, with the usual result that they wore it as adults, which made it the fashion. The jacket buttoned high up the chest, and could be worn with the brand-new turn-down shirt collar of the 1850s, or with the established high starched collar. Of course, the elderly stuck to high collars and regarded turned-down collars as a disgrace, but they still crept in. In the 1850s Lord Henry Lennox wore the turned-down version for shooting, and in 1863 the Prince of Wales wore it on his Scottish holiday at Balmoral, which made it permissible out of town. Given the overlaps of generations, however, there were still grandfathers in the 1850s and 60s who still had a strong Regency air, with top hat, high collar and cravat, blue coat with brass buttons, skin-coloured kneebreeches and boots or gaiters, like Earl Bathurst, despite the fact that the fashion magazines pretended this generation did not exist. Turning the collar down had a big impact on cravats: it squashed them, so they had to be made narrower and thus became ties. The reign of one of the proudest neckpieces in the history of menswear was on the wane – not that cravats died out quickly, for they were still around, if growing rarer, in the 1970s. The younger tie is still with us.

Kneebreeches continued popular in the country, despite the dominance of trousers in town. The fuller form of the knickerbocker formed a suit with the new lounge jacket in matching tweed, and was worn for shooting, for walking tours, on photographic excursions and for climbing mountains. Little boys were also dressed in knickerbocker suits, of velvet in town, and tweed in the country. Rural life was responsible for many of the new styles just coming into the male wardrobe. The bowler hat invented by Mr Bowler for William Coke of Leicestershire, who wanted a low, hard hat for riding, widened its appeal. In 1860 the Windsor cricket team, with Lords Paget, Berkeley and Skelmersdale, sported low-crowned bowler hats with the club colours as the hatband. Cricket became very fashionable in the 1860s at country house-parties, so a costume had to be invented. The Wilton House cricket party sported caps and straw hats, so there was a jumble before the striped cap became the cricketing cap, and the bowler hat became non-sporting headgear to wear with the new lounge suits (although the riding version continued for hunting, as originally conceived). These 1860 bowler hats had a very curved brim, and there was a long tussle ahead before they could be worn in town. As late as 1909 the *Tailor and Cutter* still damned them as an abomination. The 1860s saw other attempts to challenge the metropolitan top hat. There was the short top hat, the soft German felt hat, the wide-awake hat favoured by bohemian types, with a wide brim and lower crown, and there was the pillbox, while the straw boater was popular for cricket and boating; but none of them could be worn in the City.[22]

Umbrellas had entered the gentleman's wardrobe after a struggle. Although parasols dated back to antiquity, they were above all an article of the feminine wardrobe. A folding oiled-cloth umbrella had appeared in the 1760s, but when a few men carried it they were condemned as eccentric and effete. Gentlemen carried canes and riding whips, not umbrellas. By 1800, however, attitudes had relaxed and umbrellas appeared amongst the Incroyables and in the army. Captain Gronow of the First Foot Guards relates that the Duke of Wellington was astonished during the action at Bayonne on 10 December 1813 to see the guards officers putting up umbrellas because it was raining. He

65 Joseph Middleton Jopling, *The artist Sir Coutts Lindsay Bt.*, 1883. Although purists maintained that lounge suits should not appear in town, they eventually did. Their casual character and turn-down shirt collars infuriated the older generation. Sir Coutts sports a soft trilby hat made popular by Bertie, the Prince of Wales, and his trousers are creased at the side in the Prince's way. Appropriately, the artist stands outside the Grosvenor Gallery where advanced works were displayed, emphasizing that he was anti-establishment in dress and painting.

instructed their colonel: 'The Guards may in uniform, when on duty at St James's, carry them if they please; but in the field it is not only ridiculous but unmilitary.' Umbrellas could be carried on parade but not under fire.[23] This order restricted umbrellas to town for the gentlemen of the Guards, so they became part of their civilian uniform. As Edward VIII discovered when he joined the Guards, the adjutant ordered what the officers could wear when out of military uniform. It had to be a frock coat and top hat, with a tight umbrella, and what's more the adjutant would direct the subaltern to a tailor he approved of, in order to ensure the clothes were of the sharpest cut.[24] As many a prince and peer served in the Guards, they carried the tight umbrella into civilian life, and the riding whip ceased to be obligatory.

The sports jacket had appeared by 1860, which was simply the lounge suit jacket in the colour of the club. To begin with they were one colour but by the 1870s striped variations appeared as clubs proliferated. They were specifically a sporting garment not permitted for the season in town, and were adopted by other sports clubs such as rugger and rowing, for by now chivalry was being changed into muscular Christianity. It was not sufficient for a gentleman to have noble qualities; he should be strong and fit as well. In his *Euphranor, A Dialogue of Youth* of 1851, Edward Fitzgerald had complained that schoolboys were made to wade through worthy tracts for 10 hours a day, without any physical activity beyond a walk in crocodile. He advocated games at schools as part of the basic curriculum, with cricket, football, gymnastics, rowing, sailing, rugger, running and boxing, to make boys into men. He even suggested that literary types, particularly poets, were womanly, and this attitude became strongly established when public schools adopted the sports ethic. The greater the stress laid on physical prowess and playing the game honourably, the greater became the contempt for mental activities. To be learned, sophisticated and cultured were condemned as dangerously feminine characteristics for a man, which the later scandal over Oscar Wilde only seemed to prove. A gentleman should have a nodding acquaintance with literature and the arts but he should not specialize in them. The result of this attitude was the further estrangement of the British establishment from ideas, social understanding, creativity and invention, the very stuff upon which the country's success as a trading nation depended. The public-school ideal of the simple man,

an unquestioning Christian who played the game of life like a game of cricket, and had no truck with challenging ideas, was not equipped for an industrial world of ruthless competition, and that attitude has bedevilled Britain ever since. Albert, the Prince Consort, as a graduate of the university of Bonn, had no time for ignorant sporting types, but his early death prevented his cultured mind from influencing developments. The arts had received government support after uncle B. R. Haydon's long campaign, and his insistence on national schools of design, which was adopted by the parliamentary select committee in 1835. Prince Albert also campaigned for the involvement of art in industry, culminating in the Great Exhibition of 1851, but after the death of both men the arts were met with increasing contempt from the sporting gentleman of the establishment. Of course, costume was one of the arts too, so too great an interest in clothes was condemned along with the rest of creative activity. The hostility became so intense that eventually Bernard Shaw felt obliged to write a defence of artists and design entitled *The Sanity of Art*, 1908.

Many artists and writers were involved in the matter of dress reform from the 1850s onwards. The Pre-Raphaelite followers favoured looser clothes for women and historical garments for men such as medieval and Baroque styles with lots of lace. The Rational Dress Society was founded in 1881, in which year Oscar Wilde appeared at the Royal Academy's Private View in the correct black silk top hat and frock coat, but with a lily in his buttonhole and hair down to his neck, which caused many shocked looks. By 1884 Wilde was writing on the subject of male dress reform in the *Pall Mall Gazette*. A reader suggested that Regency dress should be revived, but Wilde replied that it was much too tight, and favoured the Cavalier look with a wide hat, cloak, and looser kneebreeches. He agreed with the views expressed by such artists and designers as E. Godwin, Watts, Lord Leighton, Albert Moore, Sir Edward Poynter and Sir Lawrence Alma-Tadema, that the future of dress should lie with Ancient Greek costume, as the noblest ever invented, although Godwin did concede that it would need warm combinations underneath in British weather. Wilde set his heart on the re-introduction of kneebreeches for day wear in town, declaring that trousers were boring tubes. He wore kneebreeches both in London and on his American tour, and by 1893 *Punch* was satirizing them as the mark of the intellectual. Another supporter of kneebreeches was Dr Gustav Jaeger from Stuttgart who founded his Sanitary Woollen System in 1878. He said the overlap of trousers, socks and suspenders was bad for the blood circulation. He argued that kneebreeches and stockings would allow for equal nourishment of the limbs with no overlapping. The only fabric he would permit was wool, claiming that vegetable fabrics like cotton and linen did not breathe. He advocated a wool undervest on the grounds that it kept the skin warm, allowed for the evaporation of perspiration, titillated the skin to stimulate a good blood supply, and assisted the skin's self-cleaning process of shedding dead flakes. Coats, he insisted, should be double-breasted to protect the trunk where all the blood vessels converged, and they should be kept on in hot weather as the perspiration would keep a man's weight down. Waistcoats should be abandoned, and nothing worn under the coat but the woollen shirt, which could be in a stockingnette web. A wool collar and cravat, he argued, would guard against chest complaints, and were to be commended to singers in particular. Jaeger censured tailors for inserting cotton and linen linings and pockets into woollen coats. Every garment from hat to socks should be in pure wool, and all day wear should be in the undyed hues of the original sheep's wool, that is, either white or brownish. Of artificial dyes the doctor approved only indigo and cochineal, as they were fast dyes. Dr Jaeger's views were taken seriously in educated

66 Henry Jamyn Brooks, *Private View of the Old Masters Exhibition, Royal Academy*, 1888. The artistic and aristocratic establishment insisted on top hats and frock coats for formal receptions, with black as the dominant tone. The painters present include Burne-Jones, Millais, Richmond, Frith, Alma-Tadema, Calderon, Orchardson, Leighton, Holman Hunt and Watts, with sundry marchionesses, countesses and earls. Van Dycks and Rubens grace the back wall.

circles across Germany, Scandinavia, Britain and the USA.[25] In 1883 the London businessman Lewis Tomalin obtained the rights to Jaeger garments in England and set up the Jaeger shop which is still in business in London's Regent Street and elsewhere, although it has widened its range of clothes. Jaeger clothes were featured in the International Health Exhibition at the Royal Albert Hall in 1884. One ardent disciple of reformed woollen clothes was Bernard Shaw, who astounded people by wearing undyed woollen knickerbocker suits in the centre of London, among all the frock coats and top hats. Shaw belonged to the Healthy and Artistic Dress Union founded in July 1890, whose journal *Aglaia* in spring 1894 supported Oscar Wilde's revival of kneebreeches as more comfortable and more aesthetic than trousers. Stalwarts of this movement continued to wear their woollen knickerbocker suits until the end of their days, in the mid-twentieth century, but they failed to topple trousers from their pinnacle in town. In the country, of course, knickerbockers were well established already while kneebreeches continued at court, but for wear in town trousers were simple and uncomplicated, and did not involve the buckling and buttoning involved in kneebreeches, so they were preferred by the majority of men. Since Shaw was also a Socialist he often attended meetings in his reddish-brown hygienic suit and by the turn of the century was to be involved in the question of dress for Socialists.

Professor John Ruskin in his advice to workers had advocated a 'marked simplicity' of dress as the most important ideal.[26] Another professor at Oxford, Sir Charles Oman, the historian, raised the matter of clothes when the Liberal leader Mr Gladstone visited the university in 1890. Gladstone had been up in the days when d'Orsay was king of the dandies and flashy young under-

67 Prince George, Duke of York. The determined supporter of frock coats in town, the Prince wears the modification introduced by his father the Prince of Wales, which was open in front and held by a link. The stand-up collar must be worn with it. Excellence of cut was considered the mark of true elegance. The Prince disapproved of his father's casual styles and became a stickler for correct dress himself. Note the absence of jewellery of any kind.

graduates imitated his styles, around 1830. What did Gladstone think of the changes in dress over the last 60 years? The Liberal leader was disgusted. Surprisingly enough, he was sad to see the end of the special black silk gown and tasseled velvet cap that had been the dress of undergraduates of aristocratic lineage, and which Bertie, the Prince of Wales, had worn when he was up in 1859. All academic distinction seemed to be collapsing, for in 1890 even dons were going about in mufti and only wore their gowns to lectures and dinner in hall. Gladstone stated:

It would have been impossible in my time. I remember my contemporaries, young men at Christ Church, who, when they were not out hunting, made a point of promenading the High Street in the most careful attire. Some of them kept a supply of breeches which they only wore for walking, and in which they never sat down, lest any creases should appear.

Mr Gladstone gave a lecture on Homer at the Oxford Union, and afterwards Professor Oman asked his opinion of the audience. He replied: 'In my days there would have been men present, who, with their two watch chains, their scarf-pin, their embroidered waistcoats, and their fashionably cut suits, could not have been dressed for £30: this night I did not notice a single man who could not have been dressed for £10, and the general effect was slovenly.' Evidently the expensive dandies were admired by Gladstone for their extreme smartness and it did not seem to occur to him that not every student could afford such outfits, even in 1830. Mr Gladstone clearly had a very conservative streak, for the presence of women's colleges on the fringe of the university caused him to complain that they were now too many ladies in the place. What horrified him even more was the sight of rowing men crossing the High in shorts! A gentleman should change his clothes between the river and the town.[27] There was a correct dress for the appropriate activity, but it should be kept for that activity alone.

Oddly enough, the age was less sensitive on the matter of wearing nothing at all. Men did not wear bathing costumes, and the sexes bathed at opposite ends of the beach, the men *au naturel*, the ladies swamped in shifts and hidden by the umbrella-fronted bathing cars. The baths at Bath did require men to wear canvas drawers because there was an audience, but a swimming garment for men was unheard-of. By 1869 a bathing costume had appeared when Bazille painted his *Summer Scene; Bathers*, but right into the Edwardian period not every bather wore it. When Charles Darwin's granddaughter Gwen Raverat was growing up in Cambridge she recorded that every summer Sheeps' Green and Coe Fen were pink with naked boys bathing in the river. Ladies being rowed past were expected to bury their faces in their parasols to avoid the horrible prospect, but in June 1887 Gwen peeped. She thought it a lovely sight, slender pink bodies diving from the branches of willow trees in happy innocence. She thought naked men looked splendid and could not understand why she should not know what they were like.[28] As late as 1906 men were bathing naked in Hyde

Park early in the morning, but by now some seaside authorities were starting to insist on bathing costumes for men, which made mixed bathing possible at last.

Traditional to the last, Oxford University maintained a special place for men to bathe in the nude, called Parsons' Pleasure. Lady undergraduates being punted up the Cherwell were required to disembark at this point and walk round the back, rejoining the river higher up, although on one occasion this one must confess she did not. On being dared to be punted through Parsons' Pleasure she accepted, but her cowardly escorts insisted on a disguise of sunglasses and a straw boater plus a blanket. What was revealed were two very fat dons, decidedly unappetizing, one rather weedy homosexual, and only one man whose anatomy possessed a reasonable degree of proportion. Gwen Raverat had better luck at that junior establishment in the Fens, where the whole river was being bathed in by male town and gown, 75 years before. At least she learned that men were not born with fig leaves, unlike more cloistered maidens with only statues to study.

68 Sir Leslie Ward, *Sir William Orchardson*, 1898. The Naughty Nineties saw a determined attempt to make lounge suits acceptable in town by dressing them up. The painter sports an elegantly cut three-piece with narrow trousers, spats, and a formal stiff collar to give it class. An artistic note is the cravat held by a ring, which with the watch chain and cuff links is the only article of a decorative nature, showing that the painter was flashier than the Duke of York.

Chapter Six

Edwardian Toffs and Cinematic Heroes

Edward, Prince of Wales, alias Bertie, ruled over menswear in the 1890s, for what is done at court influences the rest of polite society to follow. The rules were supposed to be precise, but Bertie could take liberties. That a man must dress well was emphasized by Mrs Humphry in her *Manners for Men* of 1897:

It is absolutely true, though in a very limited sense, that the tailor makes the man. If a man does not dress well in society he cannot be a success. If he commits flagrant errors in costume he will not be invited out very much, of that he may be certain. If he goes to a garden party in a frock-coat and straw hat, he is condemned more universally than if he had committed some crime.[1]

She stated that at the races like Sandown a tweed suit and bowler hat were in order, except when royalty was present, in which case a black frock coat and black silk topper were compulsory. Bertie himself, however, upset the system by arriving at Goodwood Races in the new Homburg hat he had introduced from Germany, and a lounge suit, just when everybody of note, from the host the Duke of Richmond downwards, was properly dressed in black. This was the signal for chaos to break out, for in 1900 Goodwood Races saw men in flannel suits, navy-blue blazers, and white duck trousers with straw boaters – sportswear at a society occasion![2] At the theatre full evening dress was supposed to be worn, but the late 1890s saw lounge suits and even sports jackets sneaking into the dress circle.

It was inevitable that the short jacket of the lounge suit should affect evening clothes, with the introduction of the dinner jacket in place of the evening tail coat. It had to be in black, of course, and was only allowed at family dinners or meals with very close friends. When Bertie was in Egypt in 1876 he invented a variation: the Serapis evening jacket in dark blue with silk facings and gold buttons bearing the Prince of Wales feathers. It was worn with the ordinary black evening trousers. He brought the Serapis jacket back to London but only wore it for family dinners at Marlborough House and Sandringham – not for dining with his mother at Windsor. A new fabric had been devised for coats, elastic twill cloth which had a matt finish. The elasticity made for an improvement in fit, so this cloth began to oust the traditional shiny broadcloth. The evening suit was still the tail coat, white shirt and tie, black or white waistcoat, black trousers, and black patent shoes or boots. A black tie was to be worn with dinner

jackets. Bertie decided to alter the evening suit by lowering the height of the waistcoat to reveal much more shirt-front, which was good news for laundries, but he himself fell victim to the problems that could arise when he dropped a blob of spinach purée on his shirt-front. His wife Princess Alexandra tried to rub it off, but in vain, and Bertie simply laughed and, dipping his serviette in the spinach jug, drew a pattern over his ruined front before retiring to change.[3] It went without saying that his valet would have freshly starched evening shirts to hand just in case.

In 1895 the Prince of Wales modified frock coats. Being portly, he asked his tailors to make an open version, lightly held by two linked buttons or else left to hang. He found it more comfortable than being buttoned up, and so a new style of frock coat came into fashion for town and Ascot. He had a strong dislike of confining clothes, for which reason he did not care for military uniforms, unlike his nephews the Emperors of Germany and Russia (although they had the figures for uniform, which Bertie did not). In fact he had the largest wardrobe in the world, but the civilian garments were outnumbered by the state robes and the uniforms of the British regiments in which he held rank, plus the uniforms of foreign forces in which he held an honorary position. Each uniform consisted of four outfits; the full dress, undress, mess kit, and overcoat, so they took up a lot of cupboard space. Moreover he had the robes and decorations of nine British orders of chivalry and 50 foreign ones. The Prince was also in the Freemasons and had his apron and regalia for that although when Queen Victoria saw him in the apron she laughed.[4] With so much ceremonial costume in his wardrobe, it is easy to see why Bertie liked to break the rules sometimes. At the country estate at Sandringham, for example, he said it was not necessary to change four times a day; twice would do, into shooting tweeds in the morning and into evening dress for dinner. The location of Sandringham, in Norfolk, gave its name to a new type of shooting suit. Finding most jackets too restrictive, the Prince asked for a fuller one to be devised, and his tailors came up with a jacket with deep pleats in the front and back which made it easier to swing the gun when shooting pheasants. He wore the Norfolk jacket with his tweed knickerbockers and this created the Norfolk suit, which became very popular in the countryside. Bertie knew full well that society would imitate. An anonymous member of the royal household enthused, 'The Prince of Wales has shown great restraint and wisdom in

69 The Prince and Princess of Wales's Party for Ascot, 1895. Bertie, on the left on the steps, and his friends, treat Ascot as a holiday event by wearing light-toned top hats and trousers with their frock coats. Queen Victoria's cousin, George Duke of Cambridge, centre, is more formal with a black top hat. However, the younger generation treat Ascot as an urban formal event. George, Duke of York, on the right of the steps behind his wife Princess May of Teck and his sister Princess Victoria, is attired completely in urban black, as is his brother-in-law Prince Alexander of Teck, by the drainpipe.

all that concerns his wardrobe. He has always been fully alive to the fact that a people is prone to model its manners and dress on the fancies and foibles of the Royal Family.'[5] Prince Albert, however, would have found insufficient restraint and too much informality. Homburg hats and bowler hats, indeed! By 1897 democratization was going too far, for country tweeds were beginning to appear in town in the morning. The sensible man would wear a morning tail coat, as that could be worn in the afternoon as well, but the chap who favoured tweeds would be obliged to change into the frock coat and striped dark grey trousers in mixed cheviot. Light trousers were still restricted to holidays, weddings and

garden parties. For the afternoon parade in Hyde Park a degree of colour was now allowed with grey or light-brown frock coats, but on Sundays all black was compulsory. When riding in the park the elderly still wore black coats and top hats but the young were riding in tweed knickerbocker suits and bowler hats, thus treating the park as if it were an extension of the country. When actually staying in the country, the clothes would depend on the formality of the occasion. If the Prince of Wales were present then lounge suits and Homburg hats for day, unless hunting was on the programme, or shooting, when hunting pink, and tweed knickerbocker suits would be necessary. Black toppers and black frock coats would be required for Sundays and trips to church. The number of garments the fashionable had to have was on the increase. Mrs Humphry wrote: 'A man's wardrobe is now almost as varied as a woman's. He has different costumes for walking, riding, driving, visiting, boating, hunting, shooting, golfing, bicycling, tennis, and cricket, dining, smoking, and lounging, football, racing, and yachting, to say nothing of uniform and Court suit, besides the now

developing motor-car costume.'[6] The stress on sports had become a mania, with even children in non-aristocratic schools being given physical instruction.

Despite his own fondness for innovation, Bertie did not permit it in others and would reprove any man who dared to disobey the rules. When Lord Rosebery arrived at Windsor Castle in plain clothes instead of full dress uniform Bertie remarked, 'I presume you have come in the suite of the American ambassador.' When Disraeli wore a diplomatic coat with his Trinity House trousers Bertie quipped, 'It won't do. You're found out!' He appeared to enjoy a party given by the Duke of Devonshire but on leaving stated that only one thing had been wrong: the Duke was wearing his Garter upside down.[7] The Prince was particularly scathing about Americans, for the *nouveaux riches* did not know how to dress, and he condemned the American fondness for bright ties, embroidered waistcoats, and ornate jewellery. However, more Americans were starting to appear in London society. The severe economic depression of 1870 had hit agriculture very badly when wheat from the new

70   The Eton v. Harrow cricket match at Lord's, 1900. The black frock coat and black silk topper remain correct dress for all society events in town during daytime. The father on the right has a black waistcoat, but the one in the centre allows himself a cream one as it is summer. The boys wear the short spencer jacket which Earl Spencer created during the Regency period when his coat tails caught fire. It did not become an important fashion for men, but short jackets were considered suitable for boys.

American cornfields began to flood into Europe. Several landed aristocrats faced a large drop in income and rushed across the Atlantic to find brides among the daughters of the new American rich. They took some upper-class attitudes there with them: 'To attend oratorios and philharmonic concerts is thoroughly bad form, indicating a tendency to be pedantic. It is much better to go to a horse show,'[8] and they brought back an American fashion for very flat hair. This was achieved by soaking the hair, then wrapping it in linen bandages to dry. The plastered hairstyle was soon sported by those who were 'in it', the latest phrase for being up-to-date. The question most often on British lips was whether a new idea was good form or not. Not overstepping the mark was the most important consideration, for a bad mistake could exile the perpetrator from polite society, although there was a lot of hypocrisy over social sins. The Prince of Wales's adultery was well known, but divorced couples were banished from the best events. Queen Victoria would not receive the Duchess of Manchester because of her long affair with Lord Cavendish, soon to be Duke of Devonshire (whom the Duchess later married, thus becoming a double duchess), but Bertie had no objections to such company. On the other hand, let a man slip up in his dress, and Bertie's dressing-down could wreck his social chances.

On one occasion the Americans tried to get their own back on Bertie by insisting that Sir William Orchardson's painting of the royal family, *Four Generations*, 1897, showed Bertie wearing brown shoes with a black frock coat, but he retorted that he never wore brown shoes in town. There was also a complaint that Bertie bought his gloves abroad, but his secretary Sir Francis Knollys replied that all the Prince's gloves were made in England. His preference was for grey with black stitching, of which he used dozens of pairs. Away from the metropolis Bertie would go native if visiting other countries. In Scotland he wore a kilt at all times, with full-dress Stuart tartan for evenings, and a heather-coloured kilt for deer-stalking. In India he wore the local hunting rig of a khaki jacket and knickerbockers, a sola topee, and the gaiters which were essential because of the swarms of leeches. He himself was prepared to vary his attire, but woe betide any man who usurped that role from him.[9]

The turn of the century was the height of Empire, with the Queen inspiring generations of men to conquer all, but now it was seen as a Christian crusade to bring civilization to the dark nations. The British did introduce some beneficial measures in the countries of the Empire, but there was little fraternization with the natives and colonial society reflected the values of the public school and the London season, with no place for outsiders. That pattern has survived, with the Indians particularly repeating the British way of life, with Indian regiments as British as can be, Indian schools emulating Eton, and an Indian season at Simla, despite Independence in the meantime. In 1901 Bertie succeeded as Edward VII, but it did not affect his fondness for relaxing the rules of costume. The German Chancellor Prince von Bülow declared that the King and Emperor was the *arbiter elegantiarum* for the whole of the civilized world. When Edward VII holidayed at Marienbad that was the signal for the top European tailors like Franz of Vienna to come in pilgrimage to spy out what His Majesty was wearing, because they would have to reproduce it for their customers. It was another example of fashion reflecting power. Britannia ruled the waves, so His Britannic Majesty's suits ruled international high society. If the King said trousers should be creased, creased they were, from New York to Buenos Aires and Tokyo. Furthermore, the telegraph system carried the information much more quickly, and the invention of film was another method of spreading the news over style. Edward VIII thought his grandfather's idea of trouser creases came from the way trousers were folded when put away, for these were side creases. Edward VII did not wear front trouser creases or turn-ups, but the generation of his son and heir, George, Duke of York, did start to do so, and in 1891 George's brother-in-law-to-be, Prince Francis of Teck, was photographed at Easton Lodge in front-pressed trousers. Queen Victoria's equerry, Fritz Ponsonby, was photographed in similar trousers when accompanying the Queen on her holiday in Nice in 1897, so gradually front creases were coming in, but they were resisted by the older generation and Edward VII did not adopt the style.

One of the King's most famous innovations was brought about by his fondness for gargantuan meals, about which Queen Alexandra complained in vain. As the royal stomach expanded, the bottom button of his waistcoat had to be left undone before it burst asunder, and once the King had made this tiny adjustment to his dress, the rest of male society copied, to show that they moved in royal circles. Leaving that button undone became an all-important social message, and was a fashion with an unpremeditated origin. There were a few members of high society who could cope with the King's well-known tendency to descend on errors of costume. When he ticked off Admiral Fisher for wearing an old suit to court, the admiral replied, 'But you have always told me that nothing really matters but the cut.' When the Prime Minister, Lord Salisbury, once wore the wrong trousers with a uniform, Lady Salisbury remarked that Bertie nearly died of consternation, but Lord Salisbury's neat excuse was that it had been a dark morning and his mind was preoccupied with subjects of less importance than dress. The King's consternation was also imminent when a Liberal government came to power in 1905.

Included in the cabinet was the first minister to have been a wage-earner, John Burns, President of the Local Government Board. The King was afraid that this non-gentleman would commit some tremendous howler when he came to court, but all passed smoothly, for Mr Burns knew where to get his court suit – at the King's own tailor, where Burns had started his career as the errand boy.[10] In fact, Edward VII was always willing to greet anybody from any background, and was friendly with the grocer Lipton and the Jewish financier Cassel, which outraged his snobbish imperial nephews the Kaiser and the Czar.

Snobbery was a theme of Hugh Stutfield's study of society in 1909, and while the King was the exception, the rest of high society could not be excused: 'Snobbery is not merely a pillar of the aristocracy, but a mainstay of British dominion, and our Imperial race cannot fail to enrol it among the cardinal virtues.'[11] It meant that those at the top of society could break the rules of dress, but those just below dared not. Thus the Mayfair set could go as they pleased, but in bourgeois Belgravia and South Kensington formality was oppressive – hence the saying 'it is always Sunday afternoon' on Cromwell Road, with black frock coats and black toppers obligatory. Of course, there were two million servants in the country to keep the upper set looking smart, but Stutfield was irritated that styles were set by the frivolous: 'Mankind, of course, always has been, and always will be, under the yoke of the butterflies in the matter of social rites, dress, entertainment, and the expenditure which these things involve'.[12] He condemned the hot news for 1909 that frock coats were to have three buttons. Advice in fashion columns on how to wear one's moustache were an impertinence, while the behaviour of the Hunt Committee in trying to impose one form of hunting habit, with threats to boycott the disobedient, was the height of arrogance and butterfly conceit. He felt things were even worse in the United States, where men in society took a back seat. American high society was the women, which resulted in a lot of butterfly decisions. This was confirmed by the American, Mrs Sherwood, whose guide on manners was written to instruct women how to civilize men as well as themselves. She wrote that no other country asked so many questions about what it was proper to do, as the United States. With so many nationalities pouring into the country, wild mistakes over correct attire were only too common. The immigrants would wear national and fash-

71 Sir Leslie Ward, *Keir Hardie*. The first Labour Member of Parliament who did not own a top hat and frock coat. He wears the black lounge suit which the Labour Party adopted as dress for Socialist man, and dares to sport a trilby hat in town.

ionable dress together at the same time, and new American men would commit such social gaffes as wearing Balmoral boots to a ball, and wearing informal garments, such as the Derby hat and the Ulster overcoat, where a top hat and frock coat were proper.[13] This respectable black uniform was not restricted to the upper class but was worn widely by all sorts of officials and dignitaries, from rate collectors to sports referees,

72 Sir Leslie Ward, *John Lumley Saville, Baron Savile,* 1908. In the country the knickerbocker, a fuller version of kneebreeches, continued to thrive, being more practical than trousers in muddy fields. It was teamed with the lounge suit jacket to form a suit and could be in checked materials and tweeds. Its use was promoted by Bertie, the Prince of Wales, who always wore it with spats.

fire-brigade inspectors, coal merchants, and municipal officers. Accordingly the etiquette books continued to pour from the press, but could be caught out by events. When Lady Colin Campbell ruled that dark-blue serge suits and mixed tweed suits could only be worn at the seaside and in the country, they were already appearing in town, and books on manners were about an ideal world which was on the decline.[14]

Edward VII was remembered as the smartest man in society. C. W. Stamper, who was appointed manager of the new royal garage set up in the royal mews in 1905, wrote: 'His Majesty was always very particular about his dress. I seldom saw him in a new suit, but his clothes were, of course, beautifully kept, and he was always smart and what is called "well turned-out". Indeed, his whole appearance was always faultless.'[15] The avoidance of clothes that were too new will be noted. A breaking-in period was necessary before suits made their public appearance. Stamper was responsible for the royal cars; a large Daimler and two big Mercedes for journeys, and a small Renault for town use only. Claret in colour, the royal motorcars did not have licence plates, so the consternation of a police constable near Shoreham who stopped the royal car for not having a number plate can be imagined. On shooting trips the carpet was taken out of the car to avoid mud, and the King used to hand Stamper a clean pair of shoes and socks in case the ones he was wearing got covered in mud and he had to change to go indoors. The King was always careful to keep his image perfect by such attention to possible difficulties, and by always having a clean change of clothes close at hand.

His heir, George V, was a believer in tradition, so he was not the person to embark on as many styles as his father had done. Moreover he had had a career in the Royal Navy, so he was disciplined and prompt, and expected rules over dress to be obeyed and not bent. In the country he followed the hunting knickerbocker suits and Norfolk suits of his father, but in town he was a stickler for correct dress and insisted on the frock coat, thus keeping that garment in use longer than it might have otherwise have been, as the lounge suit was proving so popular for much else. He enjoyed yachting, like his father, who was often seen at Cowes week, and he wore the same sporting outfit of a navy blazer and white duck trousers. George V did not set out to introduce new garments or hats, so the world had to watch for the tiniest variation which might represent a slight relaxation of the regulations. He was conservative by nature but lived when Parliament contained four parties, Conservative, Liberal, Irish Nationalist and the new Labour. The Liberals, supported by all except the Conservatives, even envisaged a decentralized state with parliaments in Wales, Scotland and Ireland, so the King was surrounded by change and new proposals.

At this time the question of correct dress for Socialist men came to the fore. As part of his concern for healthy and natural dress, Bernard Shaw invented a one-piece outfit in brown knitted wool, which Frank Harris said made him look like 'a forked radish in a bifurcated stocking'. Friends advised Shaw that he might be mobbed in such an outfit, so as an experiment Shaw wore his woollen combinations on a walk from Tottenham Court Road to Marble Arch without encountering any molestation. On the other hand, Shaw was six feet tall, and his fiery hair and whiskers added to the impression of a wild man whom no one would impede. In any case, Shaw had chosen to walk in the polite West End. The reaction might have been more outspoken among the dockers of the East End. On the first night of his *Widowers' Houses* in 1892, Shaw wore a silver-grey version in stockinet for the curtain call, as part of his campaign against evening clothes. Socialists argued that evening dress was a class livery, and Shaw was often involved in a row at the opera or theatre when he tried to get in in day clothes. The actor-manager George Alexander agreed with him, for it was too much to expect men in the city to commute home to change into evening dress and then trek back to town to go to the theatre, so Alexander excused evening dress in the stalls. The huge growth in the number of theatres in Victorian and Edwardian London meant that they could not rely simply on the unemployed aristocracy but had to attract the salaried middle class.[16] The Socialists decided that a black suit was best for them, a working suit, in fact, with a double-breasted jacket without the tails or skirts of morning coats and frock coats. This was worn by the Labour Party's first member of parliament, Keir Hardie, in 1892. The dockers wanted him to go to Westminster in a coach like other new MPs but Hardie declined, so they hired a wagonette and drove off with one cornet player. As the dockers cheered, the solitary figure in his tweed cap and working suit entered the palace populated by frock coats and silk toppers. The press made a fuss, but in fact the Speaker said nothing, for MPs in the Regency had worn much worse. Several gentlemen in the country sent Keir Hardie top hats, and orders on their tailors to get himself a frock coat, but Hardie never wore such clothes. The black suit was the uniform that Labour MPs wore as their party slowly increased in size. It is often easier to get changes in the colonies than in the mother country, and Australia had a Labour government before Britain. The Australian Prime Minister visited Keir Hardie in 1907, suitably attired in black.[17]

73 Sherrill Schell, *Rupert Brooke*, 1913. The poetic young prefer a casual look, hence the lounge suit, the hair longer than the norm, a soft turn-down collar and a gargantuan tie roughly knotted, as a gesture against the precision of formal dress. But there were still a lot of activities to which lounge suits could not be worn. Purists would maintain that they should only appear at country weekends.

Bernard Shaw wore the black Socialist suit when invited to dine with the Haldanes to meet the Asquiths, Arthur Balfour, and the ladies of The Souls artistic clique. They were all going on to a grand function later, so the men were all in white tie and tails, and the ladies in diamonds, when in walked Shaw in his black tailless suit. To save face he asserted that they were incorrectly dressed for dinner, but the memory was a sore point with him afterwards. Haldane had in fact suggested that as a compromise Shaw should wear a morning suit, but Shaw had rejected that as an upper-class uniform. He remained faithful to his natural clothes, although he gave up the combination suit in favour of Jaeger's jacket and kneebreeches in healthy wool of an undyed tone. It was the most extreme example of country wear in town – straight off the sheep.

The gentlemen who were models of good form

and wore correct dress for the appropriate occasion, were decimated during the Great War. Brought up to believe in chivalry and valorous knighthood, to lead men and always set the example, they encountered a war where leading charges against machine guns was a useless waste of lives. Young men were slaughtered in their thousands, and the post-war period was to be terribly aware of the shortage of skills, talents, and husbands that the Great War brought about. A marriageable man after 1918 was a rarity to be treasured and fought over by the ladies. Most desirable of all was that princely bachelor, George V's heir, Edward, Prince of Wales, whose easy charm contrasted greatly with his formal father. Young Edward was well aware that as heir to the throne he had a duty to fashion as courts set the style. While dressing to his own taste, he cooperated with the export

74 The Prince of Wales leaving the lookout at Mount Royal, during his tour of Canada, September 1919. After the war the informal lounge suit was made correct dress for day by the charming new Prince of Wales. He wore it with turn-ups and front creases, which his father King George V abhorred. The Prince discarded spats, and promoted turn-down collars and trilby hats, being greatly in favour of relaxing the rules.

trade by being photographed in his new clothes and accessories, so that the industry could rush photographs, samples of cloth, and examples of accessories across to the United States where men were most anxious to know what the Prince of Wales approved. Like Edward VII, his grandfather, the Prince went on wide travels to display British style as an ambassador for trade. After his visit to Argentina one native of the country did not simply place orders for British clothes but rushed to London to be fitted at the capital of menswear, and ordered 35 suits of which 20 were plus fours. The Prince of Wales did not introduce plus fours; Guards officers had them before he did, but he did promote the new garment. It was not revolutionary but an elongated version of the shooting knickerbocker, reaching to mid-calf instead of the knee. The Prince wore it for playing golf and that made it *the* outfit for golf courses worldwide. Trying to set the style, however, involved the Prince in disagreements with the King. In 1924, when he was 30, the Prince received a royal denunciation for turning up to tea in his shooting clothes, even though the family was on holiday at Sandringham, the very place where his grandfather had said four changes of attire a day were not

necessary. George V put the clock back by insisting on lounge suits for tea. He was equally reactionary over dinner. The dinner jacket had been around since the 1870s but George V would not wear it at any dinner where there were guests. In his view dinner jackets were for dining alone with the Queen, but the Prince of Wales wore the jacket a great deal, and had to remember that dinner with father meant a white tie and tails.

Prince Edward also got into hot water over the right clothes for Ascot. Whereas Edward VII

75 The Prince of Wales with cowboys, 1919. The Prince's easy charm and informality made him a very popular figure which increased the impact he made on menswear, with the middle-class young eager to imitate his example. This shot shows an unpremeditated occasion, with the Prince mounting a horse when not in riding dress. The cowboys' wide hats shade their eyes from the glare of the sun.

had enjoyed Ascot, he had treated it as a holiday occasion by wearing light-coloured trousers and topper with his black frock coat. George V disagreed, and while still a duke had gone to Ascot in urban black with shiny top hat, black frock

coat and black trousers. His brother-in-law Prince Alexander of Teck wore the same in 1895. Prince Edward, in the 1920s, felt that this was all too dreary, so he turned up at Ascot in a grey suit and topper. The King was furious and said it was out of place, besides which a remote cousin had died, so mourning should be worn in any case. He ordered the Prince to have the correct costume next day, but when he got back to St James's the Prince found that he did not own a black frock coat, so he had to rush round to his military tailors, the Dutch firm Frederick Scholte of 3 Cork Street. Scholte cut out a black frock coat on the spot, and one of his tailors sat up all night sewing the suit together, so that the Prince was able to face his father next day without being clapped in irons. Scholte was the Prince's tailor for 40 years, but he was very fussy about his clientele. Flashy youngsters, film stars and theatrical performers were not allowed, with very few exceptions. The tailor could be rather like George V, for he did not approve of wide Oxford bags, and he agreed with the King's rule that if one were spending the morning in town and the afternoon in the country, this required a change from town wear to country wear, with a morning suit early on and country tweeds later. George V detested bowler hats and, if one should enter Buckingham Palace, would explode that he was not having any ratcatcher's hats in his house. They were fit for the country alone, so the King would wear a bowler to Newmarket and Goodwood races, but never to royal Ascot, which was in the country but different.

Not surprisingly, Prince Edward wrote: 'All my life, hitherto, I had been fretting against the constrictions of dress which reflected my family's world of rigid social convention. It was my impulse, whenever I found myself alone, to remove my coat, rip off my tie, loosen my collar and roll up my sleeves'.[18] Consequently he was very fond of sports clothes because they were informal. He introduced the sleeveless pullover to wear when hunting, as he disliked waistcoats under his hunting coat. In 1922, he launched the Fair Isle sweater when playing golf at St Andrews. It was knitted in bright colours in the new taste of the Twenties, and the sweater became a bestseller, with its Hebridean makers swamped with orders. Woolly jumpers and pullovers were suddenly challenging the waistcoat which had been established since Charles II's three-piece suit. The young who had survived the war wanted to celebrate their existence, and they despised the world that had led to the Great War, including its rules over dress. The Prince of Wales shared those feelings.

The easiest way to annoy the older generation was to wear sports clothes in town, with navy blazers and grey flannel trousers instead of suits, woolly jumpers instead of waistcoats, cravats instead of ties, and front creases and turn-ups on the trousers when George V was still insisting on his father's side creases as correct. Turn-ups can be traced back to 1860 in sportswear when young men playing tennis or cricket would turn the trousers up for practical reasons. The Windsor cricket team in 1860 had two members with turn-ups. Gradually the turn-up became more common for sports clothes, and by the Edwardian era it had reached lounge suits, but it was not allowed on full-dress morning coats' or frock coats' striped trousers, nor with evening dress. The turn-up was given royal approval by Edward, Prince of Wales, who had all his suits with turn-ups by 1922. A further annoyance to established rules was to wear lounge suits in the City instead of formal frock coats, and this became very common after 1920. Where Edward VII and George V had both had beards, the young rejected that by shaving and having a clean face. Needless to say, such royal tailors as Poole and Scholte said the world was going to the dogs, and that the younger generation were a slovenly lot, the same complaint as had been made about Fox and the Whigs. The correct overcoats were the single-breasted Chesterfield, or the double-breasted fly-fronted Ulster, but Army officers found their 'British warm' so comfortable that they brought that home from the war, a bulky garment guaranteed to annoy their fathers who expected all a gentleman's clothes to be superbly tailored and sharply cut.

The advent of film and recordings gave a new importance to the actor. While a performer could be famous through the press before then, the opening of cinemas all round the country and the introduction of gramophones brought the star to a much wider audience. Noël Coward was one to benefit from the new media. His play *The Vortex* was a hit in 1924 and he was much photographed as a man-about-town. His fondness for dispensing with collars and ties set a vogue:

76 King George V at the wedding of Princess Maud to Lord Carnegie, November 1923. The King clung to frock coats for formal occasions, hardly different in type from those he wore as a young man (fig. 67), and still declined to adopt turn-ups and front creases on his trousers. The young generation, however, begs to differ by wearing morning coats. Both Edward, Prince of Wales, and the second son, George, Duke of York (right), banned frock coats when they became kings.

I took to wearing coloured turtle-neck jerseys, actually more for comfort than for effect, and soon I was informed by my evening paper that I had started a fashion. I believe that to a certain extent this was really true; at any rate, during the ensuing months I noticed more and more of our seedier West-End chorus boys parading about London in them.[19]

It was enough to give the stiff-collar brigade a stroke. What a decline in standards, no starched collars and shirts in the middle of town! Notoriety brought Coward wealth, so he improved his wardrobe:

I indulged immediately a long-suppressed desire for silk shirts, pyjamas and underclothes. I opened up accounts at various shops, happy to be able to order things without that inward fear that I might never be able to pay for them. I wasted a lot of money this way, but it was worth it. My clothes certainly began to improve, but I was still inclined to ruin a correct ensemble by some flashy error of taste.[20]

Rising stars always had to watch out for such an error, as they usually came from humble origins and had not been groomed from birth in the correct way to dress. An actor-dancer who got it right was Jessie Matthews' first husband Henry Lytton in 1928: 'He was dressed immaculately, as always. Blue pin-stripe suit, silk shirt from his Jermyn Street shirtmakers with just the correct show of snowy-white cuff, a corner of crimson silk handkerchief at his breast pocket, black shoes polished to a mirror finish.'[21] Another talented artist who bought the best wardrobe was the portrait painter Sir William Orpen. As an art student in 1900 he dressed in a bohemian style, with a fisherman's jersey, black trousers baggy at the top and narrow at the bottom, and a flat felt hat like a curate's. He became very successful, and in his best year, 1929, made £54,729, so he went all out for the gentleman's de luxe manner, with silk underclothes in blue or cerise, Savile Row suits, handmade shoes and silver-topped canes – a true figure of the artistic establishment.[22]

There was one group of people who were guaranteed to get their clothes wrong and this

77 Sir Bernard Partridge, *Enoch Arnold Bennett*, 1927. The novelist was an advocate of greater colour in lounge suits, but for evening he keeps to the rules. A stiff starched collar standing up rigidly was still compulsory despite the fact that turn-down collars had been around since the 1850s. For evening Beau Brummell's starched severity was still the rule after a century. The Prince of Wales was to chop the points off waistcoats in favour of a smooth hemline.

was, of course, the Americans. Their mistakes gave them away. In 1924 Noël Coward first saw his future business manager Jack Wilson in the front row at the Little Theatre: 'I remember remarking to Lilian (Braithwaite) that he must be an American because he was wearing a turn-down collar with his dinner jacket.'[23] The Prince of Wales shared this opinion, just as his grandfather had done. He complained that American men were too fond of loud ties, and that they mixed colours dreadfully, citing one American who wore a fawn shirt, a red tie, and green socks with a blue suit. An outfit should match, but not to the extent of another American who wore a check shirt, check tie, check socks, and even a check handkerchief with a check suit. There should be a harmony of tones, but the exact replica of every item was not good style. The Prince did approve of American seersucker suits for hot weather, but otherwise felt that the new rich in the USA were such a mixture of races that they did not know how to dress 'properly'. Of course, the British were just as mixed in origin, but they had had a thousand years to produce an agreed policy on clothes, to which Prince Edward declared his loyalty, heeding that 'notorious British convention of understatement, expressed in clothes'.[24]

Like Prince Albert, George V might have queried just what his heir meant by understatement, when he was dressing so casually compared to his father. The Prince's fondness for going out without a hat on annoyed both his father and the hat industry to such an extent that Thow Munro, Chairman of the Executive Council of the Textile and Allied Trades section at the British Industries Fair told the Prince that he was affecting their sales. Prince Edward apologized and agreed to wear more hats in the future, and in 1932 promoted the straw boater to help the hatters of Luton. This royal example improved sales.[25]

There were several attempts to increase the amount of colour in menswear in the Twenties. Young blades copied the Prince of Wales with fancy checked plus fours and jazzy jumpers, and Jack Buchanan wore a midnight-blue evening suit in André Charlot's revue *A to Z*. In 1927 the *Tailor and Cutter* expressed approval, stating that dark blue looked better than black under artificial light. Jack Buchanan also launched the double-breasted dinner jacket, for he was famous for his elegance in evening clothes. It was an effect he had had to work out, but being tall and lean he could wear evening dress superbly well, achieving an effortless ease and relaxed elegance which Americans envied. Bing Crosby sighed that one had to be as tall as Buchanan to wear tails, while Ben Lyon complained that Buchanan had literally out-shouldered him when they were both chasing the same blonde, Marilyn Miller. This was in 1925 when Buchanan introduced to Broadway the broader-shoulder model of suit which Savile Row had launched, after finding that officers who had survived the Great War

had improved their physiques. Men's suits were in fact more shapely than the tubes women were wearing, for they had a high waist with the new broad shoulder, producing a more curved silhouette just when women were trying to look more masculine and flat-chested. Hollywood, too, groomed its male stars to a feminine extent. Make-up was necessary because of the lighting, but Hollywood went as far as painting the negative to improve the star's looks, taking out spots, warts, veins, and blemishes to create an image of the perfect male which could not be achieved by ordinary man. How could the average male hope to compete when his girlfriend fell for the impossibly perfect man on the screen? The camera can be used to tell a lot of lies.

A firm advocate of more colour for men was the novelist Arnold Bennett, who wore a mauve

78 The first performance of *Midnight Follies* from New York, at the Dorchester Hotel, London, 11 October 1933. Most of the men in the audience remain loyal to full evening dress with white ties and tail coats, but a few in the background are following the Prince of Wales in wearing black ties and dinner jackets. This indicates that the dinner jacket was about to expand its role, from being for 60 years purely an outfit for private dinners, to being acceptable dress for the theatre, dining out, and even dances, largely replacing tails and white ties.

suit to the Royal Academy exhibition in 1926, and in 1930 a brown and strawberry-red mixture. Even more extreme was the artist Sickert, who favoured very loud check suits and white bowler hats, but he was regarded as a colourful eccentric and most men still took their model from Edward, Prince of Wales. Even Americans admitted that his example was the best one to follow, as Fred Astaire made clear. His first performance in London was in *Stop Flirting* in 1923. It was a great success and the Prince of Wales came round to the dressing room to congratulate the Astaires. Fred was impressed:

All the time I was taking special notice of how he was dressed – impeccably in tails. HRH was unquestionably the best-dressed young man in the world, and I was missing none of it. I noted particularly the white waistcoat lapels – his own special type. This waistcoat did not show below the dress coat front. I liked that.

I heard that Hawes and Curtis made the Prince's dress shirts and waistcoats. Next morning I was there and asked if I could get a waistcoat like HRH's. I was apologetically told that it could not be done. So I went somewhere else and had one made like it.[26]

Astaire had run into the superior attitude of royal outfitters in refusing to dress anyone from show business. However he had better luck at Anderson and Sheppard's, not the Prince's tailors, but occupying premises in Savile Row. With his new wealth Astaire rushed to equip himself with the best clothes in the world: 'It was difficult not to order one of every cloth that was shown to me, especially the vicuñas. They never wore out. I outgrew most of them.'[27] Fred Astaire was popular and was invited to the night clubs which the Prince frequented, such as the Kit Kat, the Café de Paris, Ciro's, the Embassy and the Riviera. Correct dress was white tie and tails but the Prince of Wales often turned up in dinner jacket because of his wish to make clothes less formal. That was why he devised his backless waistcoat with the lapels; this was cooler than a full waistcoat in the hot conditions of a club.

Europeans could also make mistakes over correct dress, as Arnold Bennett related. A foreigner entered an English drawing room in his overcoat. The hostess informed him that it was usual to remove the coat indoors, so the foreigner took it off, revealing his shirt sleeves. English consternation – the man was not properly dressed! He had no jacket on. Lawrence Housman, who was present, coped in a diplomatic manner by removing his jacket and sitting in his shirt sleeves for a while. He then said he was feeling chilly, so could he redon his jacket? The hostess said yes, and this enabled the foreigner to conceal his shirt sleeves with his overcoat, although the incident would have left him with the false impression that it was correct to show the shirt sleeves in an English drawing room.[28] Another continental *faux pas* was to wear bowler hats with tail coats, or Homburg hats with evening dress.

In 1925 it looked as if Oxford University had let the side down. It was very hot that summer, and Oxford undergraduates started wearing very wide trousers which were termed Oxford bags. It was another insult to the Old Guard, who wore beautifully slim trousers with an elegant line. The young went to the opposite extreme by being wide and untidy. According to one of the culprits, Harold Acton, they were trying to be historical. 'Our Victorian Revival had left its mark on local fashion and interior decoration. Broad trousers were now worn everywhere, but high necked jumpers of all tints and textures were worn with them.'[29] While it was true that Victorian trousers had been a little wider than Edwardian and Georgian ones, the undergraduates overdid the width, but they did make an impact and by 1930 trousers in general were $17\frac{1}{2}$ inches round the bottom.

Astonishingly enough, the king, George V, actually made a significant alteration in 1926. Hitherto he had always opened the Chelsea Flower Show, an important event in the London season, in the regulation black frock coat, but that year he arrived in a black morning coat, striped trousers and without spats! High society was stunned. How long could frock coats survive if the old King stopped wearing them? The answer was 10 years, for as soon as the Prince of Wales became Edward VIII in 1936 he abolished frock coats at court, and replaced them with morning coats as the correct dress for the season, Royal Ascot, and royal weddings (wearing one himself when he subsequently married Mrs Simpson). The frock coat had had a very good run since the English frock became common wear in the early eighteenth century two hundred years before, but men were now used to wearing short jackets, and the frock coat felt too much like an overcoat by comparison. Even George V could see that with lounge suits becoming respectable wear in town, the long frock coat was an anachronism which only appeared when he had required it.

The demands of the court were met by several

79 Walter Sickert, *Self Portrait, c.* 1935. The artist was a co-founder of the Men's Dress Reform Party in 1929, which wanted more colour and variety for men's clothes, but their advocacy fell largely on deaf ears. Sickert's white bowler hats and screamingly loud check suits were laughed at. The Prince of Wales was the best man to watch for hints where fashion was going.

suppliers. The hatter to Edward VII and George V was Herbert Johnson of 38 New Bond Street. Ede, Son, & Ravenscroft of 93–4 Chancery Lane, founded in 1689 and still in business, supplied court dress and official robes. Burberry's at 30–31 Haymarket sold court dress, military uniforms, civilian fashions and sportswear. Fimin & Sons, 108–9 St Martin's Lane, were contractors to the Army and the Navy, and also sold club dress and liveries, in addition to being the royal embroiderers and button- and buckle-makers. Doré & Sons of 25 Conduit Street supplied court dress and military tailoring, while the Wilkinson Sword Company at 27 Pall Mall sold steel court swords. Men attending court in kneebreeches were advised to wear cotton stockings underneath their black silk stockings to conceal the flesh.[30]

An attempt to alter menswear was launched in 1929 when Dean Inge of St Paul's and Sickert, the painter, founded the Men's Dress Reform Party. It complained that menswear was too dull, a strange opinion considering just how jazzy casual wear had become. They disliked suits and wanted to bring back kneebreeches for day, and to replace tailored jackets with cardigans. Above all, they wanted colourful blouses rather than stiff shirts, and liked floral prints rather than plain. In 1932 they produced their reform shirt in scarlet, green, navy, black, white, fawn or grey, but it was not taken up by the masses. They copied the Prince of Wales who wore neither floral shirts nor red ones. He made the lounge suit acceptable for many daytime occasions, and his were famous as the best-made suits in the world. In the end even his father came round and actually wore a blue lounge suit on his visit to the Chelsea Flower Show in 1934, because his son's suits looked so smart, and that was what George V cared about.

From the political point of view the Thirties was the decade of the coloured shirt. Garibaldi had worn a red shirt back in the 1860s and this was adopted by the Communists. The Fascists favoured black shirts with high collars, and the pacifists chose nature's green. Gentlemen stuck to white shirts. Intellectuals wore sweaters or open shirts with no ties. They also took up humble corduroy from the farmworker, to show their solidarity with the underprivileged, and sported corduroy trousers, usually in brown. Fashion took notice and corduroy was used for sports clothes like mountaineering breeches, ski outfits, hiking, and motorcycling outfits. The tough fabric had taken nearly 150 years to reach high society; now even the Prince of Wales wore

80 Philip Steegman, *William Somerset Maugham*, 1931. Among intellectuals and holiday-makers the tie was being left off, which outraged the older generation who saw it as a sign of moral weakness. More people were travelling, however, and workers were to receive holidays with pay, so clothes had to allow for different climates.

it in the Tyrol.

To cope with the increasing informality, Savile Row devised the four-piece suit with jacket, trousers, waistcoat and plus fours, so that the jacket could be worn with two types of trousers in the same material. The dominant colours for lounge suits were dark grey, dark blue and black, in true Protestant modesty, and this sobriety enabled the suit to appear at theatrical matinées and afternoon concerts. The undress of the 1850s was becoming the full dress of the 1930s for daytime. A gentleman still needed to change for dinner or dancing, and he began the day in his silk dressing gown and pyjamas, so the number of changes had not decreased.

Cruises were now very popular among the rich, and the transatlantic liners were the last word in luxury, but a lot of luggage was needed. 'It was the time when twenty pieces of hold luggage were the absolute minimum for social survival, and when even a gentleman required a wardrobe or innovation trunk in the corridor outside his stateroom to hold the four changes of clothes he was expected to make daily on an eight- or nine-day passage.'[31] Hollywood included the English gentleman in some of its pictures and the liners conveyed Ronald Colman, Leslie Howard, Jack Buchanan, Noël Coward, and later Cary Grant, deliberately to show the Americans how to dress and behave on stage and screen. Even Gary Cooper, born in Montana, came of English stock and was educated in England, so the English model was not restricted only to English natives. Yet at the very same time Hollywood was bringing forward an American model of man, celebrating detectives, criminals, and backwoodsmen, who did not know the rules of polite dressing. This tough-guy did all the wrong things, like wearing a dirty mackintosh instead of a suit, and a soft felt hat instead of a bowler, spoke with a cigarette in his mouth and did not lift his hat to ladies. He did not know any ladies. The Humphrey Bogart look was not one to win favour in high society, but below that level many a young man sought to affect something of that slouched manner. This American influence was condemned as bad, but it was not only American gangster films that worried Europeans: it was their music too. English bands always performed in dinner jackets with the bandleader in white tie and tails, but in 1933 Duke Ellington's band appeared at the Palladium in white jackets. The Benny Goodman band also wore white or cream dinner jackets, but by the end of the decade the Tommy Dorsey band with Frank Sinatra were appearing in lounge suits! This was further proof, if it were needed, that Americans did not know how to dress, but there was such a flood of films from that side of the Atlantic, and so many records, that how was one to protect the young from such pernicious influences? While the trend was towards more casual wear, the American taste for loud colours did not catch on, for the English male regards a lot of colour as unmasculine, and too showy.

The humble luggage zip was promoted in 1934, when the Prince of Wales, George Duke of York and Lord Louis Mountbatten all appeared with zips on their trouser flies. This was too avant-garde for some, and buttoned flies survived until well after the next war, for some men did not trust zips not to stick or come unstuck, but the idea had arrived although it took some time to catch on. From the trousers, zips spread to various forms of lumber jacket, while they appeared all over RAF flying jackets. They did not win acceptance on suits, for Savile Row regarded the zip as much too flashy and vulgar and stuck to buttons to fasten jackets and coats. Where the zip was installed on trousers it was concealed by the fly front.

81 Jacques-Emile Blanche, *James Joyce*, 1935. In town the three-piece lounge suit was now established as correct dress for day, and turn-down collars on shirts were gaining over upturned collars and starch. It was usual for literary persons to wear somewhat crumpled suits to indicate that their minds were on other subjects than appearance.

Silver-grey was decided on as the colour for 1935 which was George V's Jubilee year, and both sexes wore it in his honour for such events as Ascot and weddings. It was the last salute to the old sailor King who stuck to his father's side-creased trousers until the end, for he died in January 1936. The best-dressed man in the world succeeded as Edward VIII, but he could not introduce any new styles, for the court had to observe six months' mourning, so black was the dominant shade. The fashion world expected much of the new King, for he had done much to relax the rules over menswear, and the industry depended on the example he set. Like his grandfather, he was the best advertisement for British clothes there could be. Consequently the trade was shattered when it learned that its elegant King was going to abdicate to marry a divorcée.

How could he be so weak? It was enough to make a tailor shut up shop. His brother George VI was most conscientious, but he was rather conservative like George V, and had not Edward's ease and charm and informality.

Probably the most comfortable thing Edward VIII did for men in general was to give his approval to the end of Beau Brummell's starched shirts and stiff collars. He liked the soft shirt with a turn-down collar, and his example made it safe for society to follow suit. According to Noël Coward in the 1920s, the wearing of a turn-down collar with dinner jackets was an American error, but once the King was doing it, by 1936, it was correct practice. When the King went into exile he spent a lot of time in the Mediterranean and Caribbean areas where a more tropical wardrobe was needed. He set the example of dispensing with waistcoats in hot climates, and wearing white linen or silk suits with just a shirt underneath. For evening the army and navy's mess jackets, which were very short, entered civilian wear as white satin evening jackets, to which some Americans added the cummerbund. A sailor's bell-bottoms could be worn on holiday or on a cruise now that wider trousers had entered fashion, after being around outside fashion for centuries. The Art Deco movement had produced some very bright ties and socks, but the gentleman confined such explosions to the bedroom. It was all right to have a jazzy pair of silk pyjamas or a kaleidoscopic dressing gown, but such an outburst should be kept behind the bedroom door. The British clothing industry missed the King, but fortunately in 1935 a very elegant Foreign Secretary arrived on the scene in the person of Sir Anthony Eden, whose impeccable black suits and black Homburg hat became the Foreign Office style. His appearances at international conferences was an excellent illustration·of British style, and helped to offset the loss of royal example. Of course, as Duke of Windsor Edward VIII remained a newsworthy figure, but his style as an individual could not have the impact that a King could on his court and high society, where the members were obliged to copy the royal example.

The thirties regarded themselves as more masculine than the twenties. The superbly groomed male saw a rougher rival rising. Suits reflected this by giving up the fitted waist, which was seen as feminine, in favour of a looser jacket hanging straight from the broader shoulder. In the USA the effect of a broad shoulder was taken to an extreme not unlike their footballers' padding, but this was rejected in Britain and Europe as much too vulgar and clumsy. The new Fascist régimes in Germany and Italy in particular bridled at the notion that their men should need padding. Fascism presented a very arrogant type of male, much given to uniforms and black leather coats, a strutting vainglorious fantast. A better-humoured version of the arrogant male surfaced at Hollywood in the person of Clark Gable: a broad-chested type who did not take no from a woman. When in *It Happened One Night*, 1934, he took off his shirt to reveal a sleeveless athletic vest, male underwear changed and sleeved vests went out. A tough guy did not need a sleeved vest. Ever since the advent of knee-breeches knee-length drawers had dominated male underwear, but by the 1920s athletic-type shorts were coming in and the Thirties saw the brief as short as the pants of the 1480s. The Y-front appeared in 1938, dispensing with buttons. Zips did not reach this zone, for sensitive reasons. Oddly enough, however, male underwear has to please women, because the huge spread of department stores in the twentieth century make it possible for women to shop nearer home, and it is now the women who select a man's underpants, shirts, socks, and often the suit as well. Consequently the colours employed had to satisfy feminine tastes for men, which did not permit anything too exotic. In Britain women expected their men to dress well but with restraint and modesty. In 1937 the coronation of George VI did set off a range of red, white and blue underwear, but it was but short-lived. Most wives and mothers continued to buy white.

While the rumours of future conflict led to a depression in the market, the introduction of holidays with pay caused a boom in sportswear and holiday clothes, in 1938 – sports jackets and flannels, short-sleeved summer shirts with collar attached, shorts now acceptable for tennis, and swimming trunks. None of these garments could be worn in town, where the lounge suit now reigned by day, and dinner jackets or white tie and tails for evening, in the best circles. George VI followed his brother in making the morning coat the correct wear for the season. On his tour of Canada and the USA in 1939 he adopted the double-breasted suit, which had been in exis-

82 Sir Samuel Hoare, 30 August 1938. The Foreign Office look with black Homburg hat, rolled umbrella and a super-smart three-piece lounge suit, as crisply tailored as could be. The striped shirt has appeared with a white collar which 50 years later is still considered smart. The front crease in trousers was well established by 1938, but Sir Samuel scorns turn-ups, although the man behind him has them. The British were still regarded as the best-dressed men in the world, at the top of society.

83 The Joint Party Cabinet during World War II, photographed at Number 10 Downing Street. Seated, from the left, are Ernest Bevin, Lord Beaverbrook, Anthony Eden, Clement Attlee, Winston Churchill, Sir John Anderson, Arthur Greenwood, Sir Kingsley Wood. Standing, from the left, are Sir Edward Bridges, Marshal of the Royal Air Force Sir Charles Portal, Sir Archibald Sinclair, the First Sea Lord Admiral Sir Dudley Pound, Mr Alexander, Lord Cranborne, Herbert Morrison, Lord Moyne, Captain Margesson, Brendan Bracken, General Sir John Dill, Major-General Sir Hastings Ismay, and Sir Alexander Cadogan. The most stylish member of the Cabinet is Anthony Eden, who displays a double-breasted waistcoat where all the other civilian ministers are wearing single-breasted waistcoats. Although the Prime Minister, Churchill, wears a black jacket and waistcoat of a type much favoured by lawyers, he strikes a rakish note with a bow tie and untidy handkerchief. Front creases remain but turn-ups were axed by clothes rationing as unnecessary appendages. The Protestant Clothing Ethic is evident in the preference for dark tones. The time must be late afternoon, as Sir Archibald Sinclair has changed into a black tie and dinner jacket for evening, keeping up appearances despite the war.

tence all the decade, but now it received the royal accolade that meant even the most conservative men could do the same without censure. With the outbreak of war any hopes for a fashion lead by this King died. Fashion for men had to go into cold storage for the time being, and the pattern of different clothes for different times of day took a sudden blow. In the Army the formal full dress, undress and mess uniforms had to end because of the increase in manpower and the shortage of cloth. Battledress with its blouson jacket would do for all occasions, even dances and dinners. Civilian wear underwent exactly the same restriction, and the daytime suit could be worn at the theatre, and even in the evening, now that so much material and skill was required for the war effort. The more masculine thirties

now got the opportunity to prove it on the battlefield.[32]

Shortages became the norm during the war, which led in 1942 to a return of sumptuary law – clothes rationing – but this time the restrictions applied to everybody, princes and peasants, with no privileges for any one class. It was no longer a case of cloth of gold for royalty and its relations. The new King wanted to look the same as everybody else, because this was a very different war which affected the people at home as well as the troops abroad, with German bombs raining on civilian factories, docks and power stations as well as on military targets. When Buckingham Palace was hit it caused Queen Elizabeth's famous remark ' Now we can look the East End in the face,' where the docks had taken a blasting. This working together which was such a theme of the Second World War was helped by clothes rationing, for regardless of whether a man dressed at Savile Row or C&A's he was restricted to the same number of clothing coupons. The fact that the USA was not in the war to begin with turned it into a treasure house of the unobtainable. It seemed to be the home of plenty, which was shown by its launching of the ' Drape ' suit in 1943. This extremely loose fitting suit with sloping shoulders used far more material than Utility suits in Britain and would make a huge hole in a man's clothing-coupon allowance with little left for underwear and woollens. Fortunately it did not appeal to British taste either, since the beautifully tailored suit was the national pride. Looking swamped by a voluminous jacket did not flatter the wearer, so any disappointment that it was virtually unobtainable was lessened by dislike. What worried the older generation was the casual quality of so much American wear. Publicity photographs showing the bobbysoxers' idol Frank Sinatra in a crumpled lounge suit and no tie were seen as a bad influence on the young. Bing Crosby was another American star who was notorious for his liking for casual clothes. Even his wife complained that he was a bad example to his own sons and he conceded that his habit of lounging about in sweater, slacks and moccasins did not help when she wanted them to wear shirts and ties. However, Bing insisted that he put a lot of thought into his clothes and that they were good quality, but as he was colour-blind he could produce some weird combinations of tone and pattern.[33]

Back in war-torn Britain George VI set the example of make-do-and-mend by making his pre-war wardrobe last, wearing his old suits, and when shirt collars and cuffs grew shabby, replacing them with new ones made from his shirt tails. In addition he performed most of his public duties in uniform, usually naval as he had served in that service, to emphasize the fact that he was serving his country too. The palace guard was no longer mounted in bright uniforms but wore khaki and steel helmets, and household staff wore uniforms too. The King would check the palace blackout in person and also put a five-inch mark on the baths because that was all the hot water a person was allowed, royal or commoner. While he was no fashion leader, he was a fine example in a time of shortages, and by applying the limits of rationing to his own family gave a lead to the country.[34]

People who tried to cheat over their clothing coupon allowance could be fined, like the MP Lady Astor, who was fined £50 at Bow Street Magistrates' Court in 1943 for asking American friends to bring clothes over with them.[35] The Duke of Windsor showed some thought for limiting wardrobes by wearing a tartan suit that had been made for his father George V in the 1890s. This set off a fashion for tartan wear for men in the USA, with tartan dinner jackets, tartan cummerbunds and even tartan swimming trunks. It could not take off in Britain, as clothes rationing lasted until 1949. The new Labour government in 1945 tried to give all the demobbed soldiers a good demob suit; a complete outfit down to the shirt and cuff links, in as lavish a choice of materials and styles as could be managed at the time. The shortages continued after the war, with fuel cuts, bread rationing, and no sign of peace bringing wonderful fashions for all. The make-do-and-mend had to continue, reusing clothes as much as possible, with leather patches to cover the holes. There was one thing which was not rationed, and that was children. The ending of the war led to a huge increase in births now that people wanted to rebuild society. The result was the biggest number of teenagers in the years to come than society had ever seen before. That was going to have a big impact on menswear.

Chapter Seven

A sHoCK to tHe System

The advent of the teenager was a new phenomenon in society. The term 'teener' existed in the nineteenth century, but there was no concept of a separate class of youngsters. Quite the contrary: right down to the 1940s the principal desire of youths was to grow up as quickly as possible. An air of sophistication was the most desirable social asset, and the seventeen-year-old would sport adult suits and a rakish trilby, and try very hard to grow a moustache. In the working class in particular youth was something to get rid of as soon as possible. Mothers were terrified of sex lest it result in yet another pregnancy and yet another mouth to feed, with no increase in the father's pay, so as soon as any child was old enough to earn, out it went, to help with the family budget. The idea of a teenage life-style was a luxury that could only come into being when the young had enough money to pay mother for their keep, and have something left over for themselves. This state of affairs arrived in the 1950s. There was a shortage of labour, Europe had to be rebuilt, and there was an enormous housing shortage because of the war damage, which meant that a youngster could find a job as soon as he left school. If he earned a good wage he could give half to his mother, and still have the rest to spend on clothes, records, drink, and motorbikes. A new economic force was coming into being; the teenage market, which saw the rise of special magazines, shops, records, and even radio stations all aimed at a specific group which had not existed before. This was, of course, a luxury of European and North American cultures, for in the rest of the world children were still needed as wage-earners for the family. The established system whereby the court launched fashions faced a new challenge just at the moment when it had no Prince of Wales to set the lead in styles. When Elizabeth II succeeded in 1952 her heir was still in his infancy, while her consort was a naval man with no great interest in clothes. Thus the royal family lacked a member to carry on the work of Edward VII and Edward VIII to help British exports, right at the moment when the teenage market was beginning to flourish. The lead was temporarily passing out of royal hands, but as soon as a stylish Prince of Wales appears in the future men will be only to happy to copy him, so it cannot be seen as a permanent loss.

A number of men in high society tried to fill the gap. After the drabness of war and rationing, they wanted to bring some colour into menswear. In March 1950 Gordon Beckles hailed 'The Return of the Beau' in *Harper's Bazaar*.

He criticized Mr Churchill for his fondness for boiler suits – not a stylish fashion for a former Prime Minister to promote, but fortunately others gave a lead. A Mr Trubshawe favoured a return to the Edwardian mode, and wore a high-fronted jacket of Edwardian type, a high collar, a tie with a tie pin, and a moustache. The new Edwardian line was slim, with jackets longer to the top of the thigh, and narrow trousers. Overcoats were narrow with flap pockets and velvet collars. Gentlemen who introduced more colour were Mr Anthony Wysard, who wore a purple waistcoat with his grey suit, and Mr Simon Elwes, who had a burgundy velvet smoking jacket with satin revers and cuffs. Cecil Beaton was wearing bright waistcoats in mustards, yellows and reds. For evening moiré and sprigged brocade waistcoats were appearing. Mr Alec Guinness liked coloured cuffs to match but the effect was too much like a bandsman or a waiter. Jack Buchanan stuck to his midnight-blue evening clothes but a new touch was bejewelled buttons on his waistcoat. The Marquess of Milford Haven and Lords Sefton and Scarsdale were counted among the best-dressed men in town, but what was sadly lacking was a central figure. Savile Row's hopes to turn the Duke of Edinburgh into a stylish gentleman were not meeting with success. In 1949 the Duke turned up at the Perth Ball in a dinner jacket and odd shoes, instead of evening dress, and as he was still a serving officer in the Royal Navy he kept disappearing to sea just when society wanted him for an event. 'The world is looking to us to set the pace in men's fashions,' Beckles insisted, but without an elegant Prince of Wales or Prince Consort to take the lead, how was it to be achieved, for who else was so newsworthy as a prince?[1]

The answer came from far below, and much sooner than high society expected. By 1953 working-class young men in south London were wearing high society's Edwardian look. This was astounding. While the urban poor had always copied their superiors, it took a generation or two. Savile Row suits were famous for their durability, so one had to wait until the owner died and his valet acquired his wardrobe by right, when he would sell it to the second-hand clothes trade. Only then would the poor begin to be able to acquire a top fashion, but now here were youngsters who could actually afford to copy an upper-class style only three years after its launching. Their lordships in St James's were appalled. Why, they would have to change the fashion every five minutes if they were to keep

84 The Labour Party's Five Left-Wingers at the 50th Annual Conference at Scarborough, 30 September 1951. The lounge suit remains correct dress for conferences, but only Aneurin Bevan, second from left, has remained loyal to the black Socialist suit. Harold Wilson and Tom Driberg have opted for tones of grey while Ian Mikardo has chosen stripes. The double-breasted style introduced in the 1930s is still present. Barbara Castle has followed the New Look for women.

ahead of such instant competition! The combined spending power of this new generation could actually outsell Savile Row. The Teddy Boy look spread round the country very quickly, and it exaggerated the original model by lengthening the jacket even further to mid-thigh, taking the velvet collars off overcoats and putting them on suits, and narrowing the trousers even further, but also wearing ungentle-manly crêpe-soled shoes. Hair was worn longer than among the aristocracy in the DA style, thoroughly drenched in Brylcreem. The young men of the working class were actually creating a fashion of their own! Those at the top of society might sneer at the lack of taste displayed but the new style was big business. In 1957 John Stephens opened a boutique for men in a scruffy backstreet called Carnaby. By 1966 there were 17 boutiques in the street, of which no less than 13 were for menswear. They did not care what Savile Row and the court considered correct dress, for the young had money and these new shops designed specifically for them. The previous essential approval of royalty to secure a style was now ignored, and John Stephens launched fashions for men straight into the street.

By now, however, imperial power had moved to the United States. Europe was weak from the war, and Britain could no longer afford to rule an Empire, so inevitably an American influence on clothes became more strongly marked. Rock music burst forth with Bill Haley and the Comets in *Rock Around the Clock* in 1955. The film reached England in 1956 and next year the Comets came over on tour. The group wore those dreadful tartan dinner jackets that the Americans had gone overboard for, but Savile Row was thankful that the Duke of Edinburgh did not give the garment his blessing. The young went wild, dancing in the cinema aisles, but the big impact on dress came along after the Comets. Elvis Presley in *Jailhouse Rock* wore a denim suit, and this sparked off a fashion for denim among the fans and an increasing demand for jeans. Here was a pop star launching a fashion, instead of a prince or stage hero, and it was a fashion which completely ignored opinion among the pundits. The elevation of working fabric into fashion was not new because corduroy had made that step already. What was new was that there were more customers for it.

The term denim jeans is a tautology, for both words mean a twilled cotton fabric. 'Denim' is a contraction of *serge de Nîmes*, and denim breeches were on sale in England in 1695. By the nineteenth century denim was used mainly for overalls. 'Jeans' is a sixteenth-century cotton like fustian which was also used for working garments. In 1885 *Harper's Magazine* spoke of jeans-clad mountaineers, who were clearly wearing tough cotton working clothes.[2] In the USA the terms denim and jeans got mixed up. Jeans came to mean trousers made of that fabric, thus being jeans jeans, which was clarified by speaking of denim jeans, even though they originally meant the same thing. The firm of Levi Strauss made jeans for American miners, and American cowboys wore them too. City people could see jeans aplenty in the silent movies when cowboys became a regular feature, but the garment was then still a working one, not a fashionable one. In the 1930s and 40s Bing Crosby wore jeans at Del Mar Race Track and on his ranch at Elko, Nevada, when away from the studio and dance hall. He did not wear jeans to perform in, for all his fondness for casual dress, as they were still a country and industrial garment. It was the 1950s which saw jeans being promoted as urban wear by such films as *Rebel Without A Cause* in 1955, where the clothes James Dean wore were to become a uniform for young males around the globe: jeans, T-shirt

85 Judy Cassab, *Hugh Gaitskell*, 1957. The Leader of the Labour Party shows the post-war trend towards informality by discarding the waistcoat, particularly in the summer. On the other hand, the Leader of the Conservative Party, Harold Macmillan, remained very loyal to waistcoats, having been born in 1894; he was called the Last Edwardian. The Conservative Party is still the place to find most waistcoats. Clothes are used to reflect a political stance.

and anorak. Cowboys continued to wear them, as did Robert Mitchum in *The Lusty Men*, 1952, which examined the breed in modern conditions. The adoption of jeans in Europe was a gradual process, of course. At Oxford University around 1960 correct dress was a tweed hacking jacket and cavalry twill trousers, and a shirt and tie or cravat. Leather shoes were also correct, not cowboy boots, and suede bootees were highly suspect, smacking of moral depravity. Jeans took off during the 1960s when Britain gained twenty new universities and a whole flood of students eager to challenge authority and wear their own thing.

The USA became fashionable as an ideal, for after the war it seemed confident and strong, an open society with none of Britain's hierarchies, a more mobile society. It also seemed exciting and

86 Franck Pourcel, 1959. When waistcoats are not worn something else is needed in cool weather, so the jumper joins the suit. The trend in the late fifties was towards a more slender line, with narrow trousers, and double-breasted jackets were going to yield to single-breasted ones. The low hat was termed the pork pie, and gentlemen were still expected to wear hats.

liberal, with Kinsey starting his sexual research, whereas Europe was exhausted and inhibited. The quiet confidence was soon being challenged by some Americans themselves. The 1950s were condemned as the silent generation, and the new beat generation led by such prophets as Ginsberg and Kerouac preached mysticism, rejection of the norm, self-expression. Get up and go. Where to was not defined precisely. Whichever attitude one supported, to many the USA seemed exciting, and worthy of imitation. *The Times* declared in 1958 that the British Edward-

ian revival was the most significant shot-in-the-arm since the war, and did not deign to notice jeans. The news was the very short overcoat at least an inch above the knee which Simpson's of Piccadilly said was outselling the long overcoat by 50%. The slim silhouette continued, with trousers now tapered to 17 inches. The tone for the year was schoolboys' uniform light-grey, as in Aquascutum's grey flannel single-breasted suit with three buttons to the jacket and the slim line, price 26 guineas. To top the outfit, one of Simpson's lightweight bowler hats, available in grey, tobacco and black, price £2.10s. Drip-dry shirts were now available, but the City still liked the stiff collar for professional men and Hardy Amies created a soft shirt with the collar stiffened by buckram, termed the commuter's shirt, which would stay stiff all day. Turn-ups were disappearing. Rationing had forbidden unnecessary material on a suit, and after the war, although some turn-ups survived, the new lean trouser looked best without them.[3]

By 1962 the *Woman's Mirror* was complaining that 'Men aren't what they used to be.' While the end of the Victorian paterfamilias dictating to the whole family was a good thing, modern man was leaving all the decisions to his wife. Granted, 4,000,000 wives were now wage-earners, too, but it seemed unfair to leave all the problems to them as well. Why, 50% of husbands had not even decided to ask their wives to marry them; they just 'drifted into it'. The article pleaded for the return of a stronger man, but this did not happen. With more women working, a man's economic ability to dictate was on the decline.[4]

By 1962 Britain showed that it could hit back at the flood of Americana when the Beatles achieved their first hit record. They wore longer hair, which then meant that it covered the ears, and fringes, which were widely copied. In 1963 they appeared in collarless suits by Pierre Cardin but that look did not catch on. The British did not like the French messing about with their institution, the suit, and they retained their collars. Nevertheless, the fact that the Beatles were first presented in suits showed just how careful their manager Brian Epstein was to create a respectable image which would not alarm the older generation. The Beatles conquered the USA and suddenly the foreign press became aware of Carnaby Street. It was the return of the English Dandy, they declared, amazed at the amount of colour on show, but this was an incorrect observation as Beau Brummell was opposed to lots of colour. However,

John Stephens with his Lord John boutiques, and Rupert Lycett Green, with Blades, had been children during the drabness of the war, so as young adults they felt a psychological need for something cheerful. One of the first young men to dare to wear more colour was the designer David Mlinaric of Tite Street who owned brown suits and cinnamon suits which he wore with a yellow shirt and a yellow tie. He attached frills to the front of an evening shirt and recreated the frilled shirt which was soon copied by Patrick, Earl of Lichfield. He was the Queen's cousin, and with her sons still too young to set the mode, the stylish world was delighted to have a royal relation with an interest in fashion. Lord Lichfield says: ' I just quite simply liked clothes more than most people, and by way of my position as a fashion photographer, I got very involved with the clothing world.' He admitted to the *Observer* that he spent a fortune on attire, and possessed 26 suits, mostly brown, with tweeds for the country, 50 shirts, 50 ties, innumerable polo-necked sweaters in green and beige which needed a lot of cleaning, and four suede coats. For shooting he favoured bottle-green corduroy kneebreeches and had ordered his gamekeepers to wear the same. What such a wardrobe cost was shown by the model Ted Dawson who spent £500 a year on clothes, owning 30 suits, 14 jackets, 75 shirts, and 100 ties. At Blades suits were coloured white, cream, mustard, pale grey, pink, dark blue and black, and were designed by Eric Joy. The proprietor stated that the well-dressed man should own two dinner jackets, in silk for summer and worsted for winter, a velvet evening suit, one grey suit, one black, two working suits, a lightweight tweed suit for the country, two light summer suits, a light-grey suit, and a crushproof travelling suit for aircraft and trains. For winter three overcoats were necessary, a dark one for evenings, a tweedy type for the acres, and a short coat for motoring. At least two sports jackets and about six assorted pairs of slacks completed the wardrobe, which should also contain fifty shirts and fifty ties.

Lord Lichfield argued:

A man should enjoy his clothes. A man doesn't dress for himself. He dresses to attract the girls – unlike the girls, who dress to impress each other. I have an idea all men dress to be sexy like cock pheasants in the mating season. I always dress more carefully the first time I take a girl out than the second. English girls, I think, are more adventurous in their tastes than girls of other countries and they admire adventurously dressed men.

87 Bobby Vinton, 1962. The rise of the USA as a dominant world power led to American styles gaining in importance, particularly among the young, and they were given wide display in American films with James Dean and Elvis Presley. American young rejected the suit in favour of shirts, no ties, jeans without a front crease, white socks instead of dark, and slip-on shoes instead of laced ones. Hair was cut in the manner of Tony Curtis, very short at the sides, but longer on top. This look was revived in the early eighties.

They would, of course, when he came equipped with a title and royal connections; nevertheless, only a minority of males could afford such adventurous splendour. The ordinary man with only two suits to his name could not afford to choose such impractical colours as white, cream or mustard, for they needed to be cleaned very frequently, which was expensive, and meant that half his wardrobe was at the dry-cleaners every week. Only the wealthy man, with his 20-odd suits, could ring the changes. Accordingly colour on the streets was rare, for the majority of men stuck to safe dark grey and blue which did not show the dirt. Blades was about to open a branch in New York and conceded that they would have to tone down their clothes. The tolerant British allowed a man to be unusual in his dress, but American men were more self-conscious. To them, colour and frilled shirts suggested homo-

88 The Tornados, 1962. In Britain pop groups remained loyal to suits to give themselves a respectable image. The single-breasted suit is the new look, and the velvet collars give a Teddy Boy touch, as does the high Edwardian fastening. Ties are much slimmer and so are lapels. Shirts have a curved-edge collar instead of a pointed one, and a good display of cuff with a large cuff link was considered very stylish. The hair is getting long enough to touch the ears, and fringes were a craze.

sexuality, but that charge could not be levelled against the new stylists.[5]

Marlon Brando was another filmstar to inspire a fashion. When he appeared as the Mexican leader in *Viva Zapata* it sparked off a vogue for Mexican moustaches after 1952, but it was a slow introduction. In 1967 all four Beatles, Sean Connery and designer Ossie Clark could be seen in Mexican moustaches. For the uncertain, false ones were on sale in the King's Road at £2.10s. By 1968 the debs' delights in high society were being styled the Beautiful People, who showed a strong Regency influence with high coat collars and revers, and a taste for silk cravats, but what was lacking was the stern discipline of starch. The velvet suit was particularly favoured by this set for evenings. That a film could create a fashion did not escape Simpson's, for when *The Guru* was due out in 1968 they offered a suit with high-collared Indian-type jacket and tight trousers, available in black velvet lined with purple silk, or in dark brown velvet lined with gold, priced at £38.10s. It was adopted by some but failed to oust the traditional form of evening dress which, like the Savile Row tailors, was proving more durable in changing times than many pundits anticipated. That same year hiring firms like Moss Bros could state that their turnover for evening dress had doubled over the last three years, and twice as many men were wearing evening clothes as in 1958. At the cocktail belt in Kent and in London's Putney, Wim-

bledon, Kingston, St John's Wood and Golders Green, dinner parties with dinner jackets were back in vogue. Out of town Leeds, Nottingham and Cardiff were the most conscious of stylish evening dressing. Carnaby Street's frilled shirts were influential in making evening shirts more fanciful, with tucks, ruching and discreet frills. In the ready-to-wear range dinner jackets were on sale at 16 guineas for barathea and £32 for mohair. A bespoke version would cost over £75. The white tie and tails was definitely on the way out, except at courts. When poor George Brown wore a dinner jacket and black tie in 1967 at a

89 Patrick, Earl of Lichfield. Swinging London and the Return of the Dandy, cried the international press, seeing Lord Lichfield as one of its leading exponents. The frill about the neck and on the cuffs, and the elaborate bow, mixed both Elizabethan and Regency antecedents. The look was criticized as effeminate, but it was an appropriate salute to the second Elizabethan age, with another queen regnant heading British society.

reception for King Feisal of Saudi Arabia the press were highly critical, even though very few men now owned tails, particularly not those in the Labour Party. Burton's would make a set of tails for £19 but they could be hired for £4. Special pink dress coats for Hunt Balls with par-

90 The Walker Brothers, 1965. British youth begins to reflect the dislike of suits among the American young, by wearing blazers with turtle-neck jumpers, or shirts without ties, and very narrow corduroy trousers. The high-heeled boots and the even longer hair hiding the ears emphasized the feminine trends.

ticular hunt buttons would cost £125. A trend towards making dinner jackets more like lounge suits was the news from Savile Row's Huntsman and Kilgour, and Chester Barrie had a watered-silk evening lounge suit for £80. It was claimed that at an American ball only 10% of men would be wearing a British-type black dinner jacket; the rest sported watered silks and patterned jackets with their black trousers. Chester Barrie made pale blue, bronze and purple dinner jackets, but for sale by their Italian subsidiary, appreciating that such tones would not go down well at a British rugby club dinner.[6]

In 1969 Shirley Conran interviewed some men about their approach to clothes. The boutique owner Michael Fish predicted the decline of the lounge suit in face of the Space Age tunic top, and said shirts would be long to the hip, worn outside the trousers with a large belt. It did not happen, for the simple reason that jackets were easier to put on and off than tunics, and had plenty of useful pockets. The actor Edward Woodward explained that as he had to wear very ornate costume in plays, he liked simplicity at home. He liked the tunic top in dark green Lord Snowdon wore; he had one made in charcoal worsted without a collar, to wear with his polo-necked evening shirts in pale yellow or lilac silk. The polo neck for after dark was promoted by Lord Snowdon and had a short vogue but it did not oust the traditional shirt and tie. Established styles had more durability than many young designers realized. Mr Woodward also liked conventional evening wear: 'I'm mad about dinner-jackets. I'm the only man I know who likes a dinner jacket.. Can't think why men make such a fuss about them; but I only ever feel really glamorous when I'm wearing them.' He had found velvet smoking jackets very comfortable on the stage and would like one in plum red. He favoured colour in his underpants, too, jockey pants in red and blue. The hairdresser Daniel Gavin said he and his wife liked to be well dressed. He had five Edwardian suits with raised seams made by Terry of Harrow at 60 guineas each. Colour he loved in shirts, turquoise blue or green in lawn or silk, which his wife said were a pain to wash. Underwear was chosen by the wife at Marks & Spencer. The one thing he would like just then was a long fur coat, as scruffy as an animal. Lord Rendlesham liked all black for evening, teaming a St Laurent Rive Gauche cotton safari jacket with velvet trousers and a cotton polo neck. His son Charles envied that although he could not wear it at Eton. He shopped at Take 6, a black corduroy jacket, a red

silk jersey shirt, and the newest trousers, grey worsted bell bottoms. Since 1968, the slender Edwardian trouser had been facing a threat from the flare. From the USA Tom Wolfe, chronicler of the hippie and pop scene, gave the opinion that 'There are two kinds of style consciousness. (1) You're trying to be different to be noticed and (2) you're desperately trying to be not noticed. So no one alive can say they're not clothes conscious, even hermits.' He said everybody wore a uniform, from hermits to conventional types, to hippies claiming to be different in uniform jeans.[7]

It was the old story; the young generation was dressing more casually than its parents to show that it was different and disagreed with established norms. That was common enough among the young, although by the time they had aged to forty they would discover that they were more like their parents than they would have believed possible. The hippies took this revolt to its extreme, wearing their hair as long as it would grow, and sporting T-shirts, gaudy trousers like pyjamas, or dungarees, and moccasins, while cold weather saw the Afghan sheepskin coat.

The hippies' attire reflected their unstructured and introverted philosophy, but not all youth followed suit. Those in conventional schools were still required to wear conventional school uniforms, while many rock 'n roll devotees remained loyal to their version of the Teddy Boy look, with jackets so long they were in fact frock coats back from the grave, and Tony Curtis hairstyles. Their trousers remained Edwardian-slim. Motorcyclists liked black leather; the Mods favoured tight Italian-type suits and trilby hats, black shirts and white ties. Now that the young could afford new clothes instead of hand-me-downs, they evolved several different styles. Whereas the upper and middle classes had tried to imitate royal example, the young could select several groups to identify with. The ready-to-wear firm Dunn & Co. argued that sooner or later all these butterflies would sober down, and in its advertising for November 1971 offered suits in 83 fittings and durable cloth, which were designed to be pretty timeless. 'If you can keep your suit when all around are changing theirs, then you are a man, my son.' The flared effect influenced the whole outfit. Collars and lapels grew wider, jackets were longer and touched the thigh, cuffs were flared as well as the trouser bottoms which had started to widen in the late 1960s. It had to happen because the slenderness of the Fifties and Sixties had become routine. Denim had become so popular that by 1972 leather was actually being dyed to look like washed-out denim. The designer Henry Lehr produced dyed leather suits in denim blue for £92, and blazers for £60. The year saw a serious attempt to upgrade denim into a fit material for suits, and in the entertainment and television world this had some success, with the actor Michael York buying one of Lord John's brushed denim suits, which came in pink-beige, brown and pale blue at £13.95, and the TV presenter Kenneth Allsop donning a denim-look suit in polyester and viscose from Austin Reed at £20.95.[8] Nevertheless, the woollen suit maintained its dominance. Ties became voluminous. Here the flare increased the size of the knot and made the tie much wider. They now came in knitted silk, bright satin or denim. Carnaby Street liked garish patterns on its ties, but the more stylish kept to plain colours.

The success of the Carnaby Street boutiques in boosting colour beyond the level reached by the Edwardian revival obliged established menswear firms to open boutiques. Simpson's opened Trend, Austin Reed Cue, Aquascutum Club 92, and Harrod's Way In. Carnaby Street did make men more fashion-conscious, and forced producers to show more style and colour, for the younger customer. Needless to say, most of their fathers remained loyal to their established image, and considered the latest styles too effete. Longer hair, skirted jackets, flared trousers, frilled shirts, bright colours, and even high-heeled shoes – a good two inches high – amounted to a feminine look. Then the 'unisex' style came forth, with identical T-shirts, jeans, and interchangeable pullovers and cardigans. Among the hippies the unisex look became a rigid uniform, and all those who considered themselves anti-establishment had to conform in the revolutionary norm of T-shirt, jeans and anorak, whatever the sex. Out in the shires nothing had changed, for the hacking jacket was still worn and the shooting knickerbocker or kneebreeches still existed, although Daks termed theirs 'plus twos', as they were less wide than the 1930s version. By 1975 the old blouson jacket was seen again. Before the war it was a garment of Canadian woodsmen, and Captain Molyneux launched blousons for women in 1940 as a version of that lumber jacket. During the war men had worn the garment on a wide scale. By 1975 it came into country fashion, which was where it had originated at a working level, only now it was aimed at those who visited the country for pleasure and sport.

In town the newest craze was to wear old clothes, which caused the British Clothing Manufacturers' Federation to protest in 1975 that six out of twenty British men were the worst-dressed in Europe. Army surplus had been clothing the indigent since the war, but thanks to the Arabs and the energy crisis the number of unemployed began to rise. The new poor needed old clothes as the poor had always done, but it was now given an air of fashion to display commiseration and empathy with the jobless. American buyers would snap up British rags at 6p a time and sell them in the States for £7. On the King's Road, now a rival to Carnaby Street, shops selling only old clothes stood alongside the boutiques selling new, but making it a fashion did increase the price. Back on the High Street Marks & Spencer had decided to concentrate more on menswear in general and this became the most expanding part of their trade. To the usual shirts, socks and woollens Marks & Spencer added sports jackets and suits. The firm already owned 18 branches in Canada, but in 1975 it took on the French, opening shops in Paris, Lyons and in the Belgian capital. One variation was necessary in that Frenchmen liked one vent in the jacket where the British favoured two, but otherwise their British range was equally acceptable. Prices could not be the same because the French VAT rate was higher, so a suit which cost £37 at Marble Arch cost £55 on the Boulevard Haussmann, but it still undercut French suits by £10. The French male was also seduced by navy velvet suits for 440 francs, and for day lounge suits in Prince of Wales check in grey. Surprisingly, research suggested that the ordinary French male was more sober in his tastes than French high society had been, so the colours that flourished in London had to be toned down. That the firm got things right was shown by its announcement in 1983 that it had become the biggest exporter of British clothes, to a value of £58,000,000. It was Professor Higgins in the stage and cinema versions of *My Fair Lady* who was credited with giving cardigans a new life, slim in the Sixties and now wide in the Seventies. Bulk came in, great chunky knits with huge patch pockets, in such shades as dark brown, corn, grey, and navy blue, reaching down to the thigh.

October 1976 was the date when a Chester

91 Evening dress, Austin Reed, *c.* 1972. The dinner jackets undergo elongation, as the seventies look is long to the thigh. The pleated shirt and big bow tie show the impact of the 'Sixties Dandy' style on formal wear. Cue Shop was Austin Reed's reaction to youthful boutiques, offering smart clothes of a younger style.

Cue Party Manifesto

Toe the party line. The Cue Shop Policy is to offer the smartest clothes and accessories to celebrate in:

English tailored velvet suit in black, brown, navy and green—£95. Matching velvet bow—£3.95. Pleated shirt, lots of colours—£17.50.

The Cue Shop also helps to build your formal wardrobe with a selection of jackets and slacks all in fine black crepe: jackets—£65; slacks—£24.

Double breasted satin lapels, centre vent.

Single breasted, velvet lapels, side vents.

the Cue shop
Austin Reed

AUSTIN REED

103 Regent Street,
163/9 Brompton Road,
Brent Cross Shopping Centre.

Barrie ready-made suit was priced at £1,000, entering the range of the Savile Row hand-tailored masterpieces. Savile Row replied that there would always be a demand for its quality. The rich would always come where they could buy the best, which was proved by the flood of

rich Arabs, pockets bulging with oil money, descending on London for bespoke suits, silk shirts, socks and ties, and liking in particular pale-grey outfits. Savile Row had to admit that there was a problem in recruiting labour, because fewer men were willing to sew, and to be on the safe side some of the firms started ready-to-wear lines overseas. Both the royal livery tailor, Henry Poole, and Huntsman had such labels in Japan. At Blades Lycett Green introduced a standardized range, still handmade, but cheaper than bespoke clothes for the individual. He also sold socks, shirts, ties and cashmere sweaters on the premises, so that a customer

92 Dewey Bunnell and Gerry Beckley, 1972. The American hippy look. Don't make any effort, let the hair and beard grow, wear the underwear vest, renamed the T-shirt, and jeans without any front creases. Grooming is to be resisted. The look became a uniform among the young internationally, but was strongly objected to by suited elders. The long hair received the same condemnation it had undergone in the seventeenth century for being too feminine and soft.

could purchase a complete outfit, but the old firms refused to imitate this, stating that they were tailors, not hosiers. Prime Minister James Callaghan did his bit to help by taking President Jimmy Carter some dark blue suiting with a pinstripe formed from the tiny initials JC, in March 1977. However, the Carter administration preferred a folksy image with the President often sporting a denim suit.[9] That would change come the next election.

Denim sales reached their apogee in the seventies. According to the International Institute for Cotton, sales of jeans in Britain in 1970 were 12 million pairs worth £26,000,000, which increased to 38 million pairs worth £243,000,000 in 1976. Worldwide, sales had reached to 170 million pairs worth £1.6 billion, which made Levi Strauss the biggest clothing manufacturer in the globe. Thereafter a reduction in sales began, as young men grew tired of jeans with everything, and started to return to corduroy and canvas trousers, although an overlap would last for years to come. In 1977 Austin Reed offered corduroy blousons at £49 and corduroy trousers at £16, while a corduroy jacket with quilted lining and toggle fastening cost £49. The blouson reached the waist, but other jackets were still down to the thigh, with huge patch pockets. The revival of corduroy was the first hint of a rougher look ahead when the inevitable reaction against the effeminate styles of the seventies would occur.

The old word 'punk', which Ned Ward had used in the seventeenth century to denote a gaudy prostitute, came to the fore again in 1976. The increasing economic depression caused a generation of youth to see a society which had no use for it. Some of them reacted by showing contempt and breaking as many of the social rules as they could think of. Away with cleanliness, manners, tidiness and taste. Enter dirt, scars, rags, and obscenity. The first singers of punk did not have a uniform, and wore jeans and T-shirts or else conventional shirt, tie, jumper and slacks. Their difference then was shown by cropping the hair short to distinguish them from long-haired hippies. The costume was concocted later and looked back to women's clothes in the 1930s, using Schiaparelli's Surrealist zips all over again, and Captain Molyneux's safety-pin fasteners of 1933. It showed a greater degree of sophistication than the usual working-class outfit, which suggested some art-college involvement in its development. The uniform consisted of a great deal of black leather with some denim. Badges, Nazi iron crosses, chains, and safety

pins formed the cheap jewellery, while the most effective way to illustrate one's place as a victim of society was to sport a concentration camp striped shirt. Punks made a political statement through clothing in the same way that the Whigs, the Tories, and the betrousered French revolutionaries had. Charles James Fox would have been delighted. With many members of the Punk movement being on the dole, they could not afford lavish spending on clothes, so the cheapest way to shock was to do things with their hair. Multicoloured effects, stripes, and patches flourished, to be followed by the shaved head with only a Mohican cockscomb, and by 1983 by pointed tufts in the manner of circus clowns. At the same time there were neo-Mods and rockers, skinheads, and pinheads, so the young had a variety of choices, and Britain seemed to be returning to the number of tribes she had when the Romans landed. The punk look, like the other looks of the fifties and sixties, was quickly imitated in Eastern Europe. While the Communist régimes condemned every Western style as decadent, the young loved them as obvious ways to illustrate their contempt for the ultra-conservative anti-revolutionary Communist governments, which are terrified of any innovation. In the Soviet Union there was a permanent shortage of jeans because it is a military state where the wishes of the consumer come last. Right-wing regimes also disliked jeans; when the generals took over in Turkey they banned jeans, and wore top hats and tails themselves. Clothes are used to make a great variety of political statements.

The outburst of youthful styles and attitudes had worried Noël Coward when he looked at what was happening in the United States:

In England it may be, and is, the age of the common man, but in America it is definitely the age of the crazy-mixed-up-kid. With a few notable exceptions . . . the whole nation seems to be becoming increasingly juvenile. They are such a kindly, hospitable, vital race, and their traditions are strong, but I wish they weren't so maddeningly volatile and emotionally swayed and so god-damned naïve '.[10]

He feared for a future left in hysterical hands. There was certainly a craze among older Americans to try to look young instead of growing old with dignity, so that the 1970s also saw the rise of the health fanatics. Of course, as medicine in the USA is terribly expensive, there was a good reason for trying to avoid the bills of old age and obesity. The pre-war track suit was renamed the

jogging suit and left sports fields to appear in town as some ran several miles every morning before work, and others wore the outfit all day to suggest that they were highly athletic. Before long, however, doctors were saying that so much shaking about of one's insides was not good for them, and medical arguments pro-jogging encountered medical opposition. However, perhaps the keeping-young fashion will fade out before the fact that in the 1980s the number of teenagers in the USA were outnumbered by those over 65. A mature look will surely surface as a result, which will prefer health activities more in keeping with its dignity. The youthful fling has been the main fashion since the war but all fashions end – until they are revived.

The eighties saw a swing to the conservative right in the USA, Britain and West Germany, and consequently conservative clothes were given more prominence. The new attitude was, as before, that the post-war years had been too soft, too liberal and too feminine. It was now time for sterner, harsher, more brutal policies and a return to masculinity. It will be noted that this definition of feminine as too liberal is the opposite of the Romantic definition of feminine, which found it too orderly and restrictive. The concept of the female changes as much as that of the male, but it has been the men who make the definitions. Menswear of the seventies styles was condemned as effete; the vogue for colour had gone too far, and now it was time for sobriety, simplicity and strength in dress. The lounge suit gained in importance. The shortage of jobs meant that the young man most likely to be appointed at an interview was the one who presented himself in a suit, with a shirt and tie and short hair. The message from employers to the young was 'smarten up'. It was heard. In Coventry in 1980 followers of the pop group the Specials wore tonic suits (two-tone), a revival of the shiny suits of the Americans in the Fifties, saying that punk dirt was boring and they enjoyed looking smart. The group Squeeze wore such suits for its first American tour in 1982, and more young men on the street appeared in suits. After all, the two-piece lounge suit was only just over 120 years old, so there was plenty of life in it yet, and still a long way to go before

it could match the three-piece suit at 320. Darker tones also came in, with black, dark brown and blues.

Conservatism could now be seen in Washington with the Reagan administration wearing suits instead of adopting Carter's casual air, while military men who had not been wearing their uniforms in the capital received a rebuke from the new President. The US Navy quickly ordered all officers and men to wear their naval uniforms from 1 May 1981 'to instill pride and professionalism', while the US Air Force also required such pride, and more Army uniforms appeared than had been seen for years.[11] Less conservative, perhaps, was the President's willingness to be groomed for television. As a former actor he did not object to being made up for the colour camera, while his jet-black hair though in his seventies, added to a presentation intended to convey youthful appeal. This made an impact and white hair became increasingly rare among men of his generation who would have scorned hair dyes before, but if the ex-cowboy actor could use it, so could they. The example was less imitated in Britain. While some older Britons do colour their hair, anything that smacks too much of artifice is suspect, while a well-scrubbed look was *de rigueur* for the supporters of the Iron Lady.

It is interesting to compare the awards for the best-dressed man as presented by different countries. In the USA the Custom Tailors' Guild voted Secretary of State General Haig the best-dressed man for 1981 and hoped he would do something to sharpen up the President's look. That same year the Menswear Association of Britain voted the Earl of Lichfield their best-dressed man. Like Haig, he wore suits, and this was the style both countries favoured, but Lichfield said his limit for a handmade suit was £1,000. Compared with his days as dandy, he maintained that he no longer followed fashion and kept to a conventional look. In France, meanwhile, the Club des Créateurs voted for Vitas Gerulaitis, who was known for very casual styles and claimed that his friends would not recognize him in a suit and tie.[12] The difference may be explained by the fact that the French had voted for the first Socialist government in years, so an undressed image was still permissible, whereas the USA and Britain had gone conservative and now preferred a dressed look. The waistcoat gained a new importance, for it advertised that the wearer could afford a three-piece suit, compared with the majority who could only afford a two-piece. In the bespoke world the dif-

93 Leo Sayer, 1980. The transition towards the severe eighties. The hair is less long and has undergone a feminine perm but it is more organized than in the Seventies. The front crease marks a return towards greater formality on the way, while the zip-adorned flying jacket in leather shows the tougher male the eighties promoted after the sloppy male of the previous decade.

ference in price was that a three-piece from Kilgour, French and Stanbury of Savile Row cost about £700, while a two-piece could be tailored for £200, only slightly more expensive than a Monsieur Dior ready-made suit at £160 in the summer of 1981. A bespoke ensemble of a dark-blue worsted suit for town (a two-piece), a Glen Urquart three-piece for the country, a tweed jacket, a camel overcoat and a pair of cavalry twill trousers would total £1,800 at Gieves & Hawkes.[13] Of course, it was the year when the Labour leader Michael Foot drew widespread condemnation for wearing a green coat, a plaid tie and brown shoes at the Remembrance Day celebrations; even some of his own party were annoyed that he did not wear black. There are always some people who cannot dress no matter how hard they try, of which ilk is Mr Foot, who retains the casual clothes and longish hair of the 1930s intellectual.

In the City and the professions the possession of a good suit is regarded as an investment that should last for years, so despite statements to the effect that men leave concern about fashion to their wives, where their image is concerned they go to great pains lest they incur the disapproval of their fellows. Correct dress for the appropriate occasion continues to be important. One such was the EEC summit in London in November 1981, when President Mitterand of France, Chancellor Schmidt of West Germany and other European heads had lunch with the Queen at Buckingham Palace, where all the men and the Duke of Edinburgh wore two-piece lounge suits, mainly dark in tone. In both the USA and Japan the English Look for menswear was news, for the suit is an English creation, and conservatism loves suits. Among the more inventive tailor-designers, Antony Price showed suits with broader shoulders now that masculinity was back, and baggy trousers held up by back-to-the-past braces. Mr Major of Fulham was regarded as a tailor of the highest reputation for cut, and from Hollywood to the Gulf States, men travelled to his door. He kept to the high waist of the 1920s suits and still used the four buttons at the cuff that the best tailors do. The traditional English casual style was also the rage

on the Continent, with tweed jackets, corduroy trousers, Fair Isle and Arran sweaters, striped shirts, braces, and collarless shirts. Such rough fabrics as Harris tweed and corduroy were essential to the new masculine image of toughness.

The blouson, alias the lumber jacket, made some inroads into casual wear, but walking about with the hands in the pockets in front looked rather like a revival of the peascod belly of the 1580s. The garment came in wool, cotton, and canvas at prices like £34.95 at Hepworth's, and £99 at Aquascutum and Burberry's. It was yet another example of a working garment being upgraded into a fashion, and will continue as a working garment outside. By 1983 fashion reporters were claiming that 'everybody' in the man's world was wearing them, which really means about 1 per 1,000. However, the paunch effect in front is not likely to remain stylish for long, as it ages the wearer. For those wishing to look rugged, the fur-lined flying jacket to the hips offered greater bulk, being padded and bedecked with zip pockets or studs. The rugged outdoors became the theme for casual wear in the autumn of 1983. The new masculine line was dubbed its Mountaineer look by Nashville clothes, with echoes also of the cowboy on the trail. Trousers were heavy corduroy, shirts of check came in thick brushed cotton or wool mixture, leather belts added a manly air, sweaters were heavy knits and tweed flecked yarn, and boots should be worn. Yet even here the impact of conservative formality could not be excluded, for the new corduroy and cotton trousers came supplied with front creases. Jeans had not held front creases, but corduroy can, so the American country look was being smartened up by the British crease. Come the 1990s, the front crease in trousers will attain its centenary. The new rugged man had to look smart even when 'undressed' in casual clothes.

In town, the double-breasted jacket was making a reappearance, for the new man should seem to possess some bodily bulk and solidity suggestive of a well-muscled torso beneath. In a reaction against the seventies flare of 24 inches, trousers were now slimmed down to around 14–18 inches at the bottom. The correct shirt was the classic one in blue stripes on white with a pure white collar and cuffs. It was goodbye to seventies frills, bandannas, semi-transparent cheesecloth shirts, love-beads, earrings, and long hair. The hair of the conservative eighties is short. The established suit was given the accolade in Bruce Feirstein's *Real Men Don't Eat Quiche*, as being the only outfit a 'real man'

94 The autumn/winter look 1983, by Austin Reed. Tough old agricultural corduroy comes back to reflect a more manly image. Austin Reed translate the casual blouson top into a suit, by making it double-breasted, worn with a waistcoat, shirt and tie, in earthy tones. Names like fern green, sandstone and moleskin brown underline the outdoor character. The blouson was priced at £59, the waistcoat at £18, the trousers at £26, and the three-quarter coat, right, at £69.

could wear. He certainly should not imitate ethnic groups, or wear military cast-offs, and would leave cowboy boots to cowboys and racing overalls to racing-car drivers. In short, he should dress like a British gentleman with a shirt and tie and get his clothes from his own tailor – not from Italian and French designers whose designs for men were too feminine, too fussy and, when trying to be macho, overblown. British restraint was the ideal. The real man should not be a sports fanatic but should rather embark on adventures in the tradition of the British stories written by John Buchan, Edgar Wallace, Sapper and Captain Johns.[14] Unfortunately Feirstein ruins his argument by saying that the real man's ideal is to be a James Bond. That fictional male, passively enjoying being pampered by his adoring 'Bond girls' like a baby in a cot, is hardly worthy of the active hero.

That masculinity should have to be redefined every age may seem an unnecessary extravagance. After all, a man's masculinity really depends on nothing but himself, so why should his clothes and his accessories matter? They do, because the image is important. Every society, whether clothed or naked, has its symbols to advertise status and dominance, whether they be a handmade suit from Savile Row or feathers and body paint in the Amazon Basin. They are the language defining who is who in the local hierarchy. That being so, why do the symbols need to be redefined and why should they change? They can remain fairly static in static societies, but in inventive and mobile societies there is challenge from below. Consequently the correct clothes worn at the top have to change to keep ahead, for as Pepys was well aware in the 1660s, fashion was meant to show scorn for city types and country clowns by identifying oneself with the style of the court. While the current Prince of Wales is no trendsetter, his wife certainly continues the role of the court in launching styles, and this will continue so long as there are courts at the top of society, although the degree of impact will depend on the ability of the individual royal figure to fulfil that commercial role. Since change is necessary for both status and trade, the image of a man is altered from age to age. There is no single absolute law as to what is masculine and what is not, and society expresses a preference for different types at different times. That is why we have traditional masculine looks and feminine styles between which menswear swings to and fro in the pendulum of Western society, which grows bored with a constant image.

Every so often society tends to redefine its idea of the male and the female, so there can be no absolute law as to what is masculine and what is feminine (apart, of course, from the reproductive process). Frills and long hair are not in themselves feminine, but society may see them as such, and in reaction to a period which has been considered effeminate, will rule that men must eschew such decorations. As a result, men are extremely self-conscious about their image, and feel that they must 'prove' their masculinity, although there is no such pressure on women to prove their femininity. This may explain why men set themselves dangerous and even self-destructive challenges. While they maintain that they climb vertical mountains or sail the wildest seas just because they are there, in fact they are trying to prove that they are man enough to master the difficulties involved. Such behaviour is well illustrated by American football heroes where the rule is said to be 'You Play in Pain, You Stay in Pain'. Some players drive themselves so hard that they end up as cripples.[15] They can break their knees one season, and get them repaired by surgeons, but instead of retiring while they can still walk, go back to the game for more punishment, forced to take painkilling amphetamines in order to perform, while the trainer keeps urging them to go out and kill the opposition regardless of the physical cost to themselves. It is a story of broken necks, paralysed bodies, and shattered knees, all sacrificed to prove that one group of males was more masculine than the other. In Britain the squash court is a battleground for displaced muscles, shattered ligaments and damaged eyeballs, as two males seek to annihilate one another. The destructive terminology of such 'games' illustrates the point. That is how far men will go to prove their masculinity, yet there have been periods in history when they have been quite happy to wear feminine styles for hundreds of years at a time as from the Elizabethan age down to the start of neo-classicism, when feminine qualities were defined as admirable, elegant and reasonable. Of course the next masculine period would proclaim the exact opposite.

Masculine identity explains the difficulties of marketing male toiletries. The cosmetic industry would love to double its profits by persuading men to use as many beauty products as women, but in view of male doubts places its advertising in women's magazines in order to persuade women to buy the lotions for men, in the same way that they buy the socks, shirts and underwear. It is relatively easy to persuade men to buy

95 The new business suits, Austin Reed, winter 1983. The suit gains in significance in the eighties, dividing the employed from the jobless. The man in the three-piece business suit feels established. The double-breasted suit is back, reflected in the double-breasted waistcoat, here cut off at the bottom. The classic striped shirt is the appropriate accessory for the man competing in a ruthless world. Price: £125.

themselves shaving products, but moisturizers, skin lotions, and perfume require feminine persuasion. Manly names are used, like Brut and Turbo, but one must query whether Stench and Pong would not be more appropriate in the rugged Eighties? The male market remains an area where beautification is taboo, but cleanliness, health and muscle-toning are permissible, for they suggest practical application and not mere vanity, which males are supposed to be above, according to Luther and Calvin, whose influence on the appearance and conduct of Protestant males has been immense, particularly in Britain. That influence shows no sign of disappearing. No matter how often there are attempts to introduce brighter colours and more

exhibitionistic clothes, the Protestant Clothing Ethic will return in force. It has reformed courts, and taught kings and lords to dress with more middle-class modesty and sobriety, to display good taste instead of flamboyance, and to set the standard for correct dress which is still highly influential in the world today, with politicians and heads of new countries eager to wear the British suit, as the true mark of civilization

and sophistication. The lounge suit has become the professional and correct dress for a great many activities and occasions, and now occupies the place formerly held by the frock-coat suit.

Bristol Weather Centre said the summer of 1983 was the hottest since 1659. The press declared that at last British males had taken to shorts in a big way, and both Burton's and Marks & Spencer sold out of men's shorts, but shorts for summer will only be a regular thing if hot summers become the norm. In the City, however, the Stock Exchange rule of dark suits only was still maintained, with no shorts and no suits in beige. Once again the movement had started with the workers, for it was builders' labourers who began wearing shorts for summer work during the 1970s. If a hot summer returns in the near future it may help to end the myth that men should not show their legs. They may be less smooth than the feminine version but they can still be well proportioned.

A past fashion has to be a good 30 years old before it can hope for a successful revival, and the early eighties saw many aspects of the fifties making a return in Britain, with young men wearing the DA or Tony Curtis hairstyle, and the white socks and slip-on shoes of Elvis Presley, while the grey used for décor in that decade was being revived for clothes and artefacts. Suits can now be light-grey to charcoal, with light-grey ties. Grey sweaters and jumpers go with grey corduroy trousers for casual wear, in tones reflecting the depressed economic climate. The new brutality in the air is reflected by the fashion for hard steel for watches, cuff links, tie pins and signet rings, as well as for furniture. The soft sixties and seventies with their fondness for colour and decoration have been ousted by a stripped-down, stern simplicity which regards itself as masculine and realistic, not that such qualities really have anything to do with sex, for they are characteristics of individuals. Even American medicine began to condemn the self-expression of the Seventies, stating that doing one's own thing increased blood pressure, caused tension in families, and was less healthy than a degree of reserve.[16] Was the USA admitting that its liberal ideal had gone too far, and that it should look back to the British model for clothes and lifestyle?

Menswear will continue to swing to and fro between the masculine and feminine principles, although of course those concepts are variable. Yet the majority of the basic garments involved are of respectable vintage, for all the variation that takes place. Trousers are thousands of years old, and shirts date back to antique tunics. Kneebreeches are still worn for shooting because trousers would get muddy, and they are close to 400 years old. Buttoned coats have reached 700 years. The classic British three-piece suit of coat, waistcoat and trousers or kneebreeches is 380, and the two-piece suit approaches 130. Hats, cloaks and cloth stockings have been found in pre-historic graves in Danish bogs. The humble handkerchief is nearly 600, and predates such variants as cravats and ties by centuries. Fashion may alter the silhouette, and stress length or breadth, but the constituent parts of the male wardrobe are pretty constant. Fashion in menswear consists in variations on established themes, as each new ideal tries to look different to a 'masculine' or a 'feminine' degree. As there are only two sexes to resemble, menswear seems to alternate between the two. It is the outlook of individual periods which decides how much.

96 Leisure clothes for summer 1984, Austin Reed. In casual wear the fifties look returns with the Tony Curtis/James Dean hairstyle, and the anorak, along with white socks and slip-on shoes. This zip jacket is reversible, in sky-blue and navy or rust and beige, at £45. Cotton trousers replace routine denim jeans. The knitted shirt is £12.95. The simplicity is marked, despising the guru beads and frills of the sixties and seventies.

Notes

1 A Verray Parfit Gentil Knight

1 Raphael Holinshed, *Chronicles*, 1577, reprinted 1927 (Dent & Sons), p. 27.
2 Ramon Lull, *Le Libre del Ordre de Cavayleria*, trs. William Caxton, with Adam Loutful's Scottish transcript, ed. A. Byles (Early English Text Society, OUP 1926), p. 31.
3 Christine de Pisan, *The Booke of Fayttes of Armes and of Chyvalrye*, trs. William Caxton, ed. A. Byles (Early English Text Society, OUP 1937), p. 35.
4 Philippe de Mezières, *Le Songe du Vieil Pelerin*, ed. Dora Bell (Geneva, Librairie E. Droz, 1955).
5 Stella Mary Newton, *Fashion in the Age of the Black Prince 1340–60*, (UK, Boydell Press/USA, Rowman & Littlefield 1980), p. 15.
6 Alfred Franklin, *Les Rues et les Cris de Paris au XIIIᵉ Siècle*. Collection de documents rares ou inédits relatifs à l'histoire de Paris (Paris, Librairies Willem & Daffis 1874), pp. 35–42.
7 Barbara Tuchman, *A Distant Mirror, the Calamitous 14th Century* (Macmillan 1978), p. 30.
8 Geoffrey Chaucer, *The Canterbury Tales*, trs. into modern English by J. Nicolson (W. H. Allen 1934).
9 Quoted in full in Stella Mary Newton, *op. cit.*, Appendix I.
10 James Robinson Planché, *History of British Costume* (The Library of Entertaining Knowledge, Charles Knight 1836), p. 173.
11 John Russell, *The Boke of Nurture*, ed. F. Furnivall (John Child & Sons 1868), pp. 59–64.
12 Stella Mary Newton, *op. cit.*
13 Louis Douët d'Arcq, *Comptes de l'Argenterie des Rois de France au XIVᵉ siècle* (Paris, Jules Renouard 1851), pp. 82ff.
14 *The Paston Letters 1422–1509*, a selection in modern spelling ed. N. Davis (OUP 1963), *passim.*
15 Iris Origo, *The Merchant of Prato, Francesco di Marco Datini* (Jonathan Cape 1957), intro. & pp. 256–68.
16 Albert Franklin, *op. cit.*
17 Danby Pickering, *The Statutes at Large* (Cambridge 1762); Frances Baldwin, *Sumptuary Legislation and Personal Regulation in England* (Baltimore, John Hopkins Press 1926).
18 Iris Origo, *op. cit.*
19 Barbara Tuchman, *op. cit.*, pp. 148, 425.
20 Planché, *op. cit.*, p. 151, n. 2.
21 For more information on this period see Elizabeth Birbari, *Dress in Italian Painting, 1460–1500* (John Murray 1975).

2 Renaissance Man

1 Secretary to Francesco Capello, *A relation or rather a true account of the Island of England*, 1500, trs. Charlotte Sneyd (Camden Society 1847).
2 William Brenchley Rye, *England as seen by Foreigners in the days of Queen Elizabeth and James I*, 1865, pp. xxxii ff.
3 Sebastiano Giustiniani, *Four years at the court of Henry VIII 1515–19*, trs. Rawdon Brown (Smith Elder & Co. 1854), pp. 26, 67, 85–6.
4 Edward Halle, *Chronicles 1548 containing the History of England during the Reign of Henry IV and the Succeeding Monarchs to the End of the Reign of Henry VIII* (Longman, Hurst, Rees & Orme 1809), p. 513.
5 Raphael Holinshed, *op. cit.*, p. 185.

6 Halle, *op. cit.*, pp. 518–614.

7 *Relation des Ambassadeurs Vénétiens sur les affaires de France au XVIe siècle*, recueillies et traduites par M. Tommaseo. Collection des documents inédits sur l'histoire de France publiés par ordre de Roi (Paris, Imprimerie Royale 1838), I, pp. 195, 255–7.

8 Etienne Perlin, *Description des Royaumes d'Angleterre et d'Escosse*, 1558, p. 15.

9 *Relation des Ambassadeurs Venetiens, op. cit.*, I, pp. 555–7.

10 *Ibid.*, I, p. 279.

11 *Ibid.*, I, p. 555.

12 Francis Sheppard, *Robert Baker of Piccadilly and his Heirs* (London Topographical Society publication no. 127 1982).

13 Philip Stubbes, *The Anatomie of Abuses* (Richard Jones at the sign of the Rose and Crown 1583), p. 4.

14 G. B. Nenna, *Nennio, or a Treatise of Nobility*, trs. William Jones (Paul Linley & John Flasket at the Sign of the Black Bear, St Paul's Churchyard 1595).

15 Count Baldassare Castiglione, *The Booke of the Courtyer*, trs. Thomas Hoby, intro. Sir W. Raleigh, 1561, pp. xi, 135–6.

16 Fernand Braudel, *The Structures of Everyday Life*, Civilisation and Capitalism 15th–18th Century, trs. Sian Reynolds (Collins 1981), I, p. 317.

17 Dr Martin Luther, *A Shorter Catechism*, trs. by a clergyman (London 1770), p. 25.

18 Jean Calvin, *The Institutes of the Christian Religion*, 1535, trs. H. Beveridge (Edinburgh, Calvin Translation Society 1845), p. 252.

19 Sir Thomas Elyot, *The Boke named the Governour*, 1531, ed. Henry Croft (Kegan Paul 1880), *passim*.

20 Roger Ascham, *The Scholemaster*, 1570, ed. John Mayor (Bell & Sons 1884), pp. 112–7, 133.

21 Frances E. Baldwin, *op. cit.*, p. 211.

22 Michelangelo, *The Letters*, ed. E. H. Ramsden (Peter Owen 1963), nos 143n., 150, 335, 384, 411, 412.

23 John Stow, *The Survey of London* (Elizabeth Purslow 1633), *passim*.

24 W. B. Rye, *op. cit.*, p. 13.

25 *Ibid.*, p. 71.

26 Paul Hentzner, *Travels in England*, trs. Horace Earl of Orford, 1797.

3 Effeminate and Wanton Age

1 John Donne, *Satyres, Epigrams and Verse Letters*, ed. W. Milgate (Oxford University Press 1967), Satire 1.

2 John Aubrey, *Brief Lives*, p. 46; Lucy Hutchinson, *Memoirs of the Life of Colonel Hutchinson* (Longman, Hurst, Rees & Orme 1806), p. 65.

3 James Cleland, ΗΡΩ-ΠΑΙΔΕΙΑ (*ERO-PAIDEIA*), *The Institution of a Young Nobleman* (Oxford 1607), pp. 214–16.

4 Sir John Davies, *Complete Poems*, ed. Rev. A. Grosart (Chatto & Windus 1876), vol. II, p. 43, Epigram no. 47.

5 W. B. Rye, *op. cit.*, pp. 150–3.

6 John Nicols, *Progresses of King James the First* (Nicols 1828), vol. I, pp. 597–8.

7 K. A. Patmore, *The Court of Louis XIII* (Methuen 1909), pp. 223–4.

8 Hutchinson, *op. cit.*

9 *Calendar of State Papers Domestic Series, Charles I, 1625–6*, pp. 163, 568, and *Charles I Clothing Account*, Victoria & Albert Museum Ms. 86, GG.2.

10 Thomas Dekker, *The Guls Horne Booke*, 1609, p. 6.

11 Henry Peacham, *The Compleat Gentleman*, 1622, pp. 190–1.

12 William Prynne, *The Unlovelinesse of Love-lockes*, 1628, pp. 1, 17–18.

13 John Bulwer, *Anthropometamorphosis : Man Transform'd ; or, The Artificial Changeling*, 1650, p. 263.

14 *Bibliotheca Lindesiana* vol. V, *A Bibliography of Royal Proclamations of the Tudor and Stuart Sovereigns 1485–1714*, with essay by Robert Steele (Oxford, Clarendon Press 1910), pp. 285–293.

15 John Aubrey, *Brief Lives*, p. 244.

16 Anthony Wood, *The Life and Times of Anthony Wood, antiquary of Oxford, 1623–1695, described by Himself*, collected by A. Clark (Oxford 1891), vol. II, p. 63.

17 Planché, *op. cit.*, p. 296–7.

18 John Evelyn, *Tyrannus ; or, The Mode*, 1661, pp. 11–12.

19 Samuel Pepys, *The Diary*, complete transcription ed. R. Latham and W. Matthews (Bell 1970), *passim*.

20 E. S. de Beer, 'King Charles II's Own Fashion', *Journal of the Warburg and Courtauld Institutes*, 1938–9, vol. II, pp. 104–15; D. J. de Marly, 'King Charles II's Own Fashion, The Theatrical Origins of the English Vest', *Journal of the Warburg and*

Courtauld Institutes, 1974, vol. XXXVII, pp. 378–82.

21 Anthony Wood, *op. cit.*, vol. I, pp. 509–10.

22 *Calendar of State Papers Domestic Series, Charles II*, for years 1665–1676; John Haynes, *A View of the Present State of the Clothing Trade in England with Remarks on the Causes and Pernicious Consequences of its Decay*, 1706, pp. 23–36.

23 César de Saussure, *A Foreign View of England in the Reigns of George I and George II*, trs. Mme van Muyden (Murray 1902), pp. 112–15.

24 Anthony Cooper, Earl of Shaftesbury, *Characteristics of Men, Manners, Opinions and Times*, 1713.

25 Sarah B. Osborn, *Political and Social Letters 1721–1771*, ed. Emily Osborn (Griffith Farren, Okeden & Welsh 1890), p. 23.

26 Oliver Goldsmith, *The Life of Richard Nash of Bath Esq.* (J. Newberry, 1762), pp. 32–49.

27 J. Macky, *A Journey through England* (J. Hooke 1722), pp. 94–138.

28 Sir John Nickolls, *Remarks on the Advantages and Disadvantages of France and Great Britain* (T. Osborne 1754), pp. 39–40.

29 C. Anstey, *The New Bath Guide* (Cambridge 1766), pp. 76–7.

30 Henrietta Louisa Countess of Pomfret, *Correspondence with Frances Countess of Hartford* (Richard Phillips 1805), vol. I, pp. 55–6, p. 118; vol. II, pp. 57–8.

31 Peter Kalm, *Account of his Visit to England on his Way to America*, trs. Joseph Lucas (Macmillan 1892), p. 53.

32 *Autobiography and Correspondence of Mary Granville Mrs Delany*, ed. Lady Llanover (Richard Bentley 1861), vol. I, p. 193, p. 437; vol. II, pp. 27–9, p. 72.

33 Horace Walpole, *The Letters 1735–97* (Richard Bentley 1840), vol. I, p. 240.

34 *Ibid*, vol. II, pp. 171–3.

35 Count Frederick Kielmansegge, *Diary of a Journey to England 1761–2*, trs. Countess Kielmansegg (Longman Green & Co. 1902), pp. 31, 53.

36 Philip Stanhope, Earl of Chesterfield, *The Art of Pleasing* (G. Kearsley, 1783).

37 Philip Stanhope, Earl of Chesterfield, *Letters*, vol. I, pp. 249–50.

4 Neo-Classical Nudes and Dandies

1 *Diary of Sylas Neville 1767–1788*, ed. B. Cozens-Hardy (Oxford 1950), p. 7.

2 Horace Walpole, *Letters addressed to the Countess of Ossory 1769–97*, ed. R. Vernon Smith (Richard Bentley 1848), p. 413.

3 P. J. Grosley, *A Tour of London; or, New Observations on England and its Inhabitants*, trs. Dr T. Nugent (Lockyer Davis 1772), vol. II, p. 59.

4 *The Age of Neo Classicism*, catalogue of the Arts Council Exhibition (Royal Academy of Art 1972), Hugh Honour, 'Neo-Classicism', pp. xxi–xxix, Carlo Pietrangeli, 'Archaeological Excavations in Italy 1750–1850', pp. xlvi–lii.

5 Horace Walpole, *Letters*, *op. cit.*, vol. III, pp. 72–3, 77–8, 84.

6 Horace Walpole, *Letters*, *op. cit.*, p. 183.

7 Horace Walpole, *Letters*, *op. cit.*, vol. III, p. 143.

8 P. J. Grosley, *op. cit.*, vol. I, p. 106.

9 Elizabeth Montagu, '*Queen of the Blues*', *Letters 1762–1800*, ed. R. Blunt (Constable, no date), vol. II, p. 81.

10 Sophie von La Roche, *Sophie in London 1786*, trs. C. Williams (Jonathan Cape, 1933), p. 102.

11 François Armand, Duc de La Rochefoucauld, *A Frenchman in England 1784*, ed. Jean Marchand (Cambridge 1933), p. 9.

12 *Ibid.*, p. 57.

13 John Byng, Viscount Torrington, *The Torrington Diaries 1781–94*, ed. C. Bruyn Andrews (Eyre & Spottiswoode 1934–8), vol. I, p. 88.

14 François Armand, *op. cit.*, p. 34.

15 Samuel Curwen, *Journal and Letters*, ed. G. Atkinson Ward (Boston, USA, Little, Brown & Co. 1864), p. 399.

16 Sir Nathaniel Wraxall, *The Historical and Posthumous Memoirs*, ed. H. Wheatley (Bickers & Son 1884), vol. II, pp. 267–8; vol. III, p. 361.

17 Betsy Sheridan, *Journal, Letters 1784–6, 1788–9*, ed. W. Le Fanu (Eyre & Spottiswoode 1960), p. 119.

18 Carl Philip Moritz, *Travels in England in 1782*, intro. P. Matheson (Humphrey Milford 1924), p. 49.

19 *Ibid.*, p. 53.

20 Sir Nathaniel Wraxall, *op. cit.*, vol. II, p. 269.

21 Dr John Andrews, *A Comparative View of the French and English Nations* (T. Longman 1785), pp. 66–8.

22 Dr F. A. Wenderborn, *A View of England towards the Close of the Eighteenth Century*

(G. & J. Robinson 1791), vol. I, pp. 224–5, p. 231.

23 Laure Junot, Duchesse d'Abrantès, *Memoires* (Paris, Ladvocat Librairie de S. A. R. le Duc d'Orléans, 18 vols, 1831–5), *passim*.

24 Claire, Comtesse de Remusat, *Memoirs 1802–8*, ed. P. de Remusat, trs. C. Hoey & J. Lillie (Sampson, Low, Marston, Searle & Rivington 1880), vol. I, pp. 65, 71, 234, 315; vol. II, pp. 68, 72, 99, 102.

25 Harriette Wilson, *Memoirs* (J. Stockdale 1825), vol. I, p. 223.

26 Jane Austen, *Northanger Abbey*, *The Oxford Jane Austen*, ed. R. Chapman (OUP 1933), vol. V, p. 157.

27 Jane Austen, *Emma*, *The Oxford Jane Austen, supra*, vol. 1V, p. 205.

28 Lord William Pitt Lennox, *My Recollections 1806–73* (Hurst & Blackett 1874), vol. I, p. 34.

29 Captain Jesse, *Life of George Brummell Esq.* (Saunders & Otley 1844), vol. I, pp. 62–69.

30 Prince Ludwig Pueckler-Muskau, *Tour in England, Ireland and France 1826–9*, (Zurich, Massie Publishing 1940), pp. 61, 76, 120, 127, 154, 158.

31 Lord William Pitt Lennox, *op. cit.*, vol. I, p. 207.

32 Lady Hester Stanhope, *Memoirs* (Henry Colburn 1845), vol. III, p. 90.

5 Romantic Chivalry to Muscular Christianity

1 William Connely, *Count d'Orsay, The Dandy of Dandies* (Cassell 1952), *passim*.

2 Charles Dickens, *Sketches by Boz Illustrative of Every-day Life and Every-day People* (Chapman & Hall 1839), p. 79.

3 Jane Carlyle, *Letters and Memorials*, ed. T. Carlyle & J. Froude (Longman, Green & Co. 1883), vol. I, pp. 299–300.

4 Connely, *op. cit.*, p. 492.

5 Thomas Wright, *The Habits and Customs of the Working Classes*, by a Journeyman Engineer (Tinsley Bros. 1867), pp. 189, 219.

6 Diana de Marly, *Costume on the Stage 1600–1940* (Batsford 1982), pp. 69–71.

7 Kenelm Digby, *The Broad Stone of Honour, or, Rules for the Gentlemen of England* (F. C. & J. Rivington 1822), p. 318.

8 John Manners, Duke of Rutland, *England's Trust* (J. G. & J. Rivington 1841), p. 24.

9 Peter Buchan, *The Eglinton Tournament and Gentleman Unmasked* (Simkin Marshall 1840), pp. 23–57.

10 *Ibid.*, p. 274.

11 Charles Creed, *Maid to Measure* (Jarrolds 1961), pp. 9–17. Another Englishman was in charge of women's clothes at the imperial court; see my *Worth, Father of Haute Couture* (Elm Tree Books 1980).

12 Robert Dale Owen, *Threading My Way* (USA, Trubner & Co. 1874), pp. 234–53.

13 Dickens, *op. cit.*, p. 83.

14 Mark Girouard, *The Victorian Country House* (Yale University Press 1979), pp. 263–72, and fig. 21.

15 J. Telfer Dunbar, *History of Highland Dress* (Batsford 1979), p. 145.

16 Edward VIII, Duke of Windsor, *A Family Album* (Cassell 1960), pp. 13–14.

17 Thomas Hardy, *The Dorset Farm Labourer Past and Present* (Dorset Agricultural Workers' Union 1884), pp. 8–9.

18 Captain Gronow, *Reminiscences* (Smith, Elder 1872), pp. 271–3.

19 Francis Wey, *A Frenchman sees the English in the 'Fifties*, adapted by Valerie Pirie (Sidgwick & Jackson 1935), p. 140.

20 *Ibid.*, p. 43.

21 A Member of the Aristocracy, *The Manners and Tone of Good Society* (Frederick Warne 1879), pp. 27–8, 68–81.

22 Examples of these clothes and hats can be seen in Christopher Sykes, *Country House Camera* (Weidenfeld & Nicolson 1980).

23 Captain Gronow, *Anecdotes of Celebrities of London and Paris* (Smith, Elder 1873), p. 11.

24 Edward VIII *op. cit.*, p. 57.

25 Gustav Jaeger, *Essays on Health and Culture and the Sanitary Woollen System* (Dr Jaeger's Sanitary Woollen Co. 1884), *passim*; Stella Mary Newton, *Health, Art and Reason, Dress Reformers of the 19th Century* (John Murray 1974).

26 John Ruskin, *Fors Clavigera, Letters to the Workmen and Labourers of Great Britain* (George Allen 1873), vol. IV, letter XXXVIII.

27 Sir Charles Oman, *Things I have seen* (Methuen 1933), p. 85.

28 Gwen Raverat, *Period Piece* (Faber & Faber 1952), p. 108.

6 Edwardian Toffs and Cinematic Heroes

1 Mrs Humphry, *Manners for Men*, 1897, reprinted 1979 (Exeter, Webb & Bower) p. 113.

2 A member of the Royal Household, *The Private Life of King Edward VII* (Appleton 1901), p. 251.

3 Edward VIII, *op. cit.*, p. 38.

4 Member of the Royal Household, *op. cit.*, pp. 248, 274.

5 *Ibid.*, p. 243.

6 Mrs Humphry, *op. cit.*, p. 120.

7 Giles St Aubyn, *Edward VII, Prince and King* (Collins 1979), p. 146.

8 Mrs Humphry, *op. cit.*, pp. 136–8.

9 Member of the Royal Household, *op. cit.*, p. 253.

10 St Aubyn, *op. cit.*, p. 396.

11 Hugh Stutfield, *The Sovranty of Society* (Fisher Unwin 1909), p. 192.

12 *Ibid.*, p. 103.

13 Mrs John Sherwood, *Manners and Social Usage* (New York, Harper Bros 1884), preface.

14 Lady Colin Campbell, *The Etiquette of Good Society* (Cassell 1893), p. 87.

15 C. W. Stamper, *What I Know, Reminiscences of Five Years' Attendance upon His Late Majesty King Edward VII* (Mills & Boon 1913), pp. 158, 163.

16 *Frank Harris on Bernard Shaw* (Victor Gollancz 1931), pp. 114–17.

17 Emrys Hughes, *Keir Hardie* (Lincolns-Prager 1950), pp. 58–9.

18 Edward VIII, *op. cit.*, p. 105.

19 Noël Coward, *Present Indicative* (Heinemann 1974), p. 232.

20 *Ibid.*, p. 239.

21 Jessie Matthews, *Over My Shoulder* (W. H. Allen 1974), p. 95.

22 Bruce Arnold, *Orpen, Mirror to an Age* (Jonathan Cape 1981), pp. 94, 425.

23 Noël Coward, *op. cit.*, p. 249.

24 Edward VIII, *op. cit.*, p. 119.

25 W. M. Munro, letter to *The Daily Express*, 14 February 1983.

26 Fred Astaire, *Steps in Time* (Heinemann 1960), p. 116.

27 *Ibid.*, p. 113.

28 Arnold Bennett, *The Journals* (Cassell 1932), vol. I, p. 159.

29 Harold Acton, *Memoirs of an Aesthete* (Methuen 1948), p. 146.

30 H. Graham Bennet, *Dress worn by Gentlemen at His Majesty's Court* (Harrison & Sons 1903), p. 80, and the advertisements therein.

31 Lucius Beebe, *The Big Spenders* (Hutchinson, 1967), p. 155.

32 For a year-by-year account of the period 1919–39 see *A Man's Book*, extracts from *The Tailor and Cutter*, ed. Jane Waller (Duckworth 1979).

33 Bing Crosby, told to Pete Martin, *Call Me Lucky* (New York, Simon & Schuster 1953), pp. 304–5.

34 Denis Judd, *King George VI 1895–1952* (Michael Joseph 1982), p. 186.

35 Rosina Harrison, *Rose : My Life in Service* (New York, Viking Press 1975), pp. 198–200.

7 A Shock to the System

1 Gordon Beckles, 'The Return of the Beau', *Harper's Bazaar*, March 1950, p. 70.

2 Sir James Murray, *A New English Dictionary on Historical Principles* (Oxford 1901).

3 Jill Butterfield, 'Peacock's Tail', *The Sunday Times*, 14 December 1958.

4 Jane Lockyer, 'Men aren't what they used to be', *Woman's Mirror*, 11 August 1962, p. 22–3.

5 John Crosby, 'The Return of the Dandy', *The Observer* Magazine, 1964.

6 John Fairley, 'Dress not Optional', *The Observer* Magazine, 8 December 1968.

7 Shirley Conran, 'Talking to Men about their Clothes', *The Observer*, 14 December 1969.

8 Liz Smith, 'Men in Denim', *The Observer* Magazine, May 1972.

9 Stephen Fothergill, 'English as she's bespoke', *The Observer*, 3 October 1976; *The Daily Mail*, 8 March 1977.

10 Noël Coward, *Diaries*, ed. G. Payne & S. Morley (Weidenfeld & Nicolson 1982), entry for 24 February 1957.

11 'Pentagon is back in Uniform after reported Dressing Down', *International Herald Tribune*, Paris, 2 March 1981.

12 *International Herald Tribune*, 23 October and 9 April 1981; *The Daily Express*, 14 September 1981.

13 Christopher Matthew, 'Crisp at Large, in which our hero takes a sartorial stroll down Savile Row and tries a touch of mink', *The Observer*, 25 October 1981; Suzy Menkes, 'Men's Fashion', *The Times*, 5 May 1981.

14 Bruce Feirstein, *Real Men Don't Eat Quiche : a guidebook to all that is truly masculine, special forthright True Brit edition* (New English Library 1982).

15 Richard Hoffer, 'Ex-Raider Otto still

proving NFL rule: You play in pain, you stay in pain', *International Herald Tribune*, 13 August 1981, and the film *North Dallas Forty*, 1980.

16 Christine Doyle, 'Health from America', *The Observer*, 23 October 1983.

Glossary

bowyer	bow-maker
braccia	Italian measure of arm-length
camlet/chamlet	mixed cloth like wool woven with silk
fletcher	arrowsmith
lorimer	maker of horse furniture
mark	worth 13/4*d*. or 67p
murray	purple-red
pattens	high wooden soles to keep feet out of mud
palmi	Italian measure of $7\frac{1}{2}$ inches
plunket	grey-blue
samiate	rich silk
tippet	long pointed tip of a hood
rebato	Spanish ruff support

Bibliography

ACTON, Harold, *Memoirs of a Aesthete* (Methuen 1948).

ANDREWS, Dr John, *A Comparative View of the French and English Nations* (Longman 1785).

ANON. A Member of the Aristocracy, *The Manners and Tone of Good Society* (Frederick Warne, 1879).

ANON. A Member of the Royal Household, *The Private Life of King Edward VII* (Appleton 1901).

ANSTEY, Christopher, *The New Bath Guide* (Cambridge 1766).

ARNOLD, Bruce, *Orpen, Mirror to an Age* (Jonathan Cape 1981).

ASCHEM, Roger, *The Scholemaster 1570*, ed. J. Mayor (Bell 1884).

ASTAIRE, Fred, *Steps in Time* (Heinemann 1960).

AUBREY, John, *Brief Lives*, ed. O. Dick (Penguin English Library 1972).

AUSTEN, Jane, *Northanger Abbey*, ed. R. Chapman (Oxford University Press 1933).

AUSTEN, Jane, *Emma*, ed. R. Chapman (Oxford University Press 1933).

BALDWIN, Frances, *Sumptuary Legislation and Personal Regulation in England* (Baltimore, John Hopkins Press 1926).

BECKLES, Gordon, 'The Return of the Beau', *Harper's Bazaar*, March 1950.

BEEBE, Lucius, *The Big Spenders* (Hutchinson 1967).

BENNET, Graham, *Dress worn by Gentlemen at His Majesty's Court* (Harrison & Sons 1901).

BENNETT, Enoch Arnold, *The Journals* (Cassell 1932).

BIBLIOTHECA LINDESIANA, vol. V, *A Bibliography of Royal Proclamations of the Tudor and Stuart Sovreigns* (Oxford, Clarendon Press 1910).

BUCHAN, Peter, *The Eglinton Tournament and Gentlemen Unmasked* (Simkin Marshall 1840).

BULWER, John, *Anthropometamorphosis: Man Transform'd; or, The Artificial Changeling*, 1650.

BUTTERFIELD, Jill, 'Peacock's Tail', *The Sunday Times*, 14 December 1958.

BYNG, John, Viscount Torrington, *The Torrington Diaries, 1781–94*, ed. C. Bruyn Andrews (Eyre & Spottiswoode 1934–8).

Calendar of State Papers, Domestic Series, ed. Mary Everett Green (Longman, Brown, Green, Longman and Roberts 1858).

CALVIN, Jean, *The Institutes of the Christian Religion 1535*, trs. H. Beveridge (Edinburgh, Calvin Translation Society 1845).

CAMPBELL, Lady Colin, *The Etiquette of Good Society* (Cassell 1893).

CAPELLO, Francesco, secretary to, *A Relation or rather a True Account of the Island of England 1500*, trs. Charlotte Sneyd (Camden Society 1847).

CARLYLE, Jane, *Letters and Memorials*, ed. T. Carlyle & J. Froude (Longman Green & Co. 1883).

CASTIGLIONE, Count Baldassare, *The Booke of the Courtyer*, trs. T. Hoby, 1561.

CHAUCER, Geoffrey, *The Canterbury Tales*, in modern English by J. Nicolson (W. H. Allen 1934).

CLELAND, James, ΗΡΩ-ΠΑΙΔΕΙΑ (*ERO-PAIDEIA*), *The Institution of a Young Nobleman* (Oxford 1607).

CONNELY, William, *Count d'Orsay, The Dandy of Dandies* (Cassell, 1952).

CONRAN, Shirley, 'Talking to Men about their Clothes', *The Observer*, 14 December 1969.

COOPER, Anthony Ashley, Earl of Shaftesbury, *Characteristics of Men, Manners, Opinions and Times*, 1713.

COWARD, Noël, *Present Indicative* (Heinemann 1974).

COWARD, Noël, *Diaries*, ed. G. Payne & S. Morley (Weidenfeld & Nicolson 1982).

CREED, Charles, *Maid to Measure* (Jarrolds 1961).

CROSBY, Bing, told to Pete Martin, *Call Me Lucky* (New York, Simon & Schuster 1953).

CROSBY. John, 'The Return of the Dandy', *The Observer* magazine 1964.

CURWEN, Samuel, *Journal and Letters*, ed. G. Atkinson Ward (Boston USA, Little, Brown & Co. 1864).

D'ABRANTÈS, Laure Junot, Duchesse, *Memoires* (Paris, Ladvocat Librairie de S.A.R. le Duc d'Orléans 1831–5).

DAVIES, Sir John, *Complete Poems*, ed. Rev. A. Grosart (Chatto & Windus 1876).

DE BEER, E. S., 'King Charles II's Own Fashion', *Journal of the Warburg and Courtauld Institutes*, vol. II, 1938–9.

DEKKER, Thomas, *The Guls Horne Booke*, 1609.

DELANEY, Mary Granville, *Autobiography and Correspondence*, ed. Lady Llanover (Richard Bentley 1861).

DE MARLY, Diana, 'King Charles II's Own Fashion, The Theatrical Origins of the English Vest', *Journal of the Warburg and Courtauld Institutes*, vol. XXXVII, 1974.

DE MARLY, Diana, *Costume on the Stage, reform movements 1600–1940* (Batsford 1982).

DE MARLY, Diana, *Worth, Father of Haute Couture* (Elm Tree Books 1980).

DE MEZIÈRES, Philippe, *Le Songe du Vieil Pelerin*, ed. Dora Bell (Geneva, Librairie E. Droz 1955).

DE PISAN, Christine, *The Booke of Fayttes of Armes and Chyvalrye*, trs. W. Caxton, ed. A. Byles (Early English Text Society, Oxford University Press 1937).

DE REMUSAT, Claire, Comtesse, *Memoirs 1802–8*, ed. P. de Remusat, trs. C. Hoey & J. Lillie (Sampson, Low, Marston, Searle & Rivington 1880).

DE SAUSSURE, César, *A Foreign View of England in the Reigns of George I and George II*, trs. Mme van Muyden (Murray 1902).

DICKENS, Charles, *Sketches by Boz Illustrative of Every-day Life and Every-day People* (Chapman & Hall 1839).

DIGBY, Kenelm, *The Broad Stone of Honour; or, Rules for the Gentlemen of England* (F. C. & J. Rivington 1822).

DONNE, John, *Satyres, Epigrams and Verse Letters*, ed. W. Milgate (Oxford University Press 1967).

DOUËT D'ARCQ, Louis, *Comptes de l'Argenterie des Rois de France au XIVᵉ Siècle* (Paris, Jules Renouard 1851).

DOYLE, Christine, 'Health from America', *The Observer*, 23 October 1983.

DUNBAR, J. Telfer, *History of Highland Dress* (Batsford 1979).

EDWARD VIII, *A Family Album* (Cassell 1960).

ELYOT, Sir Thomas, *The Boke named the Governour, 1531*, ed. Henry Croft (Kegan Paul 1880).

EVELYN, John, *Tyrannus; or, The Mode*, 1661.

FAIRLEY, John, 'Dress not Optional', *The Observer* magazine, 8 December 1968.

FEIRSTEIN, Bruce, *Real Men Don't Eat Quiche* (New English Library 1982).

FOTHERGILL, Stephen, 'English as she's bespoke', *The Observer*, 3 October 1976.

FRANKLIN, Alfred, *Les Rues et les Cris de Paris au XIIIᵉ Siècle* (Paris, Librairies Willem & Daffis 1874).

GIROUARD, Mark, *The Victorian Country House* (Yale University Press 1979).

GIUSTINIANI, Sebastiano, *Four Years at the Court of Henry VIII 1515–19*, trs. Rawdon Brown (Smith, Elder & Co. 1854).

GOLDSMITH, Oliver, *The Life of Richard Nash of Bath Esq.* (J. Newberry 1762).

GRONOW, Captain, *Reminiscences* (Smith, Elder & Co. 1872).

GRONOW, Captain, *Anecdotes of Celebrities of London and Paris* (Smith, Elder & Co. 1873).

GROSLEY, P. J., *A Tour of London; or, New Observations on England and its Inhabitants*, trs. Dr T. Nugent (Lockyer Davies 1772).

HALLE, Edward, *Chronicles 1548, containing the History of England during the Reign of Henry IV and the Succeeding Monarchs to the End of the Reign of Henry VIII* (Longman, Hurst, Rees, Orme 1809).

HARDY, Thomas, *The Dorset Farm Labourer Past and Present* (Dorset Agricultural Workers' Union 1884).

HARRIS, Frank, *On Bernard Shaw* (Victor Gollancz 1931).

HARRISON, Rosina, *Rose, My Life in Service* (New York, Viking Press 1975).

HAYNES, John, *A View on the Present State of the Clothing Trade in England with Remarks on the Causes and Pernicious Consequences of its Decay*, 1706.

HENTZNER, Paul, *Travels in England*, trs. Horace Earl of Orford, 1797.

HOFFER, Richard, 'Ex-Raider Otto', *International Herald Tribune*, Paris, 13 August 1981.

HOLINSHED, Raphael, *Chronicles 1577*, reprinted 1927 (Dent & Sons).

HUGHES, Emrys, *Keir Hardie* (Lincolns-Prager 1950).

HUMPHRY, Mrs, *Manners for Men 1897*, reprinted 1979 (Exeter, Webb & Bower).

HUTCHINSON, Lucy, *Memoirs of the Life of Colonel Hutchinson* (Longman, Hurst, Rees, Orme 1806).

JAEGER, Gustav, *Essays on Health and Culture and the Sanitary Woollen System* (Dr Jaeger's Sanitary Woollen Co. 1884).

JESSE, Captain, *Life of George Brummell Esq.* (Saunders and Otley 1844).

JUDD, Denis, *King George VI, 1895–1952* (Michael Joseph 1982).

KALM, Peter, *Account of his Visit to England on his Way to America*, trs. Joseph Lucas (Macmillan 1892).

KIELMANSEGGE, Frederick, Count, *Diary of a Journey to England in 1761–2*, trs. Countess Kielmansegg (Longman, Green & Co. 1902).

LA ROCHE, Sophie von, *Sophie in London 1786*, trs. C. Williams (Jonathan Cape 1933).

LA ROCHEFOUCAULD, François Armand Duc de, *A Frenchman in England in 1784*, ed. Jean Marchand (Cambridge 1933).

LENNOX, Lord William Pitt, *My Recollections 1806–73* (Hurst & Blackett 1874).

LOCKYER, Jane, 'Men aren't what they used to be', *Woman's Mirror*, 11 August 1962.

LULL, Ramon, *Le Libre del Ordre de Cavayleria*, trs. W. Caxton, ed. A. Byles (Early English Text Society, Oxford University Press 1926).

LUTHER, Dr Martin, *A Shorter Catechism*, trs. by a Clergyman, 1770.

MACKY, J., *A Journey through England* (J. Hooke 1722).

MANNERS, John, Duke of Rutland, *England's Trust* (J. G. & J. Rivington 1841).

MATTHEW, Christopher, 'Crisp at Large, in which our hero takes a sartorial stroll down Savile Row', *The Observer*, 25 October 1981.

MATTHEWS, Jessie, *Over My Shoulder* (W. H. Allen 1974).

MENKES, Suzy, 'Men's Fashion', *The Times*, 5 May 1981.

MICHELANGELO, *The Letters*, ed. E. H. Ramsden (Peter Owen 1963).

MONTAGU, Elizabeth, '*Queen of the Blues*', *Letters 1762–1800*, ed. R. Blunt (Constable, no date).

MORITZ, Carl Philip, *Travels in England in 1782* (Humphrey Milford 1924).

NENNA, G. B., *Nennio; or, A Treatise on Nobility*, trs. W. Jones (Paul Linley & John Flasket at the Sign of the Black Bear, St Paul's Churchyard 1595).

Neo-Classicism, The Age of, catalogue of the Arts Council Exhibition, Royal Academy of Art 1972).

NEVILLE, Sylas, *Diary 1767–1788*, ed. B. Cozens-Hardy (Oxford 1950).

NEWTON, Stella Mary, *Fashion in the Age of the Black Prince 1340–60* (Boydell Press/Rowman & Littlefield 1980).

NEWTON, Stella Mary, *Health, Art and Reason, Dress Reformers of the 19th Century* (John Murray 1974).

NICOLS, John, *Progresses of King James the First* (Nicols 1828).

NICKOLLS, Sir John, *Remarks on France and Great Britain* (T. Osborne 1754).

OMAN, Sir Charles, *Things I have seen* (Methuen 1933).

ORIGO, Iris, *The Merchant of Prato, Francesco di Marco Datini* (Jonathan Cape 1957).

OSBORN, Sarah, *Political and Social Letters 1721–1771*, ed. E. Osborn (Griffith Farren, Okeden & Welsh 1890).

OWEN, Robert Dale, *Threading My Way* (USA, Trubner & Co. 1874).

Paston Letters, 1422–1509, ed. N. Davis (Oxford University Press 1963).

PATMORE, K. A., *The Court of Louis XIII* (Methuen 1909).

PEACHAM, Henry, *The Compleat Gentleman*, 1622.

PERLIN, Etienne, *Description des Royaumes d'Angleterre et d'Escosse*, 1558.

PICKERING, Danby, *The Statutes at Large* (Cambridge 1762).

PLANCHÉ, James Robinson, *History of British Costume* (Library of Entertaining Knowledge, Charles Knight 1836).

POMFRET, Henrietta Louisa, Countess of, *Correspondence with Frances, Countess of Hertford* (Richard Phillips 1805).

PRYNNE, William, *The Unlovelinesse of Love-lockes*, 1628.

PUECKLER-MUSKAU, Prince Ludwig, *Tour in England, Ireland and France 1826–9*, (Zurich, Massie Publishing 1940).

RAVERAT, Gwen, *Period Piece* (Faber & Faber 1952).

RUSKIN, John, *Fors Clavigera, Letters to the Workmen and Labourers of Great Britain* (George Allen 1873).

RUSSELL, John, *The Boke of Nurture*, ed. F. Furnivall (John Child & Sons 1868).

RYE, William Brenchley, *England as seen by Foreigners in the Days of Queen Elizabeth and James I*, 1865.

ST AUBYN, Giles, *Edward VII Prince and King* (Collins 1979).

SHEPPARD, Francis, *Robert Baker of Piccadilly and his Heirs*, London Topographical Society, publication no. 127, 1982.

SHERIDAN, Betsy, *Journal, Letters 1784–6, 1788–9*, ed. W. Le Fanu (Eyre & Spottiswoode 1960).

SHERWOOD, Mrs John, *Manners and Social Usage* (New York, Harper Bros 1884).

SMITH, Anthony, *The Body* (George Allen & Unwin 1968).

STAMPER, C. W., *What I Know, Reminiscences of Five Years' Attendance upon His Late Majesty King Edward VII* (Mills and Boon 1913).

STANHOPE, Lady Hester, *Memoirs* (Henry Colburn 1845).

STANHOPE, Philip, Earl of Chesterfield, *The Art of Pleasing*, 1783.

STOW, John, *The Survey of London* (Elizabeth Purslow 1633).

STUBBES, Philip, *The Anatomie of Abuses* (Richard Jones at the sign of the Rose and Crown 1583).

STUTFIELD, Hugh, *The Sovranty of Society* (Fisher Unwin 1909).

TOMMASEO, M., *Relation des Ambassadeurs Venétiens sur les Affaires de France* (Paris, Imprimerie Royale 1838).

TUCHMAN, Barbara, *A Distant Mirror : the Calamitous 14th Century* (Macmillan 1978).

WALPOLE, Horace, *The Letters 1735–97* (Richard Bentley 1840).

WALPOLE, Horace, *Letters addressed to the Countess of Ossory 1769–97*, ed. R. V. Smith (Richard Bentley 1848).

WEDERBORN, D. F. A., *A View of England towards the Close of the Eighteenth Century* (G. & J. Robinson 1791).

WEY, Francis, *A Frenchman sees the English in the 'Fifties*, adapted by Valerie Pirie (Sidgwick & Jackson, 1936).

WILSON, Harriette, *Memoirs* (J. Stockdale 1825).

WOOD, Anthony, *The Life and Times of Anthony Wood, Antiquary of Oxford, 1623–1695, described by Himself*, collected by A. Clark (Oxford 1891).

WRAXALL, Sir Nathaniel, *The Historical and Posthumous Memoirs*, ed. H. Wheatley (Bickers & Son 1884).

WRIGHT, Thomas, *The Habits and Customs of the Working Classes* (Tinsley Bros 1867).

YORK, Peter, *Style Wars* (Sidgwick & Jackson 1983).

Index